THE YEAR AHEAD
2004

SUSAN MILLER

THE YEAR AHEAD
2004

BARNES
&NOBLE
BOOKS
NEW YORK

The Year Ahead 2004

ISBN 0-7607-4530-7

Printed and bound
in the United States of America

03 04 05 06 07 MP 9 8 7 6 5 4 3 2 1
First Edition

Designer: Midori Nakamura

This book is for entertainment purposes only.

To Susan Krakower,
for her glorious gift
of friendship

Contents

How to Read
The Year Ahead 2004

———○———

Curious people—ones like you—are always interested in ways
to live their lives more creatively. "What else is possible for
me?" they'll ask. "Am I using my talents, credentials, and life
experience to the fullest?" "Will the year ahead hold any special, happy surprises?" These are the perfect questions to ask as
you plan for the future. In *The Year Ahead 2004*, I hope to
answer many of your questions and point you in the right
direction so that you can live your next year to the fullest.

This book will give you a panoramic view of 2004. I will
also provide you with a number of imaginative ideas to make
your life more fun, loving, and productive. I will suggest certain areas that are due for an upgrade, and in some cases, you
may be surprised. Most of all, I hope you will be excited. A
new year holds so much promise and the opportunity to fulfill
dreams on many different levels.

By writing this book, I hope to open your mind to the full range of possibilities for you. However, astrology is not destiny. Even with the best aspects in your chart, you can't expect anything of value to happen without your direct involvement. The force of your will can move mountains.

Some people ask me if astrology is in conflict with traditional religion. The answer is no. In fact, your deepest religious beliefs, morals, principals, philosophies, and attitudes are all reflected in the horoscope's ninth house. Astrology acknowledges that people have free will and are not controlled helplessly by outside forces. They must take responsibility for their own lives. While we can't control all that happens to us, we can control our response to pressure, and in so doing so, we can define and shape our character and personality.

To make astrology work for you, you'll need to show the universe your intent and the depth of your commitment towards a goal. Your horoscope will suggest the right approach and the right time for action in keeping with the various cycles that are beneficial to you. Short-term trends are activated by new moons and full moons, and by the "personal planets," i.e., those that circle closely to the Sun such as Venus, Mercury, and Mars. Longer trends that allow you to create substantial changes over longer periods of time are set up by Jupiter or Saturn; the outer planets, such as Uranus, Neptune, and Pluto; and the year's eclipses.

Astrologers believe in the concept of "as above, so too below." By that they mean that there is a relationship between the activities of the planets and human activity on Earth. Most people admit they see a relationship between full moons and human behavior, but astrologers see this phenomenon in much greater depth and detail.

There is no question in my mind that the universe wants us to succeed. Full moons bring situations to a head and debris to the surface so that we can clean house. New moons indicate the right moment to plant seeds for future growth. Certain aspects in our chart bring feedback and an opportunity to correct the course we're on. Other aspects bring obstacles to test our resolve, force us to commit to our goals, or help us to move forward. Blessings are often disguised as challenges, and it is up to us to recognize them for what they are.

Good energy always attracts more good energy. If you act courageously, prepare thoroughly, work passionately, and are honest and ethical, you will overcome obstacles and ultimately achieve your dreams. If there is anything I want to impart to you it is this: life rewards action.

Try not to make decisions out of fear but out of conviction. Also, listen to your intuition, even if you have no reason to believe it is right. Your intuition is the voice of your heart, and it will protect you. You can hone your intuition by paying attention to it, trusting it, and by using it. Also, make sure to take your goals seriously: others around you will too.

While you read your copy of *The Year Ahead 2004*, I hope you will do so with a calendar handy to mark down certain dates or periods during the year. Some readers might find it helpful to have a yellow magic marker nearby to underline certain passages for later reference.

Keep in mind that the universe doesn't work on calendar years like ours. The cosmos begins new cycles in the right season, at the right time, not necessarily when our calendar says January 1. For example, in this coming year, one of the most important moments of change will occur in late September, when Jupiter enters Libra. Eclipses will also shake things up in May and November, and those will mark other key points of the year. So don't be disappointed if January or February does-n't bring an entirely new scenario immediately—all will come in its own good time.

After you have read *The Year Ahead 2004*, you may want to supplement your annual forecast with my detailed monthly forecasts from my web site, Astrology Zone (*http://astrology-zone.com*). Every month I post about 100 pages of original material, to be divided among the twelve signs. If you get your monthly forecast, you will have the most detailed description of upcoming trends to plan your initiations. My site also offers many supplemental articles on other aspects of astrology and how it can help you. All the content on my site is free.

THE IMPORTANCE OF YOUR RISING SIGN

To read your year ahead accurately, you should read for your rising sign as well as your birthday Sun sign.

The rising sign, which is also called the ascendant, is the point in your horoscope that corresponds to the Earth's eastern horizon. It is the zodiac sign that was shining on that horizon line at the moment of your birth. In astrology this critical piece of information forms the basis of a large part of your personality development, and it sets up much of the critical timing in your chart. Most people have a different rising sign from their birthday sign. However, if you were born at dawn, the Sun was rising over the horizon, so your Sun sign would be the same as your rising sign. Have you ever heard some-one refer to his or herself as "a double Pisces" or "a double Scorpio"? This is someone with the same Sun and rising signs.

Every two hours the rising sign changes into a new sign of the zodiac. Within that two-hour period, the degree of the ris-ing sign continually changes to a different mathematical degree. Since every tiny detail matters in astrology, that would mean that even twins would have very different charts. This is why astrologers need to work with an exact-to-the-minute time of birth.

To get an accurate picture of who you are and to accurately time upcoming events, you need to make sure to blend both your Sun sign and rising sign. One or the other will provide only half the picture.

GETTING YOUR CHART DONE ON LINE

If you don't know your rising sign, you can find it by casting a horoscope chart to the exact time, day, month, year, and place of birth. There are a number of web sites that will calculate your rising sign for free. Just do a search, and try out several sites. One site that many people love is *http://astro.com*, so you may want to start there.

On my site, *http://astrologyzone.com*, I don't offer a free service, but you can order a personalized book (printed on demand) that gives in-depth information about your horoscope, written in easy-to-understand, non-technical terms. The hardcover, illustrated book, which is printed only for you, is called *My Personal Horoscope* and is available in English and French. For details, please go to *http://astrologyzone.com* and click on the yellow and purple icon of My Personal Horoscope located on the home page.

THE NATURE OF ASTROLOGY

Astrology can help you on many levels. It can show when you are repeating damaging patterns or how best to deal with upcoming challenges. Astrology can also pinpoint any latent talent you might have and tell you how to best develop it. Astrology can also predict expansive and rewarding trends and show how to best take advantage of them. It is also excellent at suggesting the perfect time for action, and for putting expectations into proper perspective.

You're limited only by your imagination. Open your mind, ask lots of questions, and information will be revealed to you. Cast a wide net, and then consider all of your options—astrology will help you with that process.

When you're considering a course of action, you will probably first think of only the obvious solutions. This is common. However, if you take your time and work with your horoscope, more original and creative responses will emerge. Those ideas are often the best ones because they don't represent knee-jerk reactions, but express the truest course of action for you.

For example, let's say your money is tight because you just lost your job. You could either cut back on your spending, or find a means to earn more money. There is no correct answer. If the aspects in your astrological chart are good, you can probably command more money in your next job than you dreamed. If your aspects are poor at the time, you may need to take a more conservative approach—holding out for a larger salary may not be the smartest idea.

Give twelve people the same problem and you will get twelve different responses—that's what makes life interesting. That's true of good opportunities, too—some people will jump at the chance to do something new, while others will hang back. I can't predict what you will do, but I will tell you the environment you'll be entering. I can also tell you if conditions will change and, if so, how they will change and when. You can learn about yourself by watching how you respond to new experiences. Ultimately, you will come to understand as I have that the act of living is a highly creative endeavor and that life is always a beautiful work in progress. We are never done maturing—even in old age.

Here is a lovely truth to hold in your heart. On the day you were born, the star pattern overhead was truly unique, and those eight planets plus the Sun and Moon will never occupy the same placements ever again. You were born for a reason, and the year ahead represents a precious resource: time. You cannot save it, or buy more of it. Use it to your best advantage. Everything begins with your desire to succeed! Happy New Year, dear reader.

A Warm Welcome to 2004

―――○―――

The year ahead will be colored in soft, pastel shades. We're
not due for a vivid, bold year like 2003, but 2004 will be
remarkable in that it will bring an unusual amount of harmony
among the planets. Although no year can be said to be completely stress-free, at least 2004 won't bring any major
upheavals or unusual tensions. With a well-balanced year
before you, it makes sense to take full advantage of what's on
tap while it is there for the taking!

Last year heralded the beginning of a whole new epoch
because three outer planets—Uranus, Saturn, and Jupiter—
changed signs. This year only one major planet will be moving
into another sign, which will be Jupiter, the planet of happiness and good fortune. The big outer planets don't change

zodiac signs often, but when they do, they create shifts in our lives that we can't help but notice. How comforting it will be to have a stable year ahead that will allow us to build on what we started in the last year, without constant interference from any angry planets.

The past few years have certainly been fraught with tension, mainly due to a very public, messy row that broke out between Saturn and Pluto in mid-2001. Their dispute raged for 18 months, until May 2003, when Saturn and Pluto reached a peak point of conflict. Astrologers hoped that this would mark the end of it, but neither Saturn nor Pluto moved very far from their original opposition point, and therefore remained within shouting distance for an additional year. And shout they did. Even though the highest point of this aspect was reached in May 2003, their dispute didn't officially end until they separated far enough—ten degrees—in June 2003. After being bombarded with two years of pressure from these two Titans of the solar system, the peacefulness that followed in the second half of 2003 may have seemed to you as bordering on miraculous. No other disputes on the scale of a Saturn/Pluto conflict are due in 2004, and, in case you are wondering, Saturn and Pluto will not face each other again in similar fashion for three more decades. Wonderful!

With the planets behaving in a peaceful manner in 2004, you will have a chance to regroup, rebuild your dreams, and strengthen your confidence. You will also be able to follow your own agenda without having to worry about being blown off course. In recent years, disruptive planets forced us to pay attention to issues that were suddenly present, which meant that our dreams and goals were put on hold. With a more stable and peaceful year ahead, the time may be right to go back to those dreams.

However, if there is anything I have learned being an astrologer, it is to not make broad generalizations. There will always be exceptions to every rule. So while most people will find this year a better, brighter year than most, I cannot see everything that is going on in your individual chart, dear reader. If you do experience stress, it may be due to the actions of Saturn, the eclipses, and the way these cosmic events manifest in your chart.

2004 will enhance themes that began last year. You may have already sensed that 2003 was a marker year for you. With three planets changing signs, important seeds were sown. For some, last year's beginnings may still be too new or too subtle to notice. For others, the changes that occurred in 2003 came on like gangbusters, so it was easy to see the shifts. A lot depended on the positions of the planets in your own chart. No matter what you experienced, 2003 was to be a year in which the line in the sand was drawn: update your outlook or risk being left behind.

How to Judge Your Year Ahead

There are two considerations to make when planning for a new year. First we need to see if the major outer planets—the ones I listed at the start of this chapter—will be supportive or challenging to the rest of the planets in the solar system. As I mentioned, in 2004, these planets will be remarkably friendly to one another.

Secondly, we need to ask how will the planetary configurations affect your own natal planets in their unique positions. Although I don't have your personal chart in front of me, I *can* tell you how your Sun will be affected, and I can delineate how the rest of the planets will relate to the Sun in your horoscope. The Sun is a major player in any horoscope chart, as it points to the divine spark of your personality, your ego, and your drive to succeed.

Should you find yourself in a stressful position this year, I will offer ideas in this book to help you deal with it. We study astrology to anticipate all kinds of situations so we're ready for them. I can offer you several possible solutions and once you are armed with your list of options, you can choose the one that fits your personal style. In astrology, there is no one right or wrong answer, only one that is right for you.

Remember that even in the darkest situations, there are almost always some rather superb aspects operating concurrently, and that positive energy can be enlarged. You will need to prepare just as carefully to take advantage of positive, rewarding aspects as you would difficult ones. You will want to cast a wide net to capture all the cosmic goodies that are due you!

THE OUTER PLANETS IN 2004

To get a feel for the coming year, we look to the position of the outer planets—Pluto, Neptune, and Uranus, as well as the planets next in the planetary line up, Saturn and Jupiter.

Saturn and Jupiter are in a unique position to give a year its structure, because they orbit neither too quickly nor too slowly, but just fast enough to give us a feeling of a beginning, middle, and end to important life chapters. Jupiter orbits one sign for a year, while Saturn takes about two years to fully move through one zodiac sign. Jupiter expands, and Saturn constricts. The symbolism of their astrological glyphs says it all: Jupiter is spirit triumphing over matter (reality), and Saturn is matter triumphing over spirit. They are opposites, but work well together, for too much expansion, too quickly can be just as bad as too much constriction. As you read about the planets below, pay special attention to Saturn and Jupiter to provide key news.

PLUTO, THE PLANET OF TRANSFORMATION, CAN NOW BE YOUR FRIEND

Pluto is the planet that is considered a law unto itself. It is so powerful that when it is in contact with other planets, it tends to dominate the conversation. Pluto's main job is to transform whatever it touches from the inside out, and to help us see our inner power to make these changes in ourselves possible. Pluto has an all-or-nothing quality, so when Pluto touches a planet (or your natal Sun sign) things change quite dramatically. However, Pluto never works in sudden ways, thank goodness. Pluto's changes are gradual, but forceful. A well-aligned Pluto is always of enormous help—Pluto can truly move mountains.

Pluto is also the symbol of roots or buried treasure, so its job is to bring things to light. It can either expose the jewel that is hidden below or bring to light little-known truths that have festered in darkness for too long.

Many people mistakenly think Pluto is a harsh planet. Quite the contrary—Pluto can be your best friend. It's just that over the past few years Pluto behaved badly, and in so doing, gave itself a bad name. Luckily, Pluto is going to be your friend in 2004.

Pluto remains in Sagittarius in 2004, a journey this planet began in 1995. Pluto can take anywhere from 13 to 25 years to travel through a sign, depending on the speed of its elliptical orbit. This year, we find Pluto a little more than halfway through Sagittarius, as Pluto is not due to leave this sign until 2008. Sagittarius is a publishing and broadcasting sign, and so Pluto's long visit has made the world a great deal smaller.

Pluto in Sagittarius also affects religious dogma and moral and ethical beliefs. Morals and ethics will continue to be a source of public discussion, as they have been since Pluto entered Sagittarius in 1995. Sagittarius will not stand for pretentiousness, cheating, or hypocrisy, so Pluto will continue to reveal the inconsistencies or misbehavior of corporations and individuals.

NEPTUNE TO REMAIN IN AQUARIUS UNTIL 2012

Neptune began touring futuristic, electronic Aquarius in early 1998. Neptune has a lot to do with image and symbolism, so since then we've seen an indication of how easily technology, through the Internet, television, or air travel, can shrink a world community into a global village. Photography and music, the two areas ruled by Neptune, will continue to be the universal currency that unites people around the world. Now that music, photography, film, and TV have become digitized, it has taken on the electronic effects of Aquarius. Cultural ideas will no longer remain in one corner of the globe, but will spread like lightning to everyone, and will apply to a wide variety of situations. The idea that information should be free to all is an Aquarian notion. Aquarius—basically democratic in spirit—illustrates this point with the Internet, in which there is the potential for equal access for one and all.

Neptune will remain in Aquarius until early 2012, so there will be no changes in this area of your chart. Gone are the 1980's, when Neptune was in the more ambitious and money-and-status sign of Capricorn. Back then, all that mattered was the type of car you drove, the designer label you wore, the title on your business card.

Ever since Neptune entered Aquarius in 1998, values shifted. Something new and extraordinary occurred—suddenly it was cooler to be smart than rich. Aquarius is not a materialistic sign, so the idea of less being more became popular. Flashing logos and status symbols became tacky. Ideas and opinions set you apart, not the things you owned. Capricorn, an earth sign, deals with the things you can see and touch, while Aquarius, an air sign, is more interested in ideas.

Independence is a hallmark of Aquarius, but having a strong connection to community is also valued. So while we all want to be thought of as unique individuals, with Neptune remaining in Aquarius, enjoying a feeling of intellectual connectedness with others remains just as important. This is achieved through very Aquarian ways: the Internet, television, or through other means of creating a sense of community.

URANUS, PLANET OF SURPRISE, ARRIVES IN PISCES

Last year, Uranus made headline news when it moved out of Aquarius, a sign it had occupied for seven years, and into Pisces on March 10, 2003. Uranus had not occupied Pisces since the years 1919–1927, so only a few people alive today can remember this time. Even those who were alive during those Roaring Twenties were probably still quite young, so Uranus in Pisces will be a fresh experience for everyone. When a major planet like Uranus changes signs it is an exciting development because it shakes up the system we are accustomed to, and allows for new areas of growth.

This is *especially* true of Uranus. Uranus's job is to sweep away old, outmoded structures suddenly and swiftly, and replace them with something more relevant for the future. The hard part is that we have to decide what will replace these tired old structures, which is rarely an easy or quick decision. Uranus likes to test your resourcefulness and ingenuity.

Uranus is famous for lightning-like movements, creating and ending situations without warning. That is why it is called the "Great Awakener." While at times this planet's effect can be jarring, Uranus often triggers sudden epiphanies and moments of sheer brilliance. Ultimately, Uranus teaches us that change is good, and that we should learn to embrace it, for change is the single constant we can count on in our universe. As soon as we learn this simple lesson of Uranus, our lives will be easier.

When a major planet like Uranus changes signs, it is common for opinions, politics, music, art, and other signposts of the times to shift. Now that Uranus is posited in the imaginative and lyrical sign of Pisces, Uranus is poised to create a beneficial influence for the arts. Past ages of Uranus in Pisces produced magnificent breakthroughs in cultural arts, including literature, painting, sculpture, theater, architecture, music, and fashion. We are on the brink of another watershed era in this decade.

Last year Uranus entered Pisces on March 10, 2003, and remained in that sign until September 15 of that year, when Uranus retrograded back into Aquarius to make an appearance at a farewell party the other planets had planned for him. After all, Uranus will not be back to Aquarius for another 84 years! Then, on December 30, 2003, Uranus moved back into Pisces and unpacked his bags for a long stay—specifically, Uranus will remain in Pisces until 2011. How symbolic it was that Uranus hurried into Pisces to punctuate 2003, but will begin 2004 at his desk, fully ready for business in time for the new year. Uranus is sure to launch 2004 in style.

While in Aquarius, Uranus was happy—Uranus is the ruler of Aquarius, so that sign is considered his home base. The colors of Aquarius are neon and acidic—as lively as the half of grapefruit that we eat in the morning or as shockingly elegant as a fuchsia ball gown. If you know an Aquarian, you can practically see their brain light up when they have an idea. No wonder Uranus loved being in that sign!

With Uranus in Pisces, the colors and mood of society will shift to reflect this new sensibility. Pisces rules gentler, watery shades: multi-toned watercolor blues, violets, and sea greens. Accordingly, the feel and tenor of the times will soften as well. Aquarius is intellectual and sometimes a bit devoid of emotion—"dry," so to speak. But Uranus in Pisces is capable of countering the Aquarius cool, detached, intellectual sensibility with tremendous passion and an unfathomable depth of heartfelt emotion. It is no accident that the Sistine Chapel and the Mona Lisa were painted during a Uranus in Pisces phase.

Will Uranus be just as happy in Pisces? Oh yes! Thanks to a mutual reception between Neptune and Uranus, you can bet Uranus will express its highest powers in Pisces!

URANUS AND NEPTUNE WILL BE IN MUTUAL RECEPTION, A WONDERFUL BONUS FOR ONE AND ALL!

We are lucky in that in the coming year—and indeed throughout this decade—we will enjoy a very rare "mutual reception" between Uranus and Neptune, considered in astrology to be quite a blessing.

A "mutual reception" occurs whenever two planets visit the sign that the other one *rules* simultaneously. Neptune, the planet that rules Pisces, will be *visiting* Aquarius. Meanwhile, Uranus, the planet that *rules* Aquarius, will be *visiting* Pisces. Neptune in mutual reception with Uranus will mitigate Uranus's jarring side effects, and provide us with a softer landing. In turn, Uranus will see to it that Neptune has a sharper and more far-reaching visionary focus. Both planets are highly creative: Uranus is associated more with the sciences, while Neptune, with the arts.

This rare cooperation between Neptune and Uranus increases the chances that Uranus's visit to Pisces will give a stronger-than-usual boost to the arts. Uranus in Pisces alone would certainly encourage creativity, but in mutual reception with Neptune, the planet that happens to rule the arts? Wow, now that's potent!

Uranus takes 84 years to go around the Sun while Neptune takes 214 years. That is why a mutual reception between this pair is so exceedingly rare. As you see, we are quite lucky to have this situation! While this will have the most benefit for Pisces and Aquarians, every sign will benefit from this wonderful interaction between Uranus and Neptune.

WITH URANUS IN PISCES, FOCUS IS ON SPIRITUALITY AND THE ARTS

When Uranus toured Aquarius from 1995 to 2003, society put enormous emphasis on science, technology, and industrial progress, specifically the Internet and electronics. Now the pendulum will swing in the other direction, toward spirituality and the arts. Like Aquarius, Pisces is not a materialistic sign. You can expect even greater emphasis on quality of life, close relationships, and one's inner spiritual development with Uranus in Pisces.

Pisces is a sign that rules religion, theology, and our belief system, so the philosophical search for meaning in our lives will become deeper and more powerful. With Uranus in Pisces, traditional religions may update their doctrines to become more current. Religion will be discussed on an international level in a way we haven't yet seen. We will also need to broaden our understanding of other cultures' spiritual beliefs. Religion and spirituality will also become more significant on a personal and private level.

We noted earlier that Pluto in Sagittarius will focus on religion and morals, but in a more intellectual, less emotional, heartfelt way. It is common in astrology for differing trends to be operating at the same time—both will form part of the cosmic soup that is being cooked up. Sagittarius is a sign that learns about the world through debate and through what one reads and hears, but Pisces senses the changing currents in the air by osmosis. Both on an emotional and intellectual front, the topics of religion, morals, ethics, theology, and metaphysics will move increasingly to the forefront of our minds.

Now that Uranus is in Pisces, intuition, ESP, and other "fuzzy" areas, also ruled by Pisces, are not likely to be as swiftly dismissed by critics. Society will be more inclined to investigate these little-understood areas of human experience.

Pisces rules influences from the East, so there may be greater interest in learning about Asian culture, especially the cuisine, Eastern medicine such as acupuncture, and fitness, such as tai chi and the martial arts.

Pisces is one of the most creative and mysterious signs in the zodiac. Pisces focuses on the subconscious mind, the place from which many of our ideas spring forth. Older cultures tell us that not everything can be understood within our lifetime. Pisces, the sign that is comfortable with ambiguity, understands this, and relies on dreams and honed intuition to point the way. Pisces knows that facts are often inaccurate or biased, so Pisces will rely on their gut feeling to make decisions.

There is a universal, caring quality about Pisces, and a willingness to sacrifice for the good of others. Another trend, which will emerge over the next seven years, is a renewed sense of idealism on a global level, especially among the young, who will, through volunteer work, help the unfortunate (Uranus rules youth).

Thanks to Uranus in Pisces, the oceans of the world—considered by many to be the next great frontier—will become a source of major interest from the scientific community. Also watch for a breakthrough in the scientific understanding of what happens to our body when at rest, an area ruled by Pisces. Those who suffer from a sleep disorder may learn something new which can help them.

The social sciences—social work, psychology, psychoanalysis, and other humanitarian disciplines—should also advance under this trend, with Uranus in compassionate Pisces.

We will feel the effects of Uranus, not only on a societal level, but also on an intimate, personal level. Look to the area of life that Uranus will touch in your chart (to be found in your sign's chapter). Whatever area of your chart Uranus is in, you can be sure it will be revolutionized. If you've struggled with old, stubborn situations that were impossible to change, just wait until Uranus has time to work its magic. A dream you've had for a long time may suddenly seem possible. If so, go for it!

SATURN TO REMAIN IN CANCER UNTIL JULY 2005

Saturn entered Cancer on June 3, 2003, and will remain in this sign until July 16, 2005. A visit to a sign by Saturn is rare; Saturn takes 29 years to circle through all 12 signs of the zodiac and we get only two or three visits from Saturn to the house of our horoscope during our lifetime. A typical visit to each house, which rules an area of life, lasts approximately two years.

Saturn rules the maturity we gain as we take on responsibilities and learn life's lessons. Saturn teaches us the value of sacrificing to meet big goals, often ones we assumed were beyond our reach. Saturn also shows us that success comes only through meticulous preparation, arduous effort, and enormous dedication. Saturn's rewards are considerable, so it's worth it to meet any challenge Saturn has in mind. Saturn will never ask more of you than you are capable.

Saturn, the taskmaster planet, coaches us to become better versions of ourselves, but this boot camp experience can be hard to endure. However, this year we're in luck. Ancient astrologers noticed that when Saturn was in the sign that was opposite to the sign it ruled (and Saturn rules Capricorn) Saturn was "in its detriment." Now that Saturn is in Cancer, six months from its home base, Saturn will be in detriment from 2004 to the first part of 2005. As a result, Saturn will exert a weaker signal in Cancer. This is good: we generally don't like it when Saturn is operating on high!

However, the danger here is that Saturn in its detriment is more likely to emphasize its more negative vibrations. So, for example, in food/family/shelter-oriented Cancer, Saturn could expose problems with tainted food. Or there could be an increase in eating disorders between now and July 2005. Should this happen, however, we will be prepared to cope with these issues.

Cancer rules food, so Saturn in Cancer will focus on the need to eat in a healthier manner. Expect developments in the areas of food production and distribution over the next two years to make food safer and fresher. Fat-filled fast food will become even more of a no-no, if that is possible! Smart fast-food marketers will make swift adjustments to cater to a swelling consumer demand for healthier choices. (Jupiter in Virgo will bring a similar trend, as you will see in the next section. When two planets encourage development in the same direction, the trend is sure to be a big one.) The dietary needs of the poor, the elderly, and children—whether in the school system or in day care centers—will also be on the national agenda.

Saturn in Cancer will place more emphasis on family relationships, particularly with one's parents. If your relationship with
your mother or father (or both) has been stormy, this transit may
challenge you to confront the situation and make peace. Cancer
also rules emotions, so while you may find it hard to open up
(Saturn tends to constrict feelings, especially in Cancer) it will
be an eye-opening experience if you do. You must exchange
information with others—whether with the person who is
troubling you, or others who may be in a position to help—to
solve this long-standing difficulty. If you are fortunate to have a
solid relationship with your parents, Saturn may instead, during
this trend, ask you to help one of them in a substantial way, such
as to care for a parent if he or she isn't feeling well.

Cancer is a water sign, so the safety of our water supply
will also be discussed. Also with Saturn in Cancer, cruise ships
may experience a downturn in tourism. They may be forced to
become more creative to drum up business.

Cancer rules housing, so the presence of Saturn may
depress the market, which has been booming over the last few
years. Indeed, interest rates may climb again as Saturn in
Cancer will make it more difficult to find—and afford—a new
house, co-op apartment, or condominium.

Be careful about buying in a neighborhood where valua-
tions may be inflated. Some neighborhoods may see a decline
in property value, as Saturn tends to constrict real estate prices
while in Cancer. If looking to buy, you may find that what you
see is small and expensive. If this is true, look again after
Saturn leaves Cancer, which will be in July 2005.

Hotels and restaurants fall under Cancer, so the hotel industry
may undergo reorganization. Saturn's presence suggests mergers
might consolidate some big hotel or restaurant chains. If hotels
and restaurants (like the Cancer-ruled industries of cruise lines,

home décor, and kitchen supply) can survive this shakeout period, those that do will be all the stronger for it.

In medicine, expect research and development to advance in the area of breast cancer, as Cancer rules the breasts. Women should be careful to get mammograms during Saturn in Cancer (this year through mid-2005).

The United States is a Cancer country, for it is "born" on July 4. President George W. Bush is also a Cancer, born July 6. With Saturn in Cancer, there will be increased belt-tightening. Saturn forces us to make the most of available resources, and that will mean making some hard choices. (Jupiter in discriminating Virgo will echo this theme in a different way; see below.)

Don't expect this country to come out of its current economic difficulties quickly. Saturn will hold things down until at least July 2005. Saturn works slowly for a reason—its job is to see that we do things the proper way. Saturn insists that certain procedures and standards of excellence are adhered to, for it is never satisfied with a "band-aid" fix. After this Saturn period, things will be back on track, stronger than ever. Don't be anxious—just follow a prudent and conservative course.

Saturn toured Gemini from late 2000 through mid-2003. Now that Saturn is out of Gemini, the communications industry will thrive and prosper again, proving that certain sectors can do well despite the problems that other industries may encounter in the next 18 months. Book, magazine, newspaper, and Internet publishing should start to thrive again. Tech stocks should climb too, but without the bubble that made them previously unstable. The advertising industry, lately in the doldrums, will perk up, and public relations firms should see a fresh crop of new business. Air travel, so hard hit by Saturn in Gemini, should regain its footing, much to the amazement of many industry observers.

Saturn often tests the strength of purpose of people and organizations, but if an endeavor is sound, it can weather any storm. While no one likes to have to undergo the rigors of a market correction, it does have value in revealing which companies and individuals are fittest. We know those organisms that are highly adaptable will thrive. These hearty survivors are not necessarily the strongest specimens, but are the most willing to make quick adjustments when gale storm winds start kicking up. The overriding message is flexibility, a theme that will grow in importance in the upcoming months.

BREAKTHROUGHS IN HEALTH, HEALING, AND THE LITERARY FRONT THANKS TO JUPITER IN VIRGO

Jupiter is the planet of good fortune and happiness, so it is often a strong indicator of bountiful opportunity in the year ahead. Everyone always wants to know where Jupiter will be in their charts!

The big news this year is the visit of Jupiter to two signs, Virgo and Libra.

Virgo is known to be a very discriminating sign, so with Jupiter moving through it this year, Virgo will take the power of Jupiter and focus it into very narrow, precise applications. This is a contradiction for Jupiter, as it likes to work on a huge, panoramic scale. Still, Jupiter's power will not decrease; it will become only more focused. Jupiter will help us use our resources wisely and to find practical applications for our dreams and aspirations. Don't expect helium-filled ideas to fly during the first nine months of 2004—they will be too lightweight to be taken seriously. Instead, Jupiter in this sign will demand an earthy, pragmatic, hands-on approach. Jupiter in Virgo is not flamboyant, nor is it wasteful. Make sure during this time to present your ideas with plenty of facts and charts to support your position.

Jupiter in Virgo also tells us to be selfless and nurturing and to realize that the best reward is to help those desperately in need of assistance.

This coming year, you will likely see movies and books with juicy, complex plots. How refreshing! Virgo is considered a strongly literary sign, so, for example, if a film has special effects, it had better have a smart story line as well! Audiences will demand it.

There may be strong technical advances during this time. Anyone who has ever written or seen computer code knows that one needs a precise, detailed, and eagle-eyed Virgo mind to excel in fields like that!

Virgo rules nursing and certain healing arts, and happily, Jupiter will foster the expansion of these fields. Recent news stories have chronicled how dearly we need more hospitals, nursing homes, rehabilitation facilities, as well as qualified nurses and nurses' aides to tend to the infirmed. Jupiter's job is to expand everything it touches, so there's hope that qualified professionals will be found and compensated fairly for their work.

Natural, homeopathic remedies also fall under Virgo, as this sign is associated with the softer, more caring side of healing. Massage therapy, aromatherapy, Reiki, and acupuncture are due for expansion in 2004.

Fitness and eating in a lighter, healthier way will get an additional boost in 2004, with Jupiter in Virgo. With this extra help, I wouldn't be surprised if healthy fast-food restaurants began to appear. It's good to keep an open mind—all kinds of new developments may come now under this influence!

JUPITER IN RETROGRADE FROM JANUARY TO EARLY MAY

As the year begins, Jupiter will retrograde on January 3, 2004. A retrograde orbit is considered a resting state, so Jupiter, the planet of good fortune, will operate at a weaker signal. Jupiter will remain retrograde until May 4, 2004. Being that Jupiter is associated with profit and financial gain, it would be wiser to incorporate or launch a new business *after* Jupiter returns to direct speed on May 4, 2004. Jupiter will not retrograde again until February 2005, so you will be free and clear.

We are lucky that Jupiter in Virgo blends exceptionally well with Saturn in Cancer. With Saturn in such good angle to Jupiter in early May and mid-August 2004, opportunities to create sturdy foundations for the future are possible. Projects and relationships you begin in early to middle 2004 should develop sturdily.

WHO BENEFITS MOST FROM JUPITER IN VIRGO? MAYBE YOU!

Naturally, when you have Jupiter in *your* sign, you are the celestial favorite. This is Virgo for most of 2004. This planet comes but once in 12 years, so this year is sure to be something special for Virgos. Other signs that will surely benefit from Jupiter in Virgo are Capricorn, Taurus, Pisces, Cancer, and Scorpio.

JUPITER IN LIBRA FROM SEPTEMBER 25, 2004, WILL USHER IN A ROMANTIC AND SOCIAL MOOD FOR ONE AND ALL

If Jupiter in Virgo concentrates on hard work, focus, and the value of selfless service to others, Jupiter in Libra will balance this trend by introducing a lovely relaxing period that encourages parties, dressing up, and going out. Spa treatments, elegant dinners, shopping, and similar fun activities will come to life again. Hooray!

Jupiter in Libra tells us to get things done in a relaxed social way. By mingling with others, you can advance professional and personal goals, possibly finding your soul mate or broadening your circle of friends. Joining clubs and networking are all very Libra-oriented activities, so plan to step out once Jupiter arrives in Libra, from September 24, 2004, through October 25, 2005—the first visit in 12 years.

Libra rules the clever strategist as well as the fair negotiator, judge, or mediator. The scales symbolize ultimate balance, so as soon as Jupiter enters Libra, watch for advances in the courts and judicial system, as well as in international diplomacy.

Jupiter in Libra will stimulate conversation and the exchange of ideas. People will also be in the mood to make formal agreements with partners, either in business or on a personal level (such as getting married). Libra is the ultimate sign of partnering and marriage. Agents, representatives, and specialized consultants will also do well. Libra loves an intellectual debate. In 2004 there is a good chance that an interesting public debate will surface, perhaps arising from arguments presented in high-profile (and public) litigation, or a Supreme Court case that captures the public's interest.

With Jupiter in Libra, professional matchmakers—consultants who introduce single people with compatible interests and backgrounds to one another— should begin to find success. Singles won't suffer loneliness in silence any longer— they'll be more determined to find better, safer ways to meet new and intriguing people. Internet dating may also increase (anything that increases social interaction is "Libra" in spirit), but Libra is not known to be as technology oriented as

Aquarius or Gemini. It is possible that with Jupiter in Libra, a live person—a matchmaker—would be favored over the Internet to link singles.

The demand for jewelry, flowers, perfume, cosmetics, lingerie, or other industries involved in adornment or the home decorative arts will increase, from late August 2004 through September 2005. Pastels and soft powdery colors may become fashionable—nothing too harsh for the Jupiter-in-Libra sensibility! The cultural arts will also flourish, with higher-than-usual attendance at museums, Broadway plays, and concerts, for example.

The Libras among us will enjoy the benefits of Jupiter the most, although other signs, such as Gemini, Aquarius, Leo, Aries, and Sagittarius, will benefit as well.

THE PERSONAL PLANETS, MARS, MERCURY, AND VENUS, AND THEIR AFFECT ON YOUR YEAR AHEAD

The personal planets, Mercury, Venus, and Mars, orbit close to the Sun. They move more swiftly than the outer planets, and influence us daily instead of on a yearly basis. Let's explore what these planets are up to this year and identify several sparkling dates for your calendar.

MARS, PLANET OF ENERGY, IS THE ZODIAC'S TIMEKEEPER

Mars, being the great warrior planet, tells us a great deal about our focus and drive, and, through its position in the chart, suggests where you might place your best energy. Mars also gives astrologers a good sense of the timing of events, so it is often called the zodiac's timekeeper.

This year, Mars is quick, strong, and sure, and won't dither in any particular sign for any long period like it did last year. In 2003, Mars spent a long time (six months) in Pisces and most of us were forced to focus on one main area. This occurred between June and December 2003. This will not happen this year.

In 2004, Mars zooms from Aries through Sagittarius— nine signs in all—which differs significantly from last year, when Mars visited only *five* signs. With almost double the number of houses of the horoscope to visit, Mars will provide many opportunities on a variety of fronts for you. This also suggests that productivity will be high in many areas of our lives.

However, caution is needed on the following three days: March 28, August 18, and December 31, 2004. On these days, Mars will be in a reckless mood, which means that difficulties may manifest in a physical (we may become accident prone) or emotional way (we, or others, will be temperamental). In each case, Mars is at a harsh angle to Uranus, planet of unexpected events, so exercise caution.

During this time, you may not be at fault—another driver might cut you off on the road, for example, causing your car to become nicked. On these days, be extra determined not to provoke anyone who appears hot and bothered. These are also not the best days to schedule a performance review with your boss or to speak to your lover about a matter that's been troubling you. These dates have a plus or minus of seven days, so their area of influence is quite wide. Mars will "square" Uranus on the first and last day listed, and will directly oppose Uranus on the middle day. All three days are times when we and others will be physically and emotionally unstable and more likely to make poor judgments. Make safety and serenity a priority!

FEBRUARY 26, MAY 24, AND NOVEMBER 15 ARE OUTSTANDING DAYS TO GAIN STRONG MARS ENERGY IN 2004

Mars will warmly reach out to Jupiter on February 26, making it your first outstanding day. Check your own sign's chapter to learn how best to use this date. Mars (energy) in combination with Jupiter (good fortune) is a happy circumstance. But before you head to the store to buy a lottery ticket, realize that astrology requires you to exert a little energy to uncover your luck. This would be a terrific day for an interview, presentation, or romantic date. (In terms of winning the lottery, Scorpio is the only sign favored.)

On May 24 and November 15, Mars will send a beautiful vibe to Uranus. Surprises galore are sure to keep your spirits high! Check your individual forecast to see how you can make this day work for you

VENUS CUDDLES UP TO HER COSMIC LOVER, MARS, ON TWO OCCASIONS IN 2004

When Venus and Mars are together, they always create hot and sexy sparks. For the start of new love, it's hard to beat the combination of these two planets.

Your first wonder period for love arrives April 10 through May 9. Although Mars and Venus won't actually touch during this period (this isn't actually an exact conjunction) Mars will come close enough to sniff Venus's delicate perfume and to be enticed by her beauty. If you're single or even if you are attached and looking for more attention from your main squeeze, this is the time when you might get what you want!

Venus and Mars will also cuddle in Gemini, and although this is good news for *all* signs, it will be an outstanding romantic period for air and fire signs, including Gemini, Libra, Aquarius, Aries, Leo, and Sagittarius.

Venus Is Retrograde from May 17 Through June 29, 2004, Weakening Her Powers

Venus will retrograde in the same, intellectual sign of Gemini, from May 17 through June 29. During this retrograde period, you may radically change your mind about a sweetheart or a certain financial matter. You may also need to revisit a decision you thought had been finalized.

During this Venus retrograde period, it would *not* be a good time to go on a blind date, get engaged or married, or throw a major party. Venus rules money and social events, so it is also not a good time to schedule a fund-raising benefit.

It is also *not* a good time to schedule plastic surgery or other beauty treatments, or to buy any expensive clothes or jewelry, fragrances, or cosmetics—all ruled by Venus. When it comes to beauty, you want Venus to be wide-awake!

If you are wondering, Venus did not retrograde in 2003.

Glittering Venus Days in 2004

July 16 is sure to be a wonder day to note on your calendar, when good-fortune Jupiter will give a kiss to beautiful Venus. This is a fabulous day for love, particularly for Libra and Taurus, two signs ruled by Venus.

September 2 will be nearly as special (I am splitting hairs here), as Jupiter will be at a gorgeous angle (trine) to Venus. These dates and the few days before and after them will be outstanding ones for any Venus activity—love, beauty, fun, and leisure. These dates are ideal for a vacation, shopping, having a consultation with a hair stylist, or even having your photograph taken.

November 4 is another four-star date night, when Jupiter and Venus again conjoin. Imagine having *two* of these sparkling days in one year!

December 4, however, is one of *the* best of the best romantic days of the year! Venus and Mars will finally fully engage in an intoxicating embrace—a true astrological conjunction—and it will happen in the passionate and emotional sign of Scorpio. This will be the *only* time in 2004 that these two cosmic lovers will actually touch in exact conjunction, something that didn't happen at all in 2003. This is a hot date!

The sparkling influence of December 4 will be wider than just one day. You may want to mark down the last ten days of November and the first two weeks of December for more romantic dates! This comes at the height of holiday time! Water and earth signs, including Scorpio, Pisces, Cancer, Taurus, Virgo, and Capricorn, will benefit most from this influence.

See how evenhanded the year will be? First the air and fire signs get their turn to gain Venus's favor in June, and in December, it's the turn of the water and earth signs. The universe is ultimately symmetrical—in time, we all get our turn.

THE SUN, MOON, AND MERCURY

The Sun and Moon are also critical to consider when we look at the year ahead, especially in regard to the personal planets. In this book, I discuss their effects in the chapter on eclipses. Eclipses are some of the most powerful indicators of change in all of astrology.

Mercury, the objective, brainy planet in charge of perception, communication, transportation, and commerce, will also be discussed later in a chapter called Mercury Retrograde. Although all planets retrograde, Mercury's retrograde period affects us more than any other.

Mercury's most dazzling days are perfect for signing contracts, brainstorming for good ideas, making presentations to clients (Mercury rules buying and selling), traveling, speaking to groups, or discussing important matters with someone you love.

HERE ARE YOUR BEST MERCURY DATES IN 2004:

September 28: This is a four-star day, when Mercury and Jupiter join forces and you will benefit. This will be the only day in 2004 when these two planets will be mathematically in exact conjunction. Expect it to be fantastic for all Mercury-ruled activities: writing, speaking, editing and research, coming up with ideas, selling, buying, traveling, and negotiating.

These two planets will meet in Libra, and will benefit early born Libras and all Virgos (but doubly so for those born near September 21). Gemini, Aquarius, Aries, Leo, and Sagittarius will also benefit.

January 29: Jupiter will send a golden ray to Mercury in a trine position, which is considered one of the most prized of all aspects. Again, this is an ideal day for all Mercury-ruled activities.

Capricorn, Taurus, Virgo, Gemini, Pisces, Cancer, and Scorpio will benefit.

May 23: This is the same aspect that fell on January 29. You will be articulate, intelligent, witty, and wise. The signs that benefit most are Taurus, Capricorn, Virgo, Cancer, Scorpio, and Pisces.

Another Mercury date to note is *June 25*, when you'll be concentrating well and at your persuasive best.

Surprise messages may come your way on the following dates, thanks to Uranus in elegant angle to Mercury.

January 15

May 24

The next two dates are even better:

June 22

October 17

Need to sign an agreement that can stand the test of time? Choose a date when Saturn is influencing Mercury in a positive way. You can allow two days prior to the following dates, but try not to sign *after* these dates, as the positive energy will be waning. The dates are:

February 28

May 25

June 26

September 26

November 2

A Few Parting Words

The life you create in 2004 is an outgrowth of all the decisions you've made—big ones, little ones—over the course of a lifetime. The sum total of those decisions has brought you to the place you find yourself today.

We can't be masters of our fate unless we take an active role in that process. By studying astrology, we learn that the first house of the horoscope rules your personality and strength of your character and determines much of your destiny. State your intentions to the world, for if you don't, the universe will see to it that decisions are made for you.

Astrology can help you set your compass and send you to a place of rich self-discovery. We all want to live exciting lives, where we are loved, are successful, and are using our innate talents to the fullest. You can have it all with just a little effort!

Aries

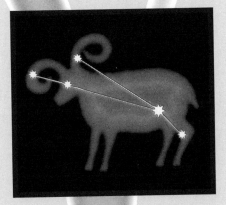

March 21–April 19

The Big Picture

This will be a far more active year than last year was for you, and for a sign as enthusiastic and energetic as yours, dear Aries, that has to be cheery news. Last year, Mars, your ruler, dallied in a very weak area of your chart for months. You had little choice but to bide your time until better conditions prevailed and you could find the right time to act. Higher-ups that you depended upon for answers were stalled, which only added to your frustration. As you begin 2004, you can finally seize the day! There is no reason to hold back.

MARS FAVORS YOU IN JANUARY, A BIG PLUS

In January, your ruling planet, Mars, will be in Aries, putting you front and center until February 3, 2004. This is the best position you've been in for two years. Mars is strong in its home base sign because, in that sign, it can exert its strongest, purest form of energy. You should feel in tiptop condition as the year begins, full of vim and vigor, and bursting with big plans and enthusiasm.

The plans you choose to initiate during January will set the tone for much of the year. Mars in Aries will set up a new cycle, and others will look to you to set the tone. Being an Aries, you will be glad to oblige. It's sure to be glorious time for you and a strong contrast to the way things were!

Ideas and projects you present and the relationships you begin in January will be poised for exceptional growth. Don't be concerned with finalizing those projects immediately—there won't be enough time, nor is it especially important. What *is* important is that you take your first steps, for in astrology, starting any new endeavor while Mars tours your sign is very favorable. Concentrate on the projects that have the most potential and that get you the most fired up. While not every project and relationship that you begin during your Mars cycle will succeed, a far higher than usual number will, which is why it's critical that you send up as many trial balloons as possible during this phase.

If you are reading your copy of *The Year Ahead 2004* later than February 3, 2004 (the date Mars will leave this glorious position of Aries), look back in your calendar to see what new relationships and projects you *did* launch during this potent period. You may have already taken all the right steps. Those endeavors are the ones to watch as you move forward.

You will have additional help from the new moon near your birthday on April 1, so all is not lost if you did not act in January. That new moon will be a critical one, and though your window of opportunity is only two weeks, it's powerful, so try to be ready for it.

HEALTH AND FITNESS:
A BIG AREA OF POSSIBLE IMPROVEMENT

One of the largest areas of focus for your year ahead will be on achieving radiant health and renewed fitness. If you've wanted to lose some added pounds and improve your looks, you will have the best year in the decade to accomplish that goal. Jupiter's move into your sixth house of health should bring you all the opportunities you need to do so. In addition, with Saturn's sharp angle to your Sun in 2004, you should be able to lose pounds more easily than any previous year. (Indeed, having Saturn in challenging angle does have its privileges, and losing weight is one of them.) Watch in September, particularly, for evidence that radiant health is within reach.

Later in the year, romance and commitment will surface as a major trend, too. If, for example, one of your goals is marriage, children, or a house or condominium, your chart shows the planets will work in your favor to ensure you have all or most of those trappings this year, or by the end of 2005. October should be a vital month for marriage or for any type of serious collaboration, including business partnerships.

WATCH HOME, PROPERTY, AND FAMILY RELATIONSHIPS

The areas of tension this year will relate to your residence, property, or a relationship with—or concern about—a close family member, most likely a parent. The universe sends certain tensions to help us grow and mature, and these areas will help you show the world that you are made of stronger stuff than anyone assumed. Saturn will be in hard angle to your Sun all year, continuing into the first half of 2005.

March-born Aries have already faced some of these tensions in 2003 and may be done (or almost done) with these challenges. Those born from March 29 to April 17 will feel these tensions in 2004. Aries with birthdays that fall after April 19 will step up to the plate for home-related challenges in the first six months of 2005. (There is a little overlap for those Aries born April 10–17 in 2004 and 2005, but no member of Aries will have Saturn any more or less than anyone else—everyone gets about six months of Saturn.)

Knowing there will a blinking yellow light in your fourth house of home and family will help you prepare for any eventuality. For example, if you know your lease on your apartment is up in mid-2004 but that you might have problems finding an apartment (now that Saturn is touring Cancer), you should start your search for a new place earlier to give yourself more time and options.

ECLIPSES EMPHASIZE LIFESTYLE, RELATIONSHIPS, AND A REORGANIZATION OF FINANCES

The eclipses this year will create possible tension but will also bring reward. Always key indicators of change, these lunar and solar events are considered the wild cards of the year's equation, for they usually bring up sudden, unanticipated conditions. They are meant to help us become more adaptable, flexible, and decisive. At eclipse time, either you make a decision or the decision is made for you by forceful conditions.

In your case, the most challenging eclipses fall in financial houses in May and late October, so it looks as though one source of income will dry up and a new source will appear, although those two events may not dovetail exactly at the same time. It is also possible that you won't have to give up your present income—it could be that you add one, although this possibility is probably less common.

One of the most important eclipses in 2004 will fall in Aries on April 19. Luckily, it is a highly friendly eclipse and will help you see yourself in a whole new light. You have been growing and maturing, but your self-image may need to play catch up. If so, this eclipse will help. Those Aries born at the end of their sign, on or near April 19, will feel this eclipse most powerfully.

Happily, the eclipse that falls on April 19 could send you off in a new direction. Your lifestyle will almost certainly change, and so could your looks and style of clothing you wear. Through it all, new skills and talents you possess will be called into play. You are always up for an adventure, and this eclipse will bring you that. You should start to see changes near your birthday, although some readers will see these shifts happening one month later, within four days of May 19. Other Aries, a smaller minority, will notice that the eclipse delivers news a month prior to the April 19 eclipse, within four days of March 19.

PLUTO, NEPTUNE, AND URANUS WILL BE FRIENDLY IN 2004

You are lucky that the three major outer planets, namely Pluto, Uranus, and Neptune, will remain in friendly positions to your Sun all year. This "band of three" will not challenge your sign in any major way. Thank your lucky stars!

This year Uranus will sharpen your intuition and your psychic ability. Don't let anyone second-guess you, dear Aries. Your sign is known to often rely on gut instinct, but now your ability to do so will be outstanding—you'll outdo yourself!

Meanwhile, Neptune will bring inspiration and encouragement from friends and from groups or clubs to which you now belong (or soon will).

In November of 2004, Neptune will be in supreme angle to Jupiter, the planet of good fortune, and will be positioned by then in your house of marriage and close alliances. This is the equivalent of having a beautiful, fragrant bouquet delivered to your doorstep by a caring universe. There appears to be someone in your life—or someone who will soon be in your life—who will inspire you to become your best version of yourself. How lovely this person's vibration will be! Aries born on April 1 or close to that date will be doubly fortunate, as the mathematical degrees of these planets will reach out and touch you.

Meanwhile, Pluto will help you open the shutters of your mind and let the light flow in. Your ideas and attitudes are reflecting a more panoramic view of the world, dear Aries, and if in the past you sprouted the views of your parents or friends, in 2004 your opinions will more likely reflect your own thoughts and life experiences. Pluto's effect should be quite exhilarating and expansive in 2004. Those best poised to take advantage of this will be Aries born April 8–11.

In early August, Pluto and Jupiter will oppose one another, which suggests you may team up with a powerful person who will act as a catalyst for bigger things for you. (If self-employed, you may, alternatively, form a joint venture with a global company.) You also may be asked to update an important long-term project. This project may go back to something you started back in 1994–1995.

If you are not enthusiastic about this extra work, you will need to decide, in early August, whether to stay with the project or end it. The universe wants you to spend your time on things that matter, so this aspect will help you clarify your feelings and put your energy where it will do the most good.

That's a good outline of the broad strokes of the year, but now we will explore in more depth all the areas you want to know about: love, marriage, career, home, health, fitness, and travel.

Details on the Biggest Trends of Your Year Ahead

GET SLEEK AND FIT
FROM JANUARY THROUGH SEPTEMBER 2004

If you have always wanted to be the person on those TV commercials who is shown in the sexy "after" photographs, this may be your best year to achieve that goal. Jupiter in Virgo, touring your sixth house of health for the first time in 12 years, is now in one of the very best positions in your chart to help you create the kind of lifestyle changes that will help you not only lose weight but keep it off. Jupiter is the happiness planet and in health-conscious Virgo, you will learn to focus your health-related goals with a powerful intensity.

Saturn's excellent position to Jupiter in 2004 stabilizes Jupiter's benefits masterfully near May 1 and August 17 (plus or minus two weeks for both dates). If you set up new habits and routines during that time, you can expect your results to last. Wonderful!

As an Aries, you are considered an athletic, energetic sign, for your ruler, Mars, gives you an enjoyment of competitive, strenuous sports. If you are true to your sign, you are already ahead of the game, because being active is one of the best ways to stay trim throughout your lifetime. With Mars in Aries in January, it is a good time to get the ball rolling for renewed fitness. You will soon be feeling like a million bucks!

With Jupiter touring Virgo, the sign of the harvest, you may now develop a greater interest in fresh fruits and vegetables, moving away from foods that do nothing to nourish you. Jupiter in the sixth house may also give you an interest in herbs, aromatherapy, acupuncture, and other natural forms of physical rejuvenation.

This will be your year to concentrate on getting a specialist's opinion on any chronic (or any other) medical condition that you would like to improve or even cure. Jupiter will remain in this house until September 24, 2004, so you will have nearly nine months to see progress.

Often readers ask me, "If I have health problems this year, does this mean Jupiter isn't working in my chart?" Not at all. If something does show up, you will be in the best cycle of the decade for finding a way to heal.

Dear Aries, I had your glittering health aspects—Jupiter in the solar sixth house—when I was told it would be too dangerous for me to have a second child. I was pregnant at the time, and desperately wanted a second baby. By doing some research and asking lots of questions of health professionals, I found, quite by accident, the only specialist in the world who had written a book about my rare condition: a congenital internal bleeding problem that could easily kill me in child-birth. The specialist I found worked with my obstetrician, allowing me to give birth to Diana, my beautiful second child.

Jupiter is associated with traditional medical techniques and may be able to help you, even at times when a good out-come might seem against the odds. You have every reason to be optimistic, dear Aries.

WORK ASSIGNMENTS AND ENVIRONMENT SHOULD IMPROVE NOTICEABLY IN 2004

Jupiter will help you improve not only your health in 2004 but also your working conditions, as the sixth house of the horo-scope rules both work *and* health. To be clear, the sixth house does not rule career fame, professional honors, or promotions; those are covered by the tenth house. Instead, the sixth house rules service to others, daily work projects, and team efforts. Under this type of influence, an assignment you receive could easily lead you to bigger and better things.

This would be an ideal year to hire assistants, whether in your office or at home (such as a babysitter or housekeeper). The person(s) you hire this year could turn out to be wonder-ful, and help to make *you* look better. Co-workers will likely be positive and helpful.

In 2004, you may consider buying new electronic equip-ment to make you more organized and efficient, such as a cell phone, fax machine, or computer. If so, try to make your pur-chases during the first nine months of the year—ideally, in the second half of August. Avoid Mercury retrograde periods, as it is never a good idea to buy expensive electronic items when Mercury, the planet ruling information, is out of phase (see Mercury retrograde chapter).

Aries is happiest when self-employed, so this could be the year you launch your own home-based business. The ruler of your tenth house of fame and honors (Saturn) will be posited in your fourth house of home. Even if you don't start a home-based business, it would be wise to entertain more at home in 2004, as doing so would benefit you financially. You will be cooking up lots of activity at home!

YOUR BEST DAY OF THE YEAR IS SEPTEMBER 21, 2004

Every year, we have *one* day that surpasses all others. That is usually is the day when mighty, fortunate Jupiter is precisely aligned with the Sun. Oh happy day! This year your lucky day is September 21 and will affect job and health matters because these heavenly bodies, Jupiter and the Sun, will meet in your sixth house, the area of your chart I have been describing.

You haven't had a date quite like this in 12 years, so it's sure to be something special. However, keep in mind that this date falls on a Saturday, so you will have to schedule things a bit earlier in the week, as some professionals are not available on a weekend. Try to use the days *leading* up to your lucky day—when energy is still building in strength—rather than the days *after* September 21, when the energy of this magical conjunction will be diminishing.

Below I list some ideas of how to use this fabulous cosmic energy for health and work:

○ Schedule a first appointment with a new doctor or dentist, or schedule surgery for a medical or dental procedure on the days preceding September 21. Start scheduling from September 15 onward.

○ If you simply want to get stronger or fit, join a gym on the days leading to September 21. If you already belong to a gym, you might treat yourself to a package of sessions with a personal trainer.

○ Consult with a nutritionist, sign up for a diet meal plan, or join a club like Weight Watchers. If you've been thinking of learning a new sport, this would be an ideal day to start taking lessons in a new sport or exercise routine, like pilates or tai chi.

○ Undergo a cosmetic procedure, such as having your teeth whitened or consulting with a dermatologist, that falls within the health category.

○ Plan a hiking or camping trip for the second half of September (your key date being the 21st). An active vacation would refresh and relax you, dear Aries, and you'd return home radiant.

You may get an important, lucrative new assignment on or near September 21, 2004. A day or two before that date would be a fine time to interview for a job or do a presentation for a client.

○ If you're looking for a second job to improve your cash flow, now may be the right time. This year, your second job may turn out to be more enjoyable than your main job and send you down a dramatically new path. This second job might grow out of a hobby, as hobbies are under the influence of the sixth house. Hence, you might start a business out of love for a hobby. You might recognize that your hobby has considerable profit potential and you may decide to start a business out of it! Take your ideas and passions seriously this year. Huge trees often grow from a single acorn.

Nothing we do is small or insignificant. Astrology teaches us to live in the moment and to give everything we have to make our lives the best they can be. Just as an actor with a small part can sometimes steal the show, so too can you.

Take time to look closely at a project to find something special in it that allows you develop it. You will dumbfound everyone who had perceived the project only with smallest possible parameters. You will get the last laugh when you get your promotion! Others are watching you and will be impressed with your talent, perception, and drive.

Launch Health and Fitness-Related Goals After the New Moon September 24

We already established that the period of January through September 24 should be glorious for health and work-related efforts, and that September 21 is also an amazing date for these matters this year. There will be one more extra strong period that falls within that time span that you might want to note.

Begin your fitness or medical program at the favorable new moon in Virgo on September 14 or any time in the two weeks that follow. Your strongest period will occur September 14–21. This is also true for work-related goals. You will be *very* busy in the second half of September, so have some ways to burn off steam, dear Aries, so you don't become exhausted!

While for Aries, this year won't be strong for career advancement, there will be several opportunities for you to make your big move. During those times you will need to be nimble and decisive. These opportunities will appear quickly but will disappear just as fast.

Watch the New Moon January 7 and Full Moon July 2 for Major Career Accolades

Your best bet for gaining a promotion or new prestigious job will be in the two weeks following the new moon January 7 or six months later, at the full moon, July 2, plus or minus four days.

Of the two, I like the opportunities of January best, as that new moon affords you a wider window in which to act. If you do interview for a new position in January, it will likely come with quite weighty responsibility, as Saturn opposes that new moon.

If you are still interviewing for jobs in June, the full moon on July 2 will clarify your situation and bring an answer about that position on July 2, plus or minus four days.

Your Residence, Property, or Family/Domestic Matter May Bring Added Responsibility

Last year, in June 2003, Saturn entered Cancer for the first time in 29 years and began a challenging period in regard to home, property, and family relationships. Whatever questions came up in the second part of 2003 were not quickly or easily solved. Saturn won't leave your fourth house of home until July 2005, which represents a long trend. The good news is that you won't feel Saturn's pressures the whole time, but only when Saturn is in exact mathematical hard angle to your Sun.

Some Aries already faced the toughest part of this trend last year. If you have a birthday that falls from March 21–26, you faced your hardest trials in 2003 and will have an easier time in 2004. You are, for the most part, done with the main part of Saturn's challenges and probably have made a few decisions already.

Those born from March 26 to April 16 will feel tension in 2004. If your birthday is then, by the end of the year, you too will be done with your tests.

Aries born after April 16 will be challenged more directly in 2005.

Now that you know about Saturn, you can be prepared, dear Aries. It's always better to know than be caught unaware.

There are many ways Saturn may affect you, whether this year or next.

Some readers may find that this year, it will be particularly hard to find a new apartment or house. If you need one, you may have to factor in more time to find a space you love, for the ones you see are probably too small, too dark, or too expensive for your taste.

If you are in the market to buy a house, you may also feel that the ones you find this year are not worth the asking price. Or you may find a place you love, but discover that interest rates have gone way up (ugh!) and that banks have become fussier about approving mortgages. Qualifying for one may require more paperwork than you ever imagined! Saturn in the fourth house tends to create lots of paperwork.

Conversely, if trying to sell an apartment or house, you may find too few interested buyers and you may have to decrease your asking price. If you don't want to do that, see if you can put off the sale until after July 2005—a better time to sell.

You may locate the perfect home to buy or rent, but become worried about how you will pay the higher overhead. Saturn sometimes represents burdens we take on. It may help to know that if you do take on a higher rent or mortgage, it won't always be this hard and will be more easily carried after July 2005.

If you plan to renovate this year, your chart suggests the contractor will require more time than estimated (Saturn brings delays) or that your family may be uncomfortable with all the digging and hammering going on.

Saturn can sometimes manifest its challenges through a relationship, rather than a piece of property. Hence, with Saturn in Cancer you may have difficulties with a roommate, tenant, landlord, or other professional related to your home.

Saturn is entering your fourth house, which rules the foundation of your life. It also rules your parents or relatives that raised you. If you are not moving, it may be that your parents are about to relocate, and you will need to help them pack or negotiate with a broker. You may feel wistful your childhood home will now be sold.

As another alternative, you may choose to take care of an elderly relative, most likely a parent. If you do, you would be an angel. Being old in our society is hard, and learning how to depend on others is one of life's most difficult lessons. The care you give your older relative will be accepted with gratitude, even if he or she never utters a word of thanks.

Saturn will reveal that you that you can handle many more responsibilities than you ever thought possible. Chances are, a year or two ago, you could not have handled these tasks.

My mother—a truly great astrologer—used to have philosophical discussions about the nature of Saturn when I was a child. She felt that we learn very little from times of ease, but a tremendous amount during challenging times. She felt that there are enormous opportunities during a Saturn transit. For example, this could be the year you buy your first house, and even if it requires a great deal of sacrifice to do so, you will have a great deal to show for your efforts later. Saturn shows us the value of putting off gratification today for longer-term gain and security tomorrow.

Saturn will not leave your fourth house of home until July 2005, if not a bit sooner (depending on your birthday). Saturn situations are usually a bit complex and take time to work out, requiring patience and fortitude.

Actually, *what* you tackle is not as important as *how* you handle it. In astrology we know that the way we respond to Saturn's tests ultimately defines us. Saturn's job is to teach us to be resourceful in times of difficulty, but if we deal with Saturn's tests in an honest and straightforward manner, we become stronger. Saturn has to make an indelible impression—it will not be back for 29 years in the same house of the horoscope.

SETTLE HOME-RELATED ISSUES DURING MAY AND JUNE 2004

Your best time in 2004 to handle domestic or family matters will be from May 7 to June 23. At that time Mars, your ruler, will be touring your fourth house of home. Whenever your ruler enters a house, your whole being will be completely focused on that area.

You may find that a relationship with a family member, roommate, landlord, tenant, or another person connected with home or property may become inflamed during this May-June period. If this becomes true for you, it may help to understand what Mars is trying to accomplish. Mars—in any house—needs to bring debris to the surface so you can see it, confront it, and make a decision about it. Mars will clarify and cleanse this area of your chart, bringing you options never before considered. That's the best news of all!

Love Is Looking Up

Single Aries Will Have Many Opportunities for Love
Attached Aries Will Make More of Their Union

Although 2004 won't bring Jupiter, the planet of gifts and luck, to your fifth house of love as it did in 2003, you might be better without it. Jupiter in the fifth house can sometimes come off like a pushy Aunt Edith who wants you to finally get married and have a whole crop of children she can dote on.

If you aren't quite ready to spin through all the stages of a relationship, from courtship, engagement, marriage, home, and possibly even baby in fairly short order, you may enjoy this year's pace better. It will be more leisurely and you will be able to set your own agenda. There will be plenty of opportunity for love.

If you are single and dating, and met your current sweetheart last year while Jupiter toured your fifth house—from August 2002 through August 2003—your new relationship has a strong chance of success. That was a magical time in your personal timeline. If you didn't meet anyone during that period, you will have more opportunities to do so.

If you are dating and hope to commit to your sweetie, this new cycle of Jupiter in Libra, which begins on September 25, 2004, and continues to October 25, 2005, represents the very best period in the decade to marry. If you are in a serious relationship, this energy may bring the time to exchange rings and promises. I hope it does, for if you feel certain about the depth of your love, there would be no reason to wait. This energy is simply spectacular.

If you are already married, Jupiter in your seventh house shows that your partner will do well this year and be willing to share his or her good fortune with you. You will certainly benefit from your partner's luck. This trend will extend beyond romance into the business realm, too. If you want to sign a partner, agent, publicist, or even hire an expert (also covered by the seventh house) you have an ideal time in late 2004 to do so. The urge to merge will be strong. Good!

FINDING NEW LOVE: JANUARY, FEBRUARY, LATE JUNE THROUGH EARLY AUGUST

Your first fabulous period begins instantly in January, at the start of the new year. Mars will be in your sign until February 5, signifying a fabulous period for matters of the heart. Mars will bring you a sexy presence and a certain oomph that the right love interest will notice. Suddenly you will be getting attention. Having Mars on your side will help you get things going!

Later in the year, from June 23 to August 10, Mars will heat up your fifth house of true love, a truly marvelous vibration. This could be your hottest, sexiest part of the year, perfect for taking a vacation, allowing friends to play matchmaker (or for seeing a professional matchmaker), and for attending and giving parties.

While January and late June-early August are my two favorite periods for your love life, there are other times that come in as close runners-up. Let's talk about those now, for they involve a very special relationship Venus shares with your ruler, Mars.

FEBRUARY IS SPECIAL: YOUR SOCIAL LIFE IS ON FIRE

In February, there will be a rare and special planetary event that will make a big difference in your social life. Mars and Venus will be in "mutual reception," which happens when two planets each tour the sign that the other planet rules, at precisely the same time.

Specifically, Mars, your ruler, rules Aries while Venus rules Taurus. In February, Mars will be in Taurus, and Venus will be in Aries. As you see, each one will be in the other's home base in February, and hence, you have a mutual reception. As you can imagine, having two planets in the sign the other one rules simultaneously is hard to find, but happily, this happens in February.

This is amazing news because Venus is Mars' mythological lover, and when they are together magical sparks are set off, the kind that bring new love, or engender more love among established couples. The fact that your *RULER* is involved in this mutual reception bodes well for you, dear Aries, for it says you will feel this wonderful configuration more than most.

The mutual reception will occur from February 9 to March 5, sure to be a sizzling time for love! Best of all, Venus will be in *your* sign, Aries, making you irresistible! It would also be an ideal time to think about adding a few choice pieces to your wardrobe, a sure boost to your morale.

APRIL SHOULD SPARKLE BRIGHTLY FOR ARIES LOVERS

December Is Even Brighter; Mars and Venus Cuddle Close

In April, two mythological lovers, Venus and Mars, will make sexy eye contact (although not exactly touch in alignment) in your third house of travel. This makes April a perfect time to take quick weekend getaways that could lead to that special introduction or, if attached, could rekindle an all-too-predictable relationship. These trips may be short in distance but they'll take you far in love.

On the weekend of December 4–5, this magnetic couple, Venus and Mars, will finally touch in perfect alignment in one of the sexiest and mysterious of signs, Scorpio. Your romantic possibilities will increase!

This enchanting and magical aspect will fall at quite a festive time of the year. It's a red-letter weekend, and so are the days leading up to it. Circle the last week of November and first few days of December as one of the best periods of 2004 for love.

Love Is On Hold: Venus Naps in May and June

When Venus retrogrades from May 17 through June 29 in 2004, Venus will call time out for a rest. Venus goes into hibernation for six weeks every two years and did not retrograde in 2003.

When Venus retrogrades, we are not able to access Venus' strongest powers of love and beauty because feelings are subdued. It is not advisable to schedule a first date, throw a party, get engaged, or married. It is not a good time to shop for expensive new clothes or jewelry, or to schedule cosmetic surgery. It is also not the best time to radically change or style your hair. (A bad hair day is usually just annoying to other members of the zodiac, but you consider it a four-alarm disaster. Of course, your sign rules the head and hair!)

For all these events, you'll want a strong, powerful Venus behind you. In astrology, it matters when you first begin any endeavor, for it represents the "birth" of that endeavor. With Venus fast asleep, it would be best to wait!

Tie the Knot from September 25, 2004, to October 25, 2005

When Jupiter, the planet of happiness and growth, visits Libra at the tail end of the year and continues into 2005, many Aries will be getting married. Libra rules marriage and partnerships and, during those 13 months, this visit is a fabulous development for those seeking commitment. If you've been dating someone special, Jupiter in Libra will gently nudge you down the aisle. If you do choose to wed during this phase, you will have chosen the best time in 12 years to do so!

Be sure to choose a date when Mercury will *not* be in retrograde. Marriage is a sacred contract between two people, but a Mercury retrograde phase is no time to enter into any contract.

If you are already married, Jupiter in Libra will bring good fortune and financial benefit to your marriage partner, and his or her luck will make you *both* happier than you've been in years.

If you are single and haven't met anyone you would even consider marrying up to this point, once Jupiter enters your seventh house of relationships in September 25, 2004 (to stay over a year), you will start to meet marriage material.

ALL PARTNERSHIPS BENEFIT FROM JUPITER IN LIBRA

Business success rests on the ability to form solid, serious joint ventures and relationships. With Jupiter in your seventh house of partnerships in the latter part of 2004, you will do well by forming new alliances. You may take on a business partner, agent, or publicist or you may enter into a joint venture with another company.

You may also hire an expert to help you—a new lawyer, accountant, or other specialist who will work well for you. The seventh house, so glittering for you, also rules experts we hire. Once you reach the end of September you will no longer need to do anything by yourself because you will easily locate qualified, hard-working professionals to help you.

Although you tend to be a self-starter that likes to work untethered and alone, dear Aries, this would not be the year to fly solo. By working with others you will soon find that the whole you create is greater than the sum of the parts.

ECLIPSES OF 2004 BRING A FRESH START:

Possible Marriage and a Massive Reorganization of Finances

There will be four eclipses in 2004, falling in April, May, and October.

Solar Eclipse: April 19, a Fresh Start

One of the most important eclipses of the year falls in Aries and will happen on April 19. This eclipse is vital to you if you were born on April 19 or within five days of that date. The closer you were born to April 19, the more you will feel the influence of this eclipse. (If you know your chart, you may also be affected if you have planets in the late degrees of Aries or early Taurus.) The job of an eclipse is to hurry you along from one stage of life to another, as eclipses don't generally work in slow or subtle ways.

The April 19 eclipse should be remarkably friendly, which is good news because not all eclipses are so helpful. It is also a new moon solar eclipse, and solar eclipses tend to bring about a whole new life direction. As an Aries you like to be in the driver's seat, and this eclipse will give you the energy you need to state your plans and draw up blueprints for the future. It's an exciting time, when doors will open up for you in rather magical ways. Be ready to set things in motion just after this eclipse appears.

TOTAL ECLIPSE MAY 4 IN SCORPIO BRINGS FINANCIAL REORGANIZATION, MEDICAL, OR DENTAL SURGERY

The May 4 full moon is also a total lunar eclipse and will arrive two weeks after the April 19 solar eclipse. Decisions you make will affect others, for this full moon eclipse is related to the first eclipse.

The full moon and the Sun will both be in harsh angle to Neptune, so be sure you are clear about the details of any agreement you may make at the time. Neptune has been known to cloud or veil certain facts, and if that is true for you, you may regret not having consulted an attorney at the signing. Luckily, Neptune is the only planet to act up at eclipse time—the other planets in your chart will be remarkably stable. Saturn's cheery glance at the Sun and moon suggests you could be setting up a long-term agreement that will stand the test of time.

The type of money covered by this eighth house of your horoscope rules not salary but rather commission, bonuses, royalties, severance, inheritance, prize winnings, insurance payouts, a new or refinanced mortgage, back or future taxes, loans, credit cards, child support, alimony, and other joint resources or obligations. One of these areas will likely become a major focal point and you will be focused hard on discussions that come up. It is possible you will be finalizing a divorce, child-support agreement, or division of property at the end of a business association. Because most of the planets will be friendly to one another, it appears likely you will find a workable solution.

This eclipse *may* also bring surgery or a dental procedure. Not to worry. This eclipse is your friend, so if you need a "tune-up" go for it. It would be better to wait a few weeks if your surgery is elective, for it is usually wise to allow an eclipse to deliver all its news before initiating an action. If you are operated on, it may clear up a long-term problem and possibly explain a mystery, which will all occur before you even have time to think about it. All eclipses bring truth to light, so be thankful.

New Moon Partial Eclipse
on October 14 Brings Relationship News

The next eclipse falls five and a half months later, on October 14, in your seventh house of close, committed relationships and marriage. This eclipse will change the status of your present relationship and clarify your feelings. If you are in love, this eclipse may help you make the decision to take the plunge. Conversely, if you have been teetering as a couple, this eclipse may bring a final split.

You will know you have reached a make-it-or-break-it stage with your other half, whether this be your mate, steady sweetheart, or business partner. All the planets in your house of marriage will be in hard angle to Saturn, so you will be asked to make a weighty, long-term decision, and to be pragmatic when considering your options.

Aspects like these won't allow you to put things off—eclipses push us to decide within one month, if not sooner. This is a new moon partial eclipse, signifying the start of a new direction. There is no turning back and, as with most eclipses, any decision made won't easily be reversed.

I think you will like this eclipse—Jupiter will be gliding through your relationship house at this time, offering fabulous protection and indicating you will be happy—either immediately or in a matter of months.

As I said, many Aries will decide to marry under this eclipse, and others will sign with business partners or enter into other collaborations. If that's how it works out for you, congratulations!

LUNAR ECLIPSE ON OCTOBER 28 IN TAURUS:

You May Find a New Source of Income or Discuss Possessions

The next eclipse, a total lunar eclipse on October 28, falls in Taurus, in your solar second house of salary and possessions. This is a full moon, and suggests an ending. It may be an emotional one at that.

Given that it falls in your second house of money, you may need to live up to a large financial obligation at this time. If so, even though it may not be easy to do, you will find a way. If you've suffered a loss—say, in a fire—this eclipse may bring a final settlement with the insurance company.

At the time of the October 28 eclipse, it is clear that you have searched for a way to increase your salary—this eclipse will only intensify your determination to find new sources.

This eclipse may change your source of income. If you want a new full-time job, Jupiter's position (October through December) suggests that you should consider working with a headhunter, recruiter, or agent. This person would work hard for you and come up with better options than you could find alone.

You may also finally get news about whether you were approved for a raise. If your raise is not approved, you will most likely leave. If you change jobs near the eclipse, you would be doing so for purely financial reasons, and not necessarily because you have found a job that offers additional prestige or status.

You might not have to change jobs to see a change in the source of your income. If your company merges with another firm, the logo and signature on your weekly check would change too, due to a newly formed company. Your source of revenue would be "new" but you will have never left your desk!

This is the easiest way the eclipse would affect you. As we discussed earlier, you may take on a second job at this eclipse.

If you are self-employed, you may find a new client or lose an important one. If you lose your big client, you will be able to find another, if not immediately, then within three to four months.

Full moons finish up certain conditions, often forever, so, on the October 28 eclipse you will close the door on a financial matter and I doubt you'll want to look back. Sometimes there is a sense of loss at an eclipse—the light is eclipsed—but if so, think of it as something that was meant to be, with new and better opportunities to follow. Please read the chapter on eclipses in this book for tips. You will see why you should not be blue!

Overall, the eclipses coming this year are meant to help you, dear Aries. They may speed your timetable and toss a few surprises in your path, but sometimes that is just what we need to perk us up and get us out of a rut.

Summary

The most precious gift of the universe is radiant health, and that's about to become more important than ever, dear Aries. With Jupiter in your sixth house of health, you may be astounded by the results you achieve, if you make the effort. Should you need surgery in 2004, you are protected. Seek a professional you trust.

The eclipse on April 19 may play into your transformation, as an eclipse in one's own sign has a powerful influence on how you will see yourself, and how you will hope others will perceive you, too. If you have wanted to lose weight and get fit, this is your year to do so.

Romantically, this could be a powerful, life-changing year if you have been dating someone special, for Jupiter is about to move into your seventh house of marriage, making the last four months of the year a glorious time to say "I do." If you are attached to someone special, late September or October could be a pivotal time for news.

Single Aries will find January, April, and most of all, early December magical. It's so important that you circulate during that time.

Keep in the back of your mind that you may have problems with housing this year or next. It doesn't mean you can't solve the problems you may face, but you will likely need to devote more time or money to the situation than you had anticipated. If the end of your lease is coming up, don't wait until the last minute to look at options.

Concerning your career, you will have opportunities, but the picture is more complex. With a glowing sixth house of work assignments, it seems a sure bet you will enjoy the work you do on a day-to-day basis. Co-workers will be gems, too, and if you need to hire any underlings, the ones you find will be well qualified and will support you strongly. You may have new equipment to use and bright, new surroundings.

While it may be possible to change jobs, if you do so, the chances are you'd be making a lateral move rather than a step up. If you can wait until 2005, your chances will improve. If not, your best bet is to dive into the plum assignments coming your way this year and let that work speak for itself. You will garner attention—let things happen organically. January and June offer the only windows for taking control of the situation to move up in rank, so if you're determined to get a better job, act then.

Eclipses in your financial sectors in May and October suggest you are about to change how you earn, spend, or save your money. Your income may come from a new source or there may be negotiation about your possessions, perhaps with an insurance company, or more obviously, in regard to the division of property in a divorce or business split. An eclipse in your marriage/business-partner sector in late October underscores that possibility.

As you see, you have a busy, bustling year ahead. All the changes will bring you to a new level of evolution and maturity, dear Aries. With Mars arching through *nine* signs this year, you'll have plenty of variety and much more opportunity to create the life you want this year. Enter it with gusto, for that is your most loveable quality!

Taurus

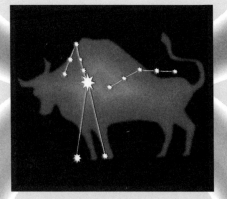

April 20–May 20

The Big Picture

This could be the year you've waited for, dear Taurus. There will be substantial change in your life, especially in matters related to love and romance, your lifestyle, and even in your perception of yourself and your abilities. 2004 could be a breakthrough year. You may not immediately realize how important this year was for you except in hindsight, when you see how far and how vast these changes have been for you.

During the first nine months of 2004, Jupiter, the great planet of happiness and luck, will brighten your fifth house of romance. Undoubtedly, Jupiter will make love a major force for you. This is both a glorious and serious development with long-range implications. You have not had any aspects this strong in romance for over a decade. You are in the process of beginning a new cycle that will last many, many years. If you've felt starved for affection, 2004 should bring a hearty feast of delights.

It doesn't matter if you are single and hope to meet someone new, or attached and are looking for more attention from your present partner—all Taurus will benefit from this new romantic influence. If you're in a relationship and feel counseling could help, this would be the year to start. This year will bring exceptional opportunities for getting the satisfaction you deserve. If you are a Taurus stuck in a hopelessly incompatible relationship—then what? The eclipses this year should help you finally find the courage to leave and to find happiness elsewhere.

At times, you may wonder if the various planets in their individual orbits are transmitting mixed messages. However, if you look closely you will see that these planets are delivering the same message: it is *finally* time for you to focus on your personal life, dear Taurus, and to have more fun.

Part of this brightening trend will be brought to you by benefic Jupiter, which will boost your magnetism. If you are not yet attached, Jupiter will increase your romantic success by placing you at the right place at the right time. Saturn will be in supportive angles to fortunate Jupiter during the critical first nine months of the year (your best period), and that indicates that a new relationship could bring the stability you crave. Saturn will also teach you how to communicate more effectively, which will also help your relationships.

The eclipses in May and November are significant because they will help you see yourself in a whole new context. You will become confident enough to ask for more for yourself—and you will get it. Relationships will be brought to the make-it-or-break-it point. If you've been in relationship limbo, you won't stay there for long.

So strong is this trend that your personal happiness will become your number one priority in 2004.

THE DIFFICULT YEARS: 1998 TO 2003

The past five years have not been easy for you. It was probably hardest from June 1998 to October 2000, a time when Saturn, the taskmaster planet, journeyed through Taurus and made a rare, once-in-29-year visit that lasted two-and-a-half years. Saturn's job is to toughen you up so you can handle more life responsibility, so during that time, Saturn sent you various challenges to strengthen your character. You gained a great deal from your experience and, although you're stronger and smarter as a result, you would *not* want to repeat those years.

Armed with those life lessons, you faced a new set of challenges from April 2001 to July 2003, when Saturn moved into Gemini. You were asked to re-evaluate your attitudes about money, possessions, and security, and on a larger scale, you were also asked to re-examine your values. Saturn's visit hit a sensitive spot in you, dear Taurus, for your sign is naturally associated with these areas. You also don't like to live by the seat of your pants—Taurus likes money in the bank, a few pieces of jewelry in the vault, and a plot of land to call your own. Yet these were the very areas that were shifting for you, and you may have felt like you were living on a moving mountain of sand.

You probably had to work quite hard for your money over the past two years, for Saturn was teaching you to understand the value of a dollar and to prioritize. For some, you may have had to forgo little pleasures to save for one big investment, like the purchase of a house, tuition for a child, or a once-in-a-lifetime vacation. For others, it may have meant taking a lower-salaried job so you could have better quality of life. That stage is, mercifully, over.

Financial constraints began to lift in the second half of 2003, when Saturn left Gemini. As you enter 2004, making money and keeping it will become an easier process. You have become a tougher negotiator since Saturn's visit to Gemini, for now you fully understand the value of your contribution to the whole and you will be less inclined to sell yourself short. You also will be less likely to pay more than you have to. These life lessons will remain with you for years into the future.

In June 2003 Saturn moved into a gentler part of your chart—your third house of communication—a place it will occupy until July 2005. In its new placement, Saturn will show you how to present your ideas in a clear and effective manner and to approach new ideas more critically. You may now learn to write or research more complex projects, or you may be trained to communicate in a new medium, such as radio or TV. The lessons you learn with Saturn in 2004 and early 2005 will be more easily assimilated than the lessons Saturn taught you in years past. Saturn will be at a far more positive angle to your Sun this year, which makes all the difference. In short, you are due for a cosmic breather. Thank goodness!

YOUR HEALTH AND APPEARANCE MAY IMPROVE RADICALLY

From late September 2004 to late September 2005, Jupiter will begin to occupy your sixth house of health for the first time in a decade. The sixth house rules the action we take to get ourselves into shape. Suddenly, in 2004, you will feel more motivated to take care of yourself. One obvious manifestation will be the desire to lose weight and get fit. If that is your goal, Jupiter will be in a position to help you see results—even if you have been frustrated before.

Jupiter will also tour a fellow earth sign, Virgo, which in itself will create a noticeable feeling of boundless energy because Virgo relates so well to your Taurus Sun.

Jupiter notwithstanding, you will still have to be careful about your health because eclipses that are falling in Taurus and Scorpio may lower your resistance to disease or bring a certain health condition to your attention. I am not saying that you necessarily *will* have a health concern this year, only that it is *possible* near eclipse time, which is in late April, early May, or mid-to-late October.

Should you encounter a problem, Jupiter will help you find highly qualified medical professionals to help. It will be the best time in over a decade to address medical matters, for Jupiter is associated with medicine and healing.

URANUS WILL LEAVE YOUR TENTH HOUSE
OF PROFESSION: YOUR CAREER WILL NOW STABILIZE

Your career finally began to stabilize last year, when Uranus moved into Pisces in March 2003. For the seven years prior to that, Uranus was in harsh angle to your Sun. You were living in a volcano for so long that you probably forgot what the words "job security" meant.

While those seven years brought some terrific opportunities and even some career breakthroughs, Uranus threw in a few devastating and unexpected setbacks as well. When it comes to career and earning a living, your sign values financial stability.

When Uranus finally left Aquarius in March 2003 (the place in your chart that was causing you havoc), you assumed you had finally made it to higher ground. You had, but only for a while. Uranus then bolted back into Aquarius six months later, in September, which was not good news for you. Uranus had suddenly returned to the same difficult position that was causing you grief before. If your birthday falls on May 15 or later, you experienced the most pronounced career gyrations in the latter part of 2003. You may have felt that you'd never see relief, but fortunately it arrived sooner than you thought.

On December 30, 2003—just days prior to the dawning of 2004—Uranus moved permanently back into Pisces, a new and very positive place for Uranus to occupy in your chart. Uranus will not return to your tenth house of career again during your lifetime. While you might miss the sudden opportunities and excitement that this planet can bring, you won't miss the stinging setbacks one bit. You are now entering a strong and stable professional cycle.

In its new placement, Uranus will enhance your friendships and contacts. How can the same planet suddenly become so positive? From now on, Uranus will be in a superb angle to your Sun—what a relief! There will be more time for fun, and the people you meet will become a source of inspiration and stimulation. Your new friends are likely to be creative types, and you won't always know what they'll do or say next—and you'll enjoy that unpredictable quality.

With Uranus now securely settled in Pisces in your eleventh house of people and friendship until 2011, you will need to change the way you do business. Instead of sending formal letters and resumes blindly to executives you have never met, you will soon discover that you will advance faster by socializing, whether at industry events or through introductions to bigwigs arranged by friends. Given that Uranus is the natural ruler of your solar tenth house of career and honors, your friends will be helpful in making the right introductions.

Those Taurus readers who will benefit most from friends, associates, and even casual acquaintances will be those born between April 20 and April 26.

The Scoop Behind the Biggest Trends of 2004

JUPITER IN VIRGO MAKES ROMANCE GLORIOUS FROM JANUARY TO SEPTEMBER

Everyone wants more romance—love makes the world go 'round! This coming year should be your wonder year for matters of the heart, dear Taurus. It doesn't matter if you are single or married, a new cycle is about to open up for you that is unlike any that you've experienced in over a decade—Jupiter's visits are *that* infrequent. The flowers in your garden are about to bloom again, dear Taurus, and when they do, the scent will be intoxicating.

As a Taurus, you have Virgo on the cusp of your solar fifth house of love, which tells me that you are very discriminating about the types you date. Good! This year, if you are single and looking for love, you will find substantial, ethical, hard-working romantic interests, with goals to match your own. You will have to do your part by circulating more, but if you do, you should see results. Your window of opportunity will last from January through September 2004.

If you are married or attached but feel your partner hasn't paid you the attention you deserve, that situation will change. Of course, you will have to be your loveable self— open, giving, compassionate, and affirming your partner's value to you—but this year, those nurturing qualities will get you the results you crave. Attached Taurus have been suffering from too little fun lately. To fix that, Jupiter will be planning more evenings out, whether to attend a concert, sporting event, the theater, or an elegant dinner. It's time for you to play!

Jupiter entered Virgo on August 27, 2003, and will stay until September 24, 2004. If you are an April-born Taurus, you may have already seen an improvement in your love life. This year, because of the recent retrograde action of Jupiter, *all* Taurus, regardless of birthday, will be included in this trend. Hooray!

WANT TO BE NOTICED?
MARS IN TAURUS WILL DO THE TRICK

From February 3 to March 21, 2004 (a period that happily includes Valentine's Day), is one area to circle on your calendar. Mars will circulate in Taurus, which will bring you exceptional energy, courage, drive, and a fantastic advantage in all of life's activities, including love. During a Mars cycle, which comes around every two years, you achieve a certain presence and are more likely to become noticed. In love, that's half the battle!

From February 8 to March 5, you will benefit from a special planetary configuration. Due to a rare "mutual reception" between Mars and Venus, you will have help from these two "cosmic lovers" of the night sky.

A mutual reception occurs when two planets each tour the sign that the other planet rules at precisely the same time. Specifically, Mars rules Aries, while Venus rules Taurus. In February, these two planets will swap home bases, which will create a mutual reception: Mars will be in Taurus, and Venus will be in Aries. Together these planets will act as one. As you may have guessed, it's hard to get a mutual reception going because each planet has an orbit of different length. We haven't had one in years.

When Venus and Mars are together they set off sexy sparks, and new love is born—or rekindled. The fact that your ruler, Venus, is involved in this mutual reception is extra-special news for you, dear Taurus, for it says you will enjoy the benefits of this stellar configuration more than most. This mutual reception will double Mars' effectiveness and do much to increase your powers of attraction.

VENUS IN MARS
WILL ENHANCE YOUR CHANCE FOR LOVE

Just as your mutual reception is ending, you get another big plus! Watch March 5 to April 3 for a lyrical Venus to jump on board to help you find love.

Unlike Mars, Venus is a very laid-back, receptive sign. And also unlike Mars, who teaches you to track down the love you want, Venus instead teaches you to do things differently—to simply attract others to you, so you won't need to work so hard. During this sterling period, accept all invitations to attend parties and meet new people.

Also, this is an ideal time to shop for additions to your wardrobe and to schedule grooming (men) or beauty treatments (women). Look great, feel great, and find love—this is the slogan for this lovely period.

Circle this in red: another spectacular period for love will occur when Mars tours your fifth house of true love, from August 10 to September 26, 2004. This could even be stronger than the periods mentioned earlier.

COMMITMENT IS YOUR MAIN FOCUS
FROM NOVEMBER 11 TO DECEMBER 25, 2004

If you have been dating someone seriously, November 11 through December 25 will be the most likely time of the year that you would get engaged or married. Perfect!

To help love along, Mars and Venus will form an exact conjunction (embrace) on December 5 in the sexy emotional water sign of Scorpio. This is the sign that rules your house of marriage, as well as all kinds of serious commitments. This hasn't happened in two years, and the implications are simply breathtaking.

December will be a standout time for you. Venus will be in your seventh house and will bring the effect of a lovely full moon to your most private, emotional affairs. Excitement will run high, and you begin to feel this aspect at the end of November. Think of December as the month that brings a double dip of pleasure!

ROMANCE TO HIT SNAGS AND BUMPS
WHEN VENUS RETROGRADES
MAY 17 TO JUNE 29, 2004

Shore Up Confidence

When Venus retrogrades, Venus naps, and that's an important cycle for you to note, because Venus is your ruler. Whenever your ruler is weak it becomes harder for you to push your agenda forward on any front, including love. Venus did not retrograde in 2003, but will in 2004.

From May 17 to June 29 it would be wise to not launch any new projects. It would be better to unveil these ideas at almost any other time, although you would be wise to avoid Mercury retrograde periods (check the chapter on Mercury retrograde for a list of dates).

When Venus moves backwards, you may have second thoughts or you may torture yourself by second-guessing your decisions. Don't lose your confidence! Your poise may wobble, but things will return to an even keel at the end of June.

During this phase, especially in love, you may feel that nothing is going the way you want, and you feel powerless to change. You may even consider taking your relationship down a notch to try to rebuild it. Venus retrograde may also bring a call from a former lover. Make no big decisions now—wait until Venus goes direct on June 29.

Try *not* to schedule your wedding or engagement during a Venus retrograde. You need a strong Venus for a wedding; the day you choose will represent the birth of your relationship and will color the years to come.

Venus also rules financial matters, and since it will retrograde in your second house of earned income, certain financial discussions could suddenly become problematic. Try to wrap up talks earlier, or else table them for discussion after June 29. Adding to the frustration, if you expect a check, it may be delayed.

Venus rules all things associated with beauty, so do not schedule cosmetic surgery—this would be the worst time to do so! You may also want to delay luxurious spa treatments. The same advice holds true if you are planning to purchase expensive new things for your wardrobe—avoid both Venus and Mercury retrograde periods. If you're planning to throw a party, launch a book, or host a charity fundraiser (to list three examples), don't do it during this Venus retrograde period.

NOVEMBER AND DECEMBER
ARE DIFFICULT FOR TROUBLED COUPLES

If you are unsure whether your sweetheart or spouse is right for you, the eclipses of April, May, and October will help clarify your situation and will force you to decide whether to stay or go.

The end of the year, November 11 to Christmas Day 2004, may turn out to be a touchy, difficult time. There may be much discussion during this period, which will help get things settled.

Why are November and December glorious for certain Taurus couples—those who want to get engaged and married—but particularly difficult for those who have been in turmoil? The answer is Mars—by then in your seventh house—a placement that will magnify both the positive and negative parts of a relationship.

Mars' job is to bring to the surface both debris and heartfelt passion, so you can see what forms the bedrock of your relationship. If your relationship is important to you, Mars will demand honesty and courage. As you later learn, the eclipses will also

speed up the process. So if you have been in a troubled relationship, everything will reach a critical phase at the end of the year.

Eclipses Will Create a New Sense of Identity

This year, the eclipses are due to fall in your sign, Taurus, and
your opposite sign, Scorpio, creating some of the year's tensions.

Several eclipses fell in the same part of your chart last year.
One eclipse that fell on May 15, 2003, might have been memorable for you. If you were born on that date, you might have
made a key decision about one close partnership. Last year's
lunar eclipse in Taurus, a full moon on November 9, might also
have been memorable, especially if you were born near May 7.
Partnership was still the topic at hand, but by then you were
clearer on what would make you happy. Each eclipse builds on
the previous one, and your transition to being a more mature
person will continue, eclipse by eclipse, to completion in 2004.

If you have been having difficulties in your relationship,
the universe will provide what's needed to give it purpose or
make you see that it's time to go. A rival or competitor may
appear; your partner may disclose certain feelings or information—these elements will change your situation in some way
to help you understand it with a renewed perspective. If you
were both together for convenience, or you were afraid to be
alone, you will no longer be able to rely on those excuses.
However, if you love the one you're with, it will be time to get
hitched. You will see all the reasons you should be together.

It is also possible that these eclipses will be felt in a business context instead of a romantic one, and, if so, you will sign
papers to either create or dissolve an alliance. The seventh
house, which is activated for you, rules contractual relationships, whether business or personal in nature.

There will be four eclipses in 2004, so let's look at how each will influence you in the year ahead.

The First Eclipse Falls on April 19: A Solar Eclipse New Moon, in the Last Degree of Aries

This first eclipse, falling on April 19, will begin a whole new lifestyle for Taurus who were born on or within five days of April 20. This eclipse suggests that this new chapter will bring some exciting new developments.

The Sun and Moon's superb angle to Jupiter, as well as Mercury's fine angle to Pluto, is the best part of this eclipse. Jupiter is based in your creative, love-oriented fifth house, which also rules children and pregnancy, so developments in this area should be excellent. It would also be a good time to make a presentation to your boss.

However, this eclipse does have mixed aspects. The harshest part of this eclipse includes two oppositions, one of Mars to Pluto, and the other of Jupiter to Uranus. The former aspect suggests that an ideological disagreement may break out between you and someone close. If so, the other person seems to be quite convinced he or she is right, and you may have to make a big effort to show this party your point of view. At times this may be frustrating. Try not to lock horns, but to use your best diplomatic skills. Money and the appropriation of funds may also be under discussion. With Pluto based in your solar eighth house, the type of money that you would discuss might be the proceeds from a marriage or business split, a mortgage, student loan, commission, bonus, settlement, insurance payout, taxes, venture capital, alimony, or child support payments. Your salary is covered in a different part of your chart and will not be affected.

Do not invest in a speculative venture near this eclipse (due to the opposition of Jupiter to Uranus). If possible, delay all-important decisions one week.

THE SECOND ECLIPSE:
FULL MOON LUNAR ECLIPSE ON MAY 4 IN SCORPIO

Relationships will be your main focus during this eclipse, with the main question being how to make your relationship more vital and loving or how to advance things to the next logical step. Perhaps you will be thinking of getting married or having a baby.

If you have been unhappy with how things have been going with your partner, you may opt for counseling or you may leave the relationship altogether. With Saturn at superb angles to the Sun, it appears that whatever your decision, it will serve you well.

There will be also be a lovely interaction of the Sun, Moon, and Jupiter, so if you are single, an exciting introduction could be in the offing.

However, simultaneously Pluto will oppose both Mars and Venus, from both financial sectors, so a dispute about money is also likely. This power struggle may stem from another part of your life, or it may be integral to your relationship.

All Taurus will feel this important eclipse. If you were born on or within five days of May 4, you will feel this eclipse in a very personal and powerful way.

Near May 4, your emotions will run from one end of the spectrum to the other. So much depends on how your relationship has been prior to this time, as an eclipse will often accelerate the direction your relationship has been heading all along. Pressures beyond your control will be operating from the outside, so whatever occurs, it is almost certain to surprise you.

This eclipse will bring mixed aspects that may go beyond the subject of your relationship, so let's study both the negative and positive signals it will emit.

Neptune, the planet of the "mist" or confusion, will be in hard angle to the Sun. Neptune is currently touring your tenth house of profession, so be sure to look closely at the terms of any new job or deal that you enter into at this time. You may be misinformed about what is expected of you or you may misunderstand some terms of the agreement. If signing a contract, have a lawyer help you, as you may later find a clause that is unclear. Jupiter will also oppose Uranus, as it did with the April 19 eclipse, so you must once again be careful not to enter any speculative ventures.

During this May 4 eclipse, Uranus (surprises) and Saturn (stability) will cooperate in a cheery manner. Your actions will bode well for your long-term security. Uranus will lend its powers of innovation, while Saturn will contribute practicality. The eclipsed Moon will allow you to integrate the best energies of both planets as you spin your plans into motion.

When this eclipse is over, your appearance may reflect the changes that have been bubbling up within you. You may start to wear a different style of clothing or style your hair in a different way, or you may relocate to a new area and adopt an entirely new lifestyle. This process of reinventing yourself will continue for the rest of the year and into 2005.

A FULL MOON SOLAR ECLIPSE IN TAURUS WILL HIGHLIGHT YOUR FEELINGS

If you were born on or within five days of April 21, you will feel the full moon solar eclipse on October 28 more keenly than other members of your sign. Like the first eclipse of the year, this one will be in your sign, Taurus, and it will make you feel very emotional.

The Sun and eclipsed Moon will be in tough angle to Neptune, which brings up the same danger of miscommunication associated with the eclipses that occur earlier this year. For example, if you're going to sign a contract, be sure to ask many questions and keep your attorney in the loop. During an eclipse like this one, the clauses that are missing from a contract may cause more problems than the ones that do. Fill in the blanks for the sake of clarity—you will be glad you did.

However, overall this eclipse will be favorable. I particularly love how Uranus and the Sun will interact at this time, suggesting a friend may have a surprise up his or her sleeve that will put a smile on your face. Any charity event or festive occasion you attend should be fun and successful. You may also receive some upbeat financial news—Mars and Pluto will interact well during this time—so you may receive that check you've been waiting for!

YOUR LUCKIEST DAY OF THE YEAR, SEPTEMBER 21, IS SURE TO BRING ROMANCE AND FUN

September 21 will be your luckiest day of the year (and everyone else's) because the Sun will conjoin Jupiter, an annual event that falls on a different part of your chart each year. This time the Sun and Jupiter will emblaze your solar fifth house of true love, creativity, children, and leisure fun.

If you were born on May 19, you win a double jackpot, because Jupiter and the Sun will meet at a mathematical degree that will perfectly align with your birthday Sun. You will also have several other planets bolstering this theme of fun and love.

Use this day to go to a party, throw your own, or ask a matchmaker to introduce you to someone new. It's also an ideal time to be on vacation. If you want to be married on a Saturday near this date, choose the prior Saturday, September 18.

This date also falls within the new moon period, September 14, which will ignite your house of love, making September a landmark month.

JANUARY TO SEPTEMBER: AN IDEAL TIME TO INVITE THE STORK

The fifth house of the horoscope (which is so good for you in 2004) covers pregnancy. If you've wanted to have a child but have hesitated, you will feel more optimistic about doing so now.

Happily, with Jupiter in this house, the pregnancy will most likely go well and the baby will be a jovial little tyke. It is one of the best times of your life to decide to have a baby.

If you have tried to conceive but haven't been successful, try again this year. See a fertility specialist without delay. You may want to try just after the most fertile new moons of 2004, assuming you can adjust your cycle to the following guidelines. You will have approximately twelve days to conceive *after* these new moons appear, with the strongest energy clustered as close to the new moon as possible.

- after February 20, when the new moon is in Pisces;
- after May 19, the new moon in Taurus;
- after July 17, the new moon in Cancer;
- after August 15, the new moon in Leo;
- after September 14, the new moon in Virgo

If you hope to adopt, I believe you will have good news to celebrate prior to the end of September, assuming you've completed the necessary applications. This trend also blesses foster parenting, too.

After September, Jupiter moves on to another part of your chart and when it does, it will end this trend. Jupiter will not be back in this area of your chart until 2015.

Should you find you are unable to conceive now or adopt, don't be blue. Check your rising sign, for you may have more opportunities in that sign.

NEPTUNE AND JUPITER HELP YOUR CREATIVITY SOAR

November 29 Is Ideal for Creativity at Work

Neptune will remain in your prestigious tenth house of career for several years, and being that Neptune is the planet of imagination, you are in a perfect position to contribute highly creative ideas on the job. Your ideas will identify you as a thinker and innovator, and an individual who should be groomed for bigger things.

Creativity is one of the truly wonderful gifts we can receive from the universe. This year take your creativity seriously, for you may be amazed with the quality of the work you turn out. I'd like you to pay special attention to your creative talents in September, October, and November 2004—all extra-special months. This is the time to polish and present your dear-to-the-heart creative projects.

The energies you will see emerge during this time may be used in your career, but you may also use this energy to develop a serious hobby to a new level. You may even decide to turn a private passion into a lucrative profit-making center. This is a strong cycle!

Neptune also rules image, so with an elevated Neptune, you may come before the public in some way, perhaps as a TV or radio personality or possibly featured in the media as a leader in your field.

On November 29, Neptune and Jupiter will be in perfect syncopation, an exceedingly rare and beneficial cosmic event. Note what transpires in the days and weeks surrounding this date. If you ever were to take full advantage of your creativity and get paid for your ideas, it's on or near this day.

AIM FOR CLARITY: NEPTUNE CAN CREATE CONFUSION ABOUT WHAT YOUR BOSS/CLIENT EXPECTS OF YOU

Be sure to have a precise job description, as Neptune occasionally can cause confusion. If you are contracted for a job, make sure an attorney checks your agreement so no clauses are open to misinterpretation.

If you were born between May 1 and May 5, you need to be extra careful to protect yourself from Neptune's misty, confusing effects this year.

If your birthday falls later than May 5, you'll still feel Neptune's influences in the future (between the years 2005 and 2012, depending on your exact birthday).

Taurus with birthdays that fall prior to May 1 already experienced their "Neptune moment" sometime in the past few years and will not feel this influence again in their lifetime. You are free and clear!

FINANCIALLY, THE ROAD AHEAD BRIGHTENS BUT REMAIN CONSERVATIVE NONETHELESS

Saturn has finally left your house of money after a two-and-a-half-year stay, so you should now be able to spend more freely.

At the same time, Pluto remains in your eighth house of other people's money, a placement Pluto has maintained for years and will remain in until 2008, This area covers investments, mortgages, credit, taxes, loans, inheritance, prize winnings—money that is not earned but comes to you in other ways. Pluto is the planet of transformation, so this type of funding is an area to watch as a possible lucrative source.

This year, Jupiter will challenge Pluto in hard aspect on August 6. At that time you may choose to restructure an existing financial arrangement or, if investing, remain conservative and not take any big risks. Keep to your goal of lowering debt on credit cards and other bills. Jupiter and Pluto are slow-moving planets, so this aspect will color your mid-year financial discussions for weeks. To help you prepare for this time, think back to any important financial investments you have made since 1994 or 1995. This year you may need to reassess that investment and decide whether you want to add any more time or money to it or just abandon it. The universe wants you to put your energies where they matter most, and the Jupiter/Pluto configuration will help you.

JUPITER'S 13-MONTH TOUR OF LIBRA REVIVES FITNESS AND HEALTH FOR TAURUS

If you have been frustrated with extra pounds that simply won't come off, this could be the year to find the formula for exercise and diet that works for you.

Jupiter's arrival in your sixth house of health and fitness in late September—and continuing for thirteen months—will show you that eating what Mother Nature intended, combined with portion control, meal timing, and exercise, can bring amazing results.

The first part of the year should be generally positive for health because Jupiter will be in Virgo, a very discriminating sign, in perfect angle to your Sun. You haven't had this benefit in years.

Once you reach September 25, things improve further, for you will be operating within your very best cycle for health, vitality, fitness, and healing in over a decade.

Should you have a chronic illness—or should there be a new medical concern—you will be able to locate the right medical professionals to help. This trend will continue into most of next year and will end on October 25, 2005.

Your best months in 2004 will span from September 25 to November 11. October will be extraordinary, with five planets crowded into your sixth house of health. That's quite a lot of energy!

PARTIAL NEW MOON ECLIPSE IN LIBRA WILL BRING A LARGE FOCUS TO WORK AND HEALTH MATTERS

The year's third eclipse will fall in Libra on October 14 in your sixth house of work and preventative health. It does not make as sharp a contact with your Sun as the previous eclipses did.

If this eclipse turns out to be vital for you, make a note of the news you hear, as eclipses next year will move into Aries/Libra, and this one might highlight an important upcoming theme for you. With more eclipses due in this family of signs in 2005, your notes may come in handy next year.

This eclipse falls in the sixth house, the part of your chart that rules work projects, and you may see major shifts in the workplace. A trusted co-worker may leave, you may be transferred to a new department, or you might get a new assignment that has big implications for your future career direction. During this time, five out of ten planets will be in this same sixth house, providing plenty of energy and news. Your company may move to new headquarters, you may get new computers or software, or your company may drastically expand or reduce staff around you.

This is a solar eclipse, suggesting a fresh start, so you may change jobs. However, if you do, it will more likely be a lateral move, not a step up to a higher position. Still, this eclipse could be very useful if you want to moonlight to increase your cash flow. Or you may take a similar job with another company to move away from a difficult situation, such as a tyrannical boss, for example. In that case, you may not mind a lateral move.

This solar (new moon) eclipse marks the very best time of 2004 to begin a fitness program, join a gym, take part in a new exercise class, or start a new sport. Initiate actions now—if you do, you will see results.

The time to try your new exercise program is just after the new moon—October 14.

Begin your weight-loss efforts just after the full moon eclipse, October 28.

If you have been troubled by a health difficulty, make an appointment with a specialist shortly after October 14.

Saturn in Cancer
Teaches How to Communicate More Effectively

Saturn is the planet that helps to transform our ideas into reality. Saturn will now be touring your third house of language, speech, and thought, and you can expect to make amazing gains in the area of communication. You may learn how to teach others, or you may become a student yourself. It will be an ideal year to take courses in communications, creative writing, library research, public relations, languages, computer software, sales, marketing, or related fields.

Saturn entered your third house in June 2003, and is set to remain there until July 2005. Since then you have gained intellectual self-discipline through the re-evaluation of your ideas and opinions. This is a long process, so you might feel unsure of your previously held opinions. This is a good sign, because it shows how seriously you are taking the re-evaluation process. You need time, so don't rush yourself.

You may also begin to write. You may write your first book or thesis for graduate school, and with Saturn involved, you will soon learn that writing these types of projects takes more than meets the eye. Saturn is all about learning the ropes, so Saturn will see to it that a guide, teacher, or boss will be at your side to teach you.

SATURN IN YOUR THIRD HOUSE
MEANS A RELATIVE MAY NEED EXTRA ATTENTION

A sister, brother, aunt, cousin, or other relative may suddenly figure more prominently in your life this year, due to Saturn's move into your third house. This part of the horoscope rules family members and places the strongest emphasis on siblings. With Saturn, the teacher planet in your third house, you may become concerned about a relative's welfare and may choose to help him or her in a significant way, perhaps financially.

If you were born with Saturn in the third house—you would have to be 28, 29, 56, or 57 years old for this to be true—Saturn's transit this year may highlight a difficult relationship you may have had with this person—most likely a sibling—during childhood. Sibling rivalry is a complex subject, but if you suddenly find you simply can't communicate with your sister or brother, it could be that Saturn is stirring up old childhood conflicts that make you emotional.

Saturn creates difficult situations like this so we can confront unresolved problems. You may find a way to break an old pattern with your sister or brother that results in a closer relationship. If you deal directly with this trend brought by Saturn, you may be surprised at the progress you make.

It is also possible that you may have no problems at all with any of your relatives. Instead, your difficulties may be with local transportation. Saturn in the third house may make traveling short distances particularly hard to maneuver. For example, you may need two cars in your household, but you find you can afford only one. Or the car you have may act up. If you are young, perhaps you long for wheels but simply can't afford the down payment to buy a car. Saturn teaches patience, so all things will come in time.

If you are to feel this aspect in terms of transportation, flying to distant cities will be easier than getting to a nearby town! Be careful with driving laws, as you could have your license suspended if you break the law too many times. Pay those past parking tickets! Saturn is a stickler about playing by the book.

Saturn in Cancer will be in fine angle to your Sun if your birthday falls between April 25 and May 17. Even if you were born outside of these dates, your birthday will still be "within orb," meaning every Taurus of every birthday will benefit this year.

Therefore, even if you encounter some difficulties, you should be able to find a good solution. Having Saturn in a supportive angle to your Sun is no small cosmic gift!

DOMESTIC PROJECTS,
INCLUDING A RESIDENTIAL MOVE OR RENOVATION ARE BEST ACHIEVED FROM JUNE 23 TO AUGUST 9

When it comes to real estate, last year and part of 2002 were outstanding. Hopefully, if you had to move, buy a new house, or make renovations, you did so in the second half of 2002 or between January and August 2003. That cycle was hard to beat. If not, you will have a superb opportunity to settle domestic matters from June 23 through August 9, 2004. It is a small window of time, so be ready to view new homes, evaluate potential buyers, or interview contractors or decorators for your home-related project. This will be your best time to apply for a mortgage, make repairs, or set in motion any other project you had planned for your home or property.

Mercury will retrograde beginning on August 9, so try to start at the front end of this period (closer to June 23), as things will slow down as you edge into August. You can certainly move during August; just try not to sign your lease, deed, or give the go ahead to your contractors in August.

Summary

Let's take all the trends and put them together so that you can see them all in one panoramic snapshot.

We spoke about how brilliantly love, romance, fun, and leisure will be highlighted for you this year, dear Taurus, and this will be true no matter if you are single or married, divorced or widowed. There is also evidence that you will have more opportunities for leisure, vacations, and creative projects. All in all, it seems certain that you will rediscover how to enjoy yourself in 2004. After having endured a difficult set of years—

spanning back to 2000—you certainly deserve a break, and happily, one is on the way!

The eclipses are the year's wild cards, and will likely create opportunities in a close, committed relationship, if you have one. A great deal depends on how things have been going, for the eclipses will push your partnership in the direction it has been heading all along. The alliance may be business or personal.

The eclipses in April, May, and October will have an influence on how you view yourself and how you want others to see you.

Your personal development will be very rapid this year—at times excitingly so—as if you suddenly became Alice in Wonderland after she drank the bottle labeled "Drink me." With arms and legs shooting out the window, it will be hard not to notice that something within you has changed.

With Uranus settling into your friendship sector through the end of the decade, you will be very stimulated by the people you will soon meet. Your pals, both new and old, will be quite instrumental in making life more fun and interesting, and helping you find career opportunities.

In the coming year you may have some concern for a relative. Or you may simply not get along too well with this person, and you will spend the year trying to find a way to converse with them in a more civilized manner. If you are concerned about the welfare of a sibling (or that of a cousin, aunt, or uncle), you may show this person you care by being more attentive or even by offering money. If you aren't getting along, you may devise some strategies to improve your relationship.

Throughout the year, your health should improve dramatically if you take some preventative measures. When Jupiter moves into your sixth house (late September through the end of your forecast period), you can finally get fit and lose weight, if this is a priority. If you are already fit, you can still benefit from this trend by setting higher goals. You can also benefit by seeking medical advice while sunny aspects shine, and although your excellent aspects will last more than a year, start immediately, as Jupiter will not be back for another 12 years to this part of your chart. Jupiter can help set up a new cycle that will last far into the future—possibly forever!

In terms of your career, 2004 will not bring any outstanding opportunities to move into a high-level job until late March-April 2005, but the changes that will occur this year may be quite welcome nevertheless. Neptune will increase your reputation for contributing visionary ideas, and at the same time, Jupiter will expand your creativity. Watch November 29, 2004, for evidence of how powerful these two planets can be when they work together. There could be a lucrative business idea that stems from a hobby this year, so see what develops.

At work, your salary should increase nicely, especially around mid-June. Pluto in your eighth house will help give you the determination to find ways to develop wealth.

On a day-to-day basis at work, things are brightening. This year you will enjoy the co-workers you interact with, the computer and other equipment you use, and the assignments you manage. The type of projects you work on should improve radically, not only due to an eclipse in Libra in October, but through Jupiter's move into the same sixth house sector from the end of September through most of 2005. Do a good job this year, and you should be in line for a promotion or new job in late March or April 2005.

As you see, it's a busy year, dear Taurus, but one that will bring solid progress on many fronts. Look forward to it, and embrace it in a wholehearted way. More happiness is due— and no one deserves it more than you!

Gemini

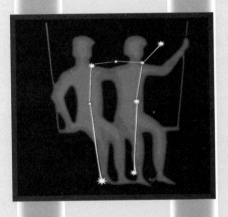

May 21-June 20

The Big Picture

As you begin 2004, you feel released and relieved. Saturn, the taskmaster planet that has put you under considerable pressure over the past few years, has moved on. It won't be back to this same difficult placement for another three decades. The new freedom you are experiencing is intoxicating. You may feel you have to make up for lost time and do the things you haven't been able to do over the past several years. However, now that you don't have so many obligations and obstacles in your way, you have a superb ability to keep to your original agenda and make your mark. Stay focused, dear Gemini, and you will rule the world.

Your Last Three Difficult Years

Gemini values being free and independent, but lately that's not what life was offering. Think back to August through October 2000 or April 2001 to June 2003. Those periods were akin to walking through glue—slow, arduous, and requiring enormous fortitude. You had to muster all your self-discipline and concentration to keep moving forward, but it wasn't easy. Saturn, the teacher planet, had set up a series of obstacles so that you would have to deliberately stop, reassess, and redirect your life's plan.

Saturn asked you to take on some hefty new responsibilities that you assumed you could never handle until you did! After a Saturn phase is over, we always feel more grown-up, no matter what our age. Saturn tends to cram a lot of tutoring into a very short span of time, so the past two and a half years probably feel like ten—you got *that* much experience!

Eclipses in your sign, Gemini, and in your relationship sign of Sagittarius added to the overall level of tension. Most people find that a Saturn visit to their sign is all they can handle, but having eclipses in your sign at the same time was a bit much. This combination of Saturn and the eclipses put every area of your life under stress: your career, money, romantic relationships, and possibly your health. The heavy cloud has lifted and soon life will feel free again.

LOOKING AHEAD, THE ROAD IS CLEAR

You should feel proud that you have fulfilled many (if not all) of Saturn's requirements and are now wiser, firmer, fitter, more energetic, better organized, and far more sharply directed than you were prior to Saturn's visit to your Sun. Like an army drill sergeant, Saturn can get results.

Saturn's pressures are gone and the eclipses, the universe's prime tool for instant, radical change, have moved on to a different family of signs. Eclipses will not be back to Gemini until 2011 and 2012, and Saturn will not be back to your sign until 2030. Unencumbered by heavy planetary artillery, you can now set your course.

First on your list may be a fresh start—a new direction, a new look, a new romance, or a rekindling of an established alliance. Your focus last year was handling massive changes in your career, at the exclusion of almost everything else. This year, you will have a chance to bring your life into better balance, by focusing on the areas of family, residence, financial management, creativity, romance, pregnancy, and child care.

Love and romance will be filled with new beginnings and new chances for happiness. In fact, it is a big theme this year.

There will also be extraordinary possibilities with your home, property, and family relationships. And Saturn—thanks to its new placement in your second house of earned income—will help you decide how to build a nest egg in 2004. Saturn, in its new mission, will help ensure that you'll have something to show for your hard work that will stand the test of time.

This is just a tiny preview, and there's much more to this year ahead! Are you excited yet? You should be!

The Major Themes of 2004

From the position of Saturn and Jupiter in 2004, you could buy a home, or reinvent an apartment or house you have now. Either way, you will appreciate your home's comfort and value. If you already own a home, you may pay off a large chunk of your mortgage this year—maybe all of it! After you get done feathering your nest, it's clear that you will be ready for love!

Romance will be one of your biggest and brightest themes this year, thanks to the position of Jupiter, and the sparkling help from Mars, Venus, and the coming eclipses. It has been more than ten years since you have had planetary energy this strong to encourage love, dear Gemini. Romance starts heating up in late March through early May, and turns white hot in October. November and early December are due to be sultry and sexy, too. Pluto will do its part to focus you squarely on a partner—you may consider marriage.

If single, you have to say goodbye to an old relationship that is simply is not panning out in order to experience new love. New faces will enter your life, and some will leave. Although this is disconcerting—particularly in April and October—you will get used to the messages the planets will be giving out, and you'll adjust rather rapidly. It may be the easiest transition you'll ever make.

If you are happily attached, this year you will take your relationship to a higher level, perhaps by getting married or by having a baby.

Career is due to bring a few big surprises, continuing a trend you began last year. There is much opportunity coming your way, and while there may be an occasional speed bump, the outlook is clearly onward and upward.

Last year Mars made you nearly career obsessed. This year, Mars will travel over the more personal sectors of your chart, to attend to the many details of living you pushed aside for lack of time. Your creativity will positively zoom in 2004, and you may start a creative venture or develop a talent to a whole new realm. There's a lucrative profit to be made from your ideas—someone's impressed with your output and wants to see you develop your talents!

We will talk about all these themes in much more detail below, so let's get to it!

ECLIPSES IN 2004 WILL HIGHLIGHT WORK, HEALTH, FRIENDS, RELATIONSHIPS, AND FUN

The eclipses, so troublesome for you in 2001 and 2002 (and possibly part of 2003 as well), have now moved out of the houses of Gemini/Sagittarius and into the next axis of Taurus and Scorpio and are also edging into Aries and Libra. These new houses are weaker than those houses that hosted the eclipses over the past few years. This is good news! Over the past few years your tension stemmed from being in transition, moving from one way of life to another. Although the process will continue this year, it will be without the overriding uncertainty that kept you on edge last year. With this greater feeling of stability, you will want to take a few risks.

In 2004, there will be four major eclipses, falling on April 19, May 4, and October 14 and 28, in the signs of Aries, Taurus, Libra, and Scorpio, respectively. Eclipses are harbingers of vast change, so we need to look closely at the houses where these eclipses will fall in your chart. The topics they bring up include love, creativity, pregnancy, and children (fifth house); friendship and group activities (eleventh house); work assignments and relationships with co-workers (sixth house); health and fitness (sixth house); and psychological rest and renewal (twelfth house).

Each of these areas will bring the possibility for change, but I suspect that this year, rather than being overwhelmed by the news these eclipses bring (as might have been the case with one or two of the eclipses last year) you will make these changes work for your benefit.

SATURN TEACHES THE PATH TO FINANCIAL FREEDOM, NOW THROUGH JULY 2005

Saturn is now bent on teaching you the merits of sound financial management. As a Gemini, you don't like budgeting—you like to spend, sometimes even impulsively—but Saturn will show you why you will want to amend some of your ways. Saturn likes to ensure that you have something to show at the end of the day for all your work. This planet's job is to crystallize ideas and thoughts into a tangible form, to engender long-range thinking, and to help you establish solid roots in whatever area it visits. Saturn also has the power to make you prosperous. Rather than resist the lessons of Saturn, give them a try—you may be surprised by the results.

You will also be better at negotiating your salary or business deals, and increasing your cash flow. Your sign tends to fall in love quickly with new ideas and concepts, but you don't always remember to protect your financial interests. Saturn will change all that by teaching you how to ask for the money you deserve.

You will also learn to put your money where it matters most (say, for a house) instead of blowing it on things that don't (like a $150 t-shirt). You might learn, for example, how to be a savvy shopper, to buy for less than retail, on eBay, or through sales. Or you may save for an expensive, beautifully tailored winter coat instead of six pairs of designer shoes you don't need.

Saturn naturally rules your eighth house of money, but will be in your second house of earned income until July 2005. Some of your income sources may shift, or you might see more money from sources that offered only small amounts previously. This has interesting implications. More of your income may be derived from areas ruled by your eighth house, namely commissions, licensing fees or royalties, or a year-end bonus.

You may also see additional income from an inheritance, tax rebates or refunds, alimony, prize winnings, gifts, or from a court or insurance settlement. As the eighth house covers credit, you may need to get a loan if you plan to undertake a big project, such as starting your own business. Try not to borrow more than you need, as it may take longer to pay it back (Saturn slows everything down).

The greatest gift from Saturn in 2004 will be that it demands you take a closer look at your values. The second house—where Saturn is based in your chart—is not just about money, but concerns our deepest priorities, as well as our inner confidence. From now until July 2005 all these areas will be under scrutiny. You have already some experience with Saturn in this part of your horoscope (in Cancer), as this planet entered this house in June 2003. The coming year will continue that trend.

Keep in mind that Saturn's position in your second house of money will be easier to host than when it was in your sign, Gemini (mid-2000 to mid-2003). Saturn used to be on one of the north/south/east/west angles of your chart and acted in a stronger, unrestrained manner. The effect was harsher than it will be now.

No one ever left a Saturn transit to the second house poorer than when they entered it, so although you may need to work harder, you may also make more money than ever before.

ROMANCE AND LASTING LOVE
A NUMBER ONE PRIORITY

This is going to be a banner year for your love life. All Gemini will benefit.

First you will have Mars and Venus, that sexy duo, working on your behalf in April by gliding into Gemini. Venus will spend an extraordinary four months in your sign! Then, Jupiter, planet of good fortune, moves into your fifth sector of true love in October for the first time in twelve years. Many planets will crowd your fifth house of love to welcome Jupiter, setting off a bonanza for matters of the heart. Neptune signals Jupiter in November, and Pluto remains in your serious commitment/marriage sector all year, turning on plenty of passion.

In the first week of December, Venus and Mars will embrace in exact conjunction, just in time for the holidays. Two eclipses will cut across your fifth and eleventh houses of social activity and love in April and October. Dear Gemini, I

see an amazing buildup of planetary energy, the likes of which
I have never seen for you!

BE READY TO CONQUER THE WORLD!
MARS IN GEMINI FROM MARCH 21 TO MAY 7, 2004

Mars in Gemini will mark the start of a new personal two-year
cycle that will be a critical and expansive period. Mars, the
great warrior planet, will give you enviable control over your
everyday affairs in a way you've not seen in ages. As a bonus,
Mars will also boost your courage and determination. You'll
have a certain presence that will allow you to make a positive
impression on others, and you won't take no for an answer.

Plan your key projects in late March through early May,
because endeavors started while Mars is in your sign tend to have
a much higher success rate than those initiated at other times.

However, you must factor in that Mercury will be retrograde within this golden period, from April 6 to April 30.
Mercury is your ruling planet, and when it retrogrades, it
sleeps and is not helpful to you. Your best time to take action
is from March 21 to April 5 and from May 1 to May 7.

Throughout Mars' visit to Gemini (whether Mercury is retrograde or not), Mars will make you more energetic, attractive, and
magnetic, and will help you attract love. Circulate, dear Gemini!

WATCH HOW VENUS AND MARS
FAN THE FIRES OF LOVE

You will be at your sexiest, most attractive best when Venus
and Mars dance together in Gemini from April 3 through May 7.
It will be one of your best periods for sparking new love or
rekindling an established relationship.

In addition, Venus, alone, will tour Gemini from April 3 to August 7, 2004, for *four* months! Venus normally remains in a sign for only one month, so this extended stay is highly unusual.

To cap off the year, these two mythological lovers, Venus and Mars, will meet again at holiday time on December 5, this time in your sixth house of work. If single, love could bloom at the office with a co-worker, so look your best! Attached Gemini will enjoy this day enormously, too. If invited to a party, go!

LOVE AND BEAUTY DIM WHEN VENUS RETROGRADES. WAIT FOR BETTER DAYS

Venus will retrograde between May 17 and July 29, and will be in a weaker state. Whenever a planet retrogrades, it asks us to become a bit more introspective and reflective. Venus in retrograde sometimes makes us a bit self-conscious or self-critical—try to not to allow this to happen. Luckily, Venus will retrograde for only a little over two months.

During this Venus retrograde period you may have second thoughts about a present relationship. Or you may hear from an old love, or be tempted to rekindle a relationship you thought was over and done.

Venus is the planet of love and beauty, so Venus retrogrades are not an ideal time to start a new relationship, get engaged or married, schedule plastic surgery, or buy expensive cosmetics. Don't throw an important party during this time and try not to shop for pricey clothes or jewelry. If you want to indulge in spa treatments or change the cut or color of your hair, do so from April 3 to May 17 or from July 29 to August 7, your very best periods. For all these endeavors, you want a strong, sure Venus behind you.

MAMA MIA!
JUPITER TO SPICE UP YOUR LOVE LIFE
SEPTEMBER 24, 2004 THROUGH OCTOBER 25, 2005!

Your wonder year for love begins the moment Jupiter, the planet of happiness and good fortune, enters your fifth house of love and romance on September 24. If you are single and looking for love or if you are attached and hoping to add zest to your relationship, this is the aspect you've been waiting for. Jupiter comes by once every twelve years, so this is truly headline news!

Those who will be first to feel it are those born from May 22 to June 8. If your birthday falls after June 8, you will feel the very best effects of Jupiter in 2005. But *every* Gemini will benefit sooner or later!

Best of all, Jupiter will be in Libra, the sign that exalts marriage. Libra is giving, kind, and very respectful of the partner, so if you are planning to wed, you could not have chosen a better aspect under which to marry. Libra also rules luxurious events, parties, jewelry, flowers, great food, and music—suddenly there will be more of these elements in your life!

Having Jupiter in your fifth house of true love is the single best aspect you could have to find new love. You will have to cooperate with this trend, however; without your intervention, things won't happen. This is a major cycle, so take it seriously! From the end of September onward, you should plan to be out and about when your chances of romantic success will reach an all-time high! Single Gemini should try new ways of meeting people. Have an adventuresome spirit—whatever you do, get out of the house!

If you are attached or married, you and your partner will find more time to do things together and plan something special. If you want to take a romantic vacation, plan it for the last third of the year and choose a spot you can discover together and call your own.

Your most romantic period will occur from September 26 to November 11, a time when you will have Jupiter *and* sexy Mars on your side. The sky's the limit for romantic experiences—Cupid and his flock of little cherubs will be out in force with their trusty bows and arrows!

But wait! There is an extra-special two-week period, starting at the new moon eclipse in Libra on October 13, which should be watched very closely. This eclipse will fall in your fifth house of true love and it will be your most outstanding period of the year, during which the status of an existing relationship may change drastically and new love can grow.

At this new moon eclipse, you will have *five* out of ten planets (including the sun and moon) in your house of true love. Dear Gemini, that is *half* the solar system crowded into one small slice of the horoscope! On top of that, eclipses almost always trigger a new direction and are some of our most powerful cosmic events. This eclipse is basically friendly, although a certain vibe from Saturn suggests you may need to make a serious long-term decision. Whatever it is, it seems to work in your favor.

If for some reason you should experience loss at the eclipse (which is not likely), know that the universe has bigger plans for you, which you may not fully understand at the time. Be patient. Sometimes it takes six months for the bigger picture to be revealed. Remember you have Jupiter protecting your love life, which adds up to considerable cosmic clout on your side.

CONCEIVE A CHILD OR ADOPT ONE
IN MID-TO-LATE OCTOBER

If you hope to have a baby, October through December would be the time to plan a pregnancy. The fifth house—so lit up in October—rules not only love but pregnancy and the plans you may make for your children.

If you already have children, they are especially protected. An older child will make you proud in the later part of the year.

If you've had problems with conception, your best time of the year will be in the days that flow from the new moon October 13. See a fertility doctor earlier in the year so you can be in a position to try at or shortly after that new moon.

If you prefer to adopt or to become a foster parent, the same rule applies—October is the month when your plan will click into place.

JUPITER ENLIVENS HOME AND FAMILY
JANUARY THROUGH SEPTEMBER 24, 2004

Having Jupiter in your fourth house of home will give you confidence and will likely bring enormous family support when you need it most. There are four sectors that are considered more important than the rest, and one of them happens to be this fourth house. This year your parents will support your dreams and will offer advice on some of your tougher life questions. In addition, Jupiter in your fourth house will make the first nine months of 2004 an ideal time to buy a house or to fix one up in a way that will allow you to make it truly your own.

You have some experience with Jupiter in Virgo, in your fourth house of home, because Jupiter entered this part of your chart last year, on August 27, 2003.

If you need to move, you should now be able to find a beautiful apartment or house with lots of light and space, thanks to Jupiter, a planet that expands everything it touches. The selling price or rent may be higher than you anticipated, but you will get solid value in return, and you will know instantly that you have uncovered a good bargain. For example, if you purchase one or two pieces of furniture these will be the ones you treasure all your life.

If you don't move, you may still find your home "growing" larger because a roommate moves out or a child goes off to boarding school or college. Also, now would be a perfect time to update your decor—it will increase your enjoyment of your home. You may also begin searching for a better lifestyle. Some people are lucky enough to have two homes, one in the city and one in the country, which might be possible for you this year. If you look for property, you will find deals that represent considerable value and will offer years of pleasure.

This trend is also about expanding the emotional attachment to your family. If you are adopted and always wanted to find your biological parents, any time *before* Jupiter enters Libra on September 24 would be an ideal time to begin your search.

If your childhood memories were not happy, this would be the year to get help so you can come to terms with your past. If you are estranged from one or both of your parents, this is the year to extend an olive branch. You may be pleasantly surprised by the response.

If you've always wanted to trace your family tree, this would be the time to start. With Jupiter in this house to guide you, you will make considerable progress.

New Moon on September 14
Brings Opportunity
for Home-Related Initiatives

Luckiest Day of the Year: September 21

If you would like to move in 2004, the first nine months are ideal for locating your beautiful new space. It's also an ideal time to sell property.

Your first date to watch is the full moon on March 6, 2004 (plus or minus four days). On that date, Jupiter will form a conjunction with the Moon in your house of home, one of a host of other sparkling aspects. During this time you should see considerable progress.

Next, circle August 10 through September 23 as one of your best periods of the year to browse for new homes, to move, or to settle any other domestic issue. However, your ruler, Mercury, will retrograde from August 9 to September 2, so wait to sign any important papers or complete any expensive purchases until after that date.

Within your golden period listed above, there is a truly outstanding week that will be triggered by the September 14 new moon. Circle the week of September 14–21 on your calendar, when home and family-related plans start to rapidly click into place. On September 21, lucky Jupiter meets with the mighty Sun in your house of home—one of your best days of the whole year!

This part of your chart also rules your parents, so if you're taking care of an elderly parent or are trying to be helpful to your mom or dad, these dates are also superb for finding the right answers to pressing questions.

Pluto: Continued Emphasis on Partnerships

Pluto has been making a long journey through your seventh house of serious, committed partnerships since 1995 and will remain there until 2008. Personal alliances like marriage and serious contract-based business collaborations are covered by the seventh house, and one or both types of partnerships may be a focus for you this year.

Any time Pluto transits the seventh house, you may feel you need a partner to help transform your life. Pluto may personify one particular individual in your life, or a series of people that seem similar in type, someone whom you've met and aligned with since 1995, particularly in business.

Having Pluto in your seventh house of partners can be a double-edged sword. On one hand, this person or company has the power to make you quite strong, secure, and influential—and you know it. However, this person's "my way or the highway" method of negotiating may grate on your nerves. It is more likely you are feeling this trend in a business alliance, but you could have a personal relationship with this person.

Because your partner is so powerful, you have not negotiated a completely evenhanded relationship with them, so this person calls most of the shots.

It is also possible your partner has adopted a lower-key, passive-aggressive approach, with sweetness on the surface, but a steely, controlling nature hidden underneath, which is often even more maddening.

Pluto has been exerting this type of influence for nearly eight years, so by now, out of necessity, you're probably good at standing up for yourself. Although these arguments may have been quite emotional—and will continue to be—you are gaining a sense of just how far you can push the envelope and

still maintain the relationship. If this personal or business relationship is not built on a sturdy foundation of mutual interest,
it may not survive this intense transit of Pluto.

Another way you may experience Pluto is in terms of a
ruthless competitor who will stop at nothing to grab a piece of
your pie. The seventh house, which is so lit up for you, is the
house of what the ancient astrologers called "open enemies."
In modern times, we call these people competitors. In this
case, your competitor will be doing you a favor by giving you a
hard time because you will emerge stronger and more confident when this episode is over. Pluto rules treasure buried
within, so you may discover traits and talents you never knew
you had.

One last parting word about Pluto—in a love relationship,
this placement can indicate enormous passion and depth of
feeling. All aspects have two sides, and the upside of Pluto in
your seventh house is its depth of emotional intensity. These
are the kinds of feelings usually seen only in the movies.

If you have a business relationship, with Pluto in your seventh house, your combined efforts with your partner can lift
you to the top of the mountain, and your success could be
truly breathtaking. So while you may wonder if you can maintain this partnership, the benefits will probably clearly out-
weigh the drawbacks.

If your birthday falls between June 10 and June 13, you
will most likely feel the strain from Pluto's position in 2004. To
relieve that pressure, be circumspect about any new
partnership, check references, and, if applicable, get the best
legal advice. If your birthday falls earlier than June 10, you've
already felt it, and if you were born later than June 13, your
challenges will occur sometime between 2005
and 2008.

REASSESS YOUR JOINT FINANCIAL TERMS AND ASSETS IN AUGUST

On August 6, Jupiter and Pluto will form a challenging "square" aspect that will force you to reassess or reorganize a joint financial arrangement.

Jupiter, being the Great Benefic, will simply ask you to re-evaluate an arrangement or project to determine whether it's worthwhile to continue or end your involvement in it entirely. You may want to think back to the starting date of your main project or alliance, which may well have been 1994 or 1995, given that an important Pluto cycle began at that time. In any case, be ready to decide (and to act if necessary) in August 2004.

NEPTUNE BOOSTS COMPASSION, CREATIVITY, AND SELF-EXPRESSION

Neptune, the planet of compassion, creativity, faith, artistic expression, and inspiration, first entered Aquarius and your ninth house in January 1998 and will remain there until February 2012. Aquarius is a deep-thinking, curious, future-oriented sign, and is highly compatible with Gemini. No doubt you've enjoyed this transit and have likely absorbed Neptune's gifts easily and naturally. The ninth house reflects dreams and goals, widening horizons, and a philosophical approach to the world. Morals, ethics, spirituality, theology, and philosophy form the pillars of this house.

This part of your chart is all about the dissemination of ideas to all four parts of the globe. The ninth house also rules a number of areas, including higher education, travel and interaction with foreigners, publishing projects, and the court system/legal pursuits. All of these fields represent areas of interest and enormous personal growth.

If your birthday falls between June 1 and June 4 (plus or minus three days), you will be in a glorious position to benefit from this year's tour of Neptune.

Over the last five years, you may have changed your career dramatically, for Neptune rules your tenth house of career status and the accolades you earn along the way. Gemini is a talented communicator, so, for example, you may have started writing books or publishing magazine articles. If so, Neptune in Aquarius will continue to help you succeed, and you will be writing more in the future. Neptune is linked to the arts, so you may have gone into painting or photography, or begun publishing art posters, or other creative products—these are fortunate areas for you.

Aquarius is a sign linked to new technology, so you could also do well with the Internet, e-books, computers, software, and related fields such as Web design. Long-distance travel and relationships with foreigners based abroad may have factored into your work in recent years and, if so, will expand in the future. You may have also decided to go back to college or grad school or become a teacher or professor. You also may become a lawyer, judge, or work within the legal system.

Neptune will also help you reflect on what your true vocation should be, with particular emphasis on how you might best serve others. Integrating your personal beliefs with what you do for a living has becoming increasingly important to you. For example, you may be less likely to tolerate being employed by a company that hurts the environment.

After Neptune's fourteen-year stay in Aquarius is completed in 2012, this planet will leave and never visit your ninth house again in your lifetime. Take advantage of the mind-and-heart-

expanding influences of this planet to help you become more
artistic, compassionate, and charitable to others, dear Gemini.

YOUR CREATIVITY TO SPARKLE
IN OCTOBER AND NOVEMBER

Creativity is truly one of the universe's greatest gifts, and often
we don't know what we're capable of until we try. Dear Gemini,
you may have talents you've not yet discovered. This year, take
your innate creativity seriously. Treat yourself to the materials or
lessons you need. If you've set aside a hobby you'd always
loved for lack of time or money, see if you can pick it up again.
If you give it your all, you'll be changed by the experience.

Keep your eye on October and November, key months to
see solid evidence of your talent. If you are in a creative job,
you may begin a big project in mid-October that could poten-
tially earn a large profit. If you take up a new hobby, it will put
a smile on your face and bring great pride, and possibly some
great reviews.

Why will October and November be so vital for engendering your creative powers? The answer is that Mars will enter
Libra on September 27 and remain in your creativity sector
until November 12. At that time, Mars will join Jupiter, Mercury,
and the Sun—four major planets—bringing light and energy to
your fifth house of creativity, and all will be in exceptionally
fine angle to Neptune, planet of the arts. This is extraordinary!

Within this period, your most important date to watch is
October 13, when the new moon eclipse will kick this powerful
energy into higher gear, an aspect that will have much longer
influence than the usual two weeks. In astrology it matters
when you start anything, so do so just after that eclipse for the
best results. Mars will make a sensational aspect to Neptune on

October 15, just two days after the eclipse arrives. If being creative is important to you, you are going to love mid-October!

Action-oriented Mars leaves this position on November 12, but on November 29, Jupiter, the planet of expansion and great happiness, will signal Neptune from what astrologers call a heavenly "trine" position, considered the most harmonious and beautiful of all planetary aspects. This is one of the year's major features, and warrants your attention. Jupiter will enlarge all of Neptune's gifts. You'll be able to express yourself in new and exciting ways, and your antenna for what the public will want will be finely tuned. Jupiter's call on Neptune won't be felt for just a day, but from the second half of October straight through November, when it will peak in strength. All this is so exciting.

SATURN HAS LEFT GEMINI
START A NEW EXERCISE ROUTINE
FROM NOVEMBER 11 TO DECEMBER 25, 2004

Saturn's visit over the past few years should have left you fitter, firmer, and trimmer. Saturn in one's own sign often causes weight loss. This planet of self-discipline may have taught you how to eat, exercise, and take better care of yourself, and if so, you enter 2004 looking trimmer and younger than you did several years ago. Future weight loss won't be quite as easy, however, now that Saturn has moved on to Cancer—but it *is* still possible.

You'll need to be especially vigilant about your waistline once Jupiter—the happy planet—moves into its position in Libra in September for a thirteen-month stay. During that time, you may be invited to many social events and will be tempted to eat more. Being that Venus rules Libra and Venus rules sweets, desserts, particularly, will entice you. Pounds may start to accumulate without your even noticing, so you might want to keep an eye on your weight.

If you hoped to jump-start a new exercise routine, do so while Mars circulates your sixth house of health from November 11 to December 25, 2004. This is your most successful time of the year to begin a more active lifestyle. The new moon in your fitness sector will fall on November 12, a superb time to kick off any exercise program, and it occurs at the very start of this dazzling fitness period.

If you are disappointed to have to wait until the end of the year to begin, you will also have an opportunity to do so during two previous months. March 21 to May 2, 2004, the new moon in Gemini, June 17 and the two weeks that follow are two periods that are nearly as good.

When I list these dates, I'm suggesting you begin your exercise program or investigate medical matters—please don't stop at the end of the phase! Don't diet until after the November 26 full moon has passed by several days. If you follow this advice, your regime will be a success! Start to exercise first; cut back on calories later.

There are two points in the year when you'll need to take preventative measures against becoming run-down. The first time is in early May, but this may be due to psychological stress rather than anything serious.

The other time arrives in late October. At that time whatever comes up will strengthen your resolve to treat your body with more tender loving care. This could be a blessing in disguise.

These are the times when two eclipses will occur in your house of physical and mental well-being. Those eclipses will arrive on May 4 and October 28, so circle those dates on your calendar. Should anything arise, it's the universe's way of telling you to attend to that issue early so you can nip it in the bud.

Finally, as we will discuss below, career shifts for May-born Gemini will be quite dramatic this year, but also possibly quite draining. If your birthday falls from May 21 to May 24, you will require more stress relief than other members of your sign. Working out at the gym or participating in a sport regularly would be a good way to offset everyday tensions.

YOUR CAREER
CONTINUES TO BRING SUDDEN SURPRISES

Circle February to Make a Big Career Move

Last year Uranus moved into your tenth house of career, a sign of massive changes to come in your professional life. If you haven't already seen these changes, 2004 could be the year you make a courageous career jump or shift into a brand-new field. Uranus rules the sciences, computers, broadcasting, the Internet, and all newly invented forms of technology (it may be developing as I write this), so your new career may fall in these areas.

Lots of opportunities will come your way, but quickly and when you least expect it. Choose carefully, as there is a danger that you might accept too many and spread yourself thin.

Now that taskmaster Saturn is no longer in Gemini, you will no longer be crushed under the weight of as many obligations and responsibilities, and will be freer to pursue more professional opportunities. Things may move so quickly that you may be tempted to retreat into your old role. Don't. You need to keep moving forward—Uranus won't have it any other way. You are not the person you once were, and your old job doesn't suit you. Quite simply, you've outgrown it.

Uranus is the planet of innovation, genius, and surprise, but also of disruption, change, and unpredictable events. The road to success won't always be smooth, but you will move into new realms, so it's logical to expect a certain number of ups and downs. Be confident that the new position you will take on will be more relevant to your future. Enjoy the adventure you're having now.

Those born from May 20 to May 28 may feel that they have reached a crisis stage in their career where something urgently needs to be done. If your birthday falls within this period, it means only that Uranus is pushing you hard to move into your new profession. Don't let this worry you—go with the flow. Uranus' job is to sweep away what is no longer relevant and help you replace it with something more vital for the future.

Look for a Job Just After the New Moon on February 20, 2004

Your three best times to change jobs will be just after the February 20 new moon, at the very end of August, and in the first few days of September. You will need to be poised to take advantage of opportunities that will occur during that time. If you don't want to change jobs during that time, wait until 2005. And while November and December will be exceptionally busy, don't be fooled—your very best period for actual advancement occurs earlier in the year, especially at that February 20 new moon and the two weeks that follow.

The eclipse on October 28 will not change your job as much as the way you do it. With this eclipse falling in your sixth house of work methods, you may learn new software, be given new computer equipment, see a certain colleague leave the company, or move to new headquarters.

Your work schedule will be particularly hectic from mid-November up to Christmas Day. You might not want to schedule too many social events during that period because chances are you'll be working late, and when you finally go home you will want to put your feet up and relax!

On August 18, Mars will oppose Uranus, so things are not likely to go your way. Why add to your stress? Lie low in the days surrounding this date and you'll be glad you did.

Summary

An amazing year lies ahead, dear Gemini. Recent years have constricted your movements and limited your options, but not 2004! Taskmaster Saturn left Gemini in June 2003, so by the time 2004 dawns, Saturn will be far enough away for you to feel freer, more optimistic, and able to consider the many new possibilities coming your way.

Personal happiness is one of the big areas of possible gain. Last year the planets almost forced you to make career your major focus, but this year you'll get to balance that preoccupation with more attention to your personal life.

Romantically, a whole stream of aspects will conspire to help you find true love. Beginning in April, Venus moves into Gemini for an astounding four-month stay—far more time than the usual orbit of one month. Like Venus, Mars will also tour Gemini in April, always considered a huge plus astrologically, because Mars increases drive, courage, determination, and attractiveness. Mars acts as a huge magnet, and helps you reel in romantic interests, money, career offers—you name it. Whenever Mars returns to your sign, it signifies the start of a new two-year cycle, so it's a critical time to make big initiations. Remarkably, Venus will be in Gemini at the same time, and when Mars and Venus are together the likelihood that love will happen increases tenfold. This never happened last year, but oh, is the universe making up for that now!

Your love life should get even hotter when benefic Jupiter enters your fifth house of true love in late September for a thirteen-month stay. Happiness, fun, and leisure will be yours, and if you didn't meet the One earlier in the year due to Mars and Venus, you will have even more cosmic help from September onward. In particular, watch October and November as important months for love!

The universe will send two major eclipses to the sectors ruling love and new people on April 19 and October 13. Eclipses sometimes require that you give up something in order to receive something new, so there may be some partings, but if so, it will be to make room in your life for something—or someone—more suited to you.

If you are in an established relationship, you will want to make something more out of your alliance, perhaps by getting married or by choosing a new goal that you can work on together, as a couple. It would be an ideal year for marriage, as Jupiter in Libra will bring special blessings to all types of partnerships (business or personal) in the last quarter of the year. If you want a baby, 2004 could make that wish come true—it is one of the best years in a decade for pregnancy. Your most likely month to hear the stork is on the way: October.

Home, real estate, and domestic goals all progress remarkably well in the first nine months of the year. If you're hoping to renovate, do so prior to the end of August and the results will rival those of *Trading Spaces*. The week of September 14 will be a dazzler for home and family-related choices. Watch September 21, when the mighty Sun will walk arm-in-arm with Jupiter, your luckiest day of the year for domestic projects and rallying family support for your dreams.

Financially, you will approach money matters differently than you have in the past. Your new mantra is "less is more." You may buy less, but what you do buy will be of far better quality and remain in your possession longer. You will have a solid chance to get your credit back in shipshape condition, too. This trend comes thanks to Saturn in Cancer, which also intends to have you re-evaluating your values. Saturn will give you an attractive earthiness and practical sense to your light-hearted persona.

2004 could bring quantum leaps in your creative powers. You may focus your creativity on a brand-new area of interest or on one that has attracted your attention all your life. There will be strong profit potential in your ideas, dear Gemini, so take your ideas seriously and influential people will, too. October and November are your biggest months to see evidence of your growing talents.

In career, things are changing radically—you may get different duties by being promoted to a completely different department of your company, or you may decide to switch to another industry. Uranus, the innovative planet that strikes suddenly and without warning, will soon show you that you can take your education and experience and use it in a completely new way.

Uranus is all about the future, and it would be pointless to resist these massive career cosmic shifts. If at times you find yourself reminiscing about "the good old days," remind yourself that your old job is more about the person you used to be rather than the person you have become.

On the road to professional success, you will have to factor in a few setbacks, but those reversals will be more than compensated by some miraculous breakthroughs, for that's how Uranus works. Take your roller coaster ride in stride.

You've got six more years of Uranus in your house of career, so this is an adventure that's not due to end any time soon.

The eclipses in Scorpio and Taurus in April, May, and October will bring changes in your workplace, but due to shifts and reorganizations of personnel, you will feel some stress. These eclipses are nowhere near as troublesome as the ones that occurred from 2000 to early 2003. To channel tension, have a sport or workout routine ready to help you relax, especially during those months. You might like the changes these eclipses bring because these will be milder and friendlier than the ones you've had before.

This year you should feel more energized and less prone to respiratory illnesses or injury to bones. You may have lost weight (a gift from Saturn when it was in Gemini). If so, be careful not to gain it back, particularly when Jupiter enters Libra during the last three months of 2004. A fitness plan begun at the new moon in November should bring outstanding results and make you proud. In all 2004 will be a year that will bring comforting balance to your life. Last year, planetary energy focused squarely on your career, so it was hard to think about anything else. This year you'll have much more opportunity to improve your personal life and will have more time to enjoy the life you worked so hard to build! You will especially enjoy the last quarter of 2004, when Jupiter visits Libra, a placement that sparkles for Gemini. Jupiter will stay in Libra through much of 2005, so you have quite an exciting ride ahead!

Cancer

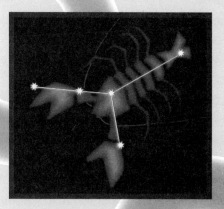

June 21-July 22

The Big Picture

This year will have more weight and purpose than most. Saturn, the planet known to bring greater responsibility, practicality, and maturity, entered Cancer in June 2003 and will remain in that sign until July 2005.

If you have been undecided about a certain life choice, this year you will learn what to do. Saturn adds to your responsibilities but also clears your path ahead. It also provides depth and authority, and makes you more pragmatic and resilient.

Between now and July 2005, Saturn will force you to make an honest assessment of yourself, your lifestyle, and your talents. Saturn will also challenge you to test your theories by putting them into practice.

Saturn can be a tough teacher because it forces us to stop deliberating and start doing. If you work with Saturn, you will receive all the structure and framework you'll need to be more sharply focused, organized, and ultimately more successful. Saturn's job is to crystallize experience, ambition, and dreams into a concrete reality. This planet will help you with discipline, which will help you to use your time wisely. This is a winning trait.

Saturn will not force you to take on any responsibilities you don't want, but what you choose may represent a dream you've always had or something you feel is the right moral choice. You will have to give it your all, at the exclusion of everything else, at least for the several months that Saturn passes in tight mathematical degree over the degree of the Sun of your *exact* birthday. The payoff will be worthy of your time and energy. With Saturn, you have to earn your rewards, but your accomplishments will stand the test of time.

Saturn's lessons almost always revolve around the wise use of time and money. Of the two, time is the more precious. This year, if you fritter away your time with activities that Saturn deems not appropriate for your age and stature, those activities will be banished. Saturn rules the concept of time, so now every minute will have to count. When Saturn visits your sign, you may feel like you're running out of time to accomplish your goals.

Life decisions almost always happen during Saturn visits. Some Cancers may marry or have children because they suddenly don't want wait before anymore. Others will buy a house because they've rented for long enough. Having Saturn visit your sign is a good thing, which you may understand either immediately or in hindsight. If you work with this planet in 2004, you will be a force to reckon with in 2005.

Uranus' move to Pisces is a major shift in 2004 and will increase your desire to learn. You will be interested in new ideas, concepts, and viewpoints that you would have never before considered, possibly through a college or graduate-level course or more likely through long-distance travel. Although your sign tends to hold tightly to opinions, you will now be exposed to outside influences that will test your thinking. Uranus in Pisces is an intuitive sign, and you will be forced to sharpen your instinct and think more critically. This new self-image will have far-reaching and upbeat ramifications for the future.

The four eclipses of 2004 will change the status of both your career and romantic life, and will most likely appear in April, May, or October. These eclipses—wild cards because they create sudden opportunities and setbacks—will be milder this year than in years past. There is nothing to fear—

you can benefit from even enforced changes. The positions of Venus and Mars—particularly at holiday time—will be telling and positive.

When it comes to your personal life, you may have to say goodbye to one or two old friends as you (and they) move on with your lives. In October, it will be impossible to ignore that you and your once-close pal have little in common. New friends will fill the gap, but this rapid change may give you pause and a pang of sadness. Cancers often dwell on the past, but in this case you really must keep your eyes on the future. The right people will be with you as you move forward.

The fourth house—ruling home and family—is under vibrant aspects from late September 2004 through October 2005. The news could not be better. Cancer is happiest when home is comfy and secure and when family relationships are harmonious. This year that wish can become a reality. You may move, renovate, paint, buy new furniture, clear clutter, or do any number of things to improve your living space. Your family will also support you during this trend.

Those are some of the broad brushstrokes of the year ahead, now let's delve into the details.

The Details of Your Year Ahead

SATURN IN CANCER IN 2004 CHANGES EVERYTHING: A NEW PRAGMATIC 'YOU' EMERGES

There is no question that Saturn in Cancer will change the way you view the world. If you have been content to live day by day, Saturn will bring on a strong yearning for stability and roots. This attitude will permeate everything you do affecting your career, money, romantic life, family, where to live, and other lifestyle considerations. By focusing on long-range, hard-to-achieve goals, Saturn will show that you will accomplish more than if you focus on smaller ones. Certain sacrifices will have to be made, but if you marshal your resources, you'll achieve what you set out to do.

We experience Saturn only two or three times in our lifetime, as Saturn takes 29 years to circle the Sun. The good news is that each time Saturn comes for a visit, you'll hopefully retain the lessons you learned in a previous cycle. You may want to see what happened in the last Saturn-in-Cancer period, which occurred from August 1973 to June 1976, assuming you were born by then and were older than 12. (If you were any younger, this planet may not have had much of an influence.) You may get a sense of what themes surfaced during that time and what might surface again.

Saturn governs rules and regulations of all kinds, and if you step over the line in the sand Saturn will punish you for the smallest infringement. Saturn may not be lenient, but it does get results. Saturn will never give you more than you can handle, although some people need a loud message from it to get the point.

Saturn periods usually coincide with the start of an important new commitment. You may start a business, get married, have a baby, publish a book, or get a master's degree. View this period as an adventurous journey into self-discovery. If you deal honestly and earnestly with challenges, you will develop into a force to be reckoned with by the end of Saturn's transit in July 2005.

Cancers born June 27 to July 19 will feel Saturn's effects the most in 2004, although all Cancers will feel

Saturn in some way. You have had six months to adjust to Saturn's new set of responsibilities, as Saturn entered Cancer in June 2003, so you may have an inkling of what lies ahead.

WHY YOU CAN FEEL UPBEAT ABOUT THIS TOUR OF SATURN

When Saturn glides into Cancer, it moves into a sign that is 180 degrees away from Capricorn, its home base. Saturn will be, as the ancient astrologers wrote, "in its detriment," meaning the planet is weak because Cancer is far away from Saturn's home base. This is good news for you—you won't see the harsher side of Saturn.

Although the usual tour of Saturn in Cancer is two years and six months, Saturn will spend only two years and one month during this tour, approximately 20 percent less time. All things considered, you're sitting pretty, dear Cancer.

JUPITER WILL INCREASE YOUR POWERS OF COMMUNICATION FROM NOW THROUGH SEPTEMBER 24, 2004

Jupiter's presence in your third house suggests that it's going to be the luckiest area of your chart until late September 2004. The third house rules communication, and because Jupiter always enhances the area it touches, you will learn to get your point across in a more sophisticated manner.

This year you may increase your powers of persuasion, your negotiation skills, or your ability to navigate the fine print of a legal contract. You may take up a new language or be asked to teach in a new area. If you are an actor, you may meet an amazing teacher who reveals your talents in ways you never thought possible. If you work in an office, your company may provide media training to help you "meet the press." Or— and this is a biggie—you may even be given your own radio or TV show! If that is a goal, go for it!

If you are a professional writer, the coming nine months could bring a huge leap in your overall status, and Jupiter will see that it is matched with impressive compensation. You may write or publish a book or screenplay. You may even launch a new career that will allow you to walk away from one you dislike. No matter what area of the communications industry you may be in, you should do well.

If you are a librarian, editor, or do research, your skills will be highly valued. If you want a more creative or investigative job, one is on the way. You may have to look for your ideal situation, but if you do, you will be rewarded.

Many Cancers have Aries, the sign of entrepreneurial effort, on the cusp of their solar tenth house of profession and, as a result, own their own business. If you do, you should consider doing a publicity campaign in March or September. You have a good chance of getting favorably written up in the press and attracting more business. If you work in advertising, sales, marketing, or public relations, expect your skills to be in hot demand.

The third house, so brilliantly lit, also rules travel, so you may be on the road much more than usual during the first nine months of the year. Uranus in Pisces will get you traveling even greater distances, so have your luggage ready, dear Cancer!

You may look into buying a new cell phone, PDA, or other gadget to make life easier. You may also buy or lease a car this year (a great time to do so), or you might add a high-speed Internet-access line to your home or office.

Contracts, leases, and other formal agreements come under the third house, so in the coming months Jupiter may help you sign a major agreement. Congratulations, dear Cancer, you are coming into your own!

SIBLINGS AND OTHER CLOSE RELATIVES ARE LUCKY FOR YOU FROM JANUARY THROUGH SEPTEMBER 2004

Siblings, cousins, aunts, and uncles come under this same third house, and thanks to Jupiter's assistance, one of these individuals may figure prominently in your life. Your sister or your aunt, for example, may take special interest in a goal you want to achieve and give you a hand. You might partner with your brother in a business, share an apartment with your sister or even buy a house together. This year, your close relatives will show you just how much they care about you.

Alternatively, your sister or brother may have very good news in their own lives. Be sure to check in often with your siblings throughout the year.

If you are estranged from a sibling and want to repair your relationship, you may be able to this year. Be the one to make the first move, and you will begin the process.

JUPITER IN LIBRA BEGINNING SEPTEMBER 24: HOME, PROPERTY, FAMILY RELATIONSHIPS SHINE FOR OVER A YEAR

Cancer rules the part of the horoscope that is devoted to home and family, so a secure and congenial home life is imperative to your happiness. The Crab, which symbolizes your sign, wears his home on his back; when life gets too difficult, he pulls his shell over his head, and privately restores himself before moving out again into the world.

Your sign is known go through great efforts to make your home and family life the very heart of your existence. If you aren't getting along with family or if the atmosphere is chaotic or upsetting, the Crab feels maimed and unable to function. Ancient astrologers wrote that the bottom of the wheel is the very foundation of the chart, and if not secure, the entire wheel will wobble and all of life will be in danger of collapse.

That's why 2004 will be such a standout year! Jupiter, the wonder planet that brings good tidings and break-throughs, will move into Libra and your fourth house of home—the very part of the chart Cancer rules—on September 24, 2004, and will remain there for thirteen glorious months.

The last quarter of 2004 would be a fantastic time to buy or sell real estate or renovate your present home. If you rent, you will also be in luck. Look for a beautiful, big apartment with lots of light, big closets, and a view. Don't settle for a less-than-perfect space. If you need a loan or advice from your parents, this would be the time to ask. If you're estranged from them, Jupiter will help you get your relationship back on track. Extend an olive branch to your mom or dad in mid-September or October, your best time of the year to do so.

This would be an ideal time to trace your genealogy (a very Cancer-oriented hobby), as Jupiter's position will help you. Start doing your research early in the year, because by September or October you may have a breakthrough.

Residential, Domestic, and Family Quests
Progress From Mid to Late October

Changes at home are very likely near October 14, thanks to an eclipse that will highlight this area of your chart. This will be a new moon eclipse, suggesting a fresh start. Saturn is in hard angle to this eclipse, so you may be jittery about the scale of your undertaking, but other positive elements of this eclipse will help you move forward anyway. Many planets will be crowded into your fourth house of home, so changes will be under way.

If you need to make any domestic or family-related decisions, watch the period starting September 26 through November 10, 2004, with special emphasis in October. Mars will be touring your fourth house of home and will open a big window of opportunity.

Protect Health Throughout 2004
While Saturn Hovers Over Your Sun

You will need to protect your health during Saturn's visit to Cancer, as Saturn may drain your vitality. Be sure to eat right and get enough sleep—Saturn sometimes makes us feel tired for no apparent reason. Be proactive about scheduling medical checkups. This is a critical year to get a flu shot, and keep in mind that it takes about a month for the vaccine to become active in your system. Other sensitive areas are your bones and teeth (Saturn depletes calcium) and your stomach. Eating disorders could also become a problem, as Cancer rules the upper digestive system.

At first you won't like Saturn because he will seem like the army sergeant who makes you get up at dawn, run five miles, and do push-ups before breakfast. However, if you work with Saturn you will become healthier than you've ever been. If you were born June 21-27, you experienced its hardest aspects in the second half of 2003, but you still should be proactive. If you were born June 27-July 7 you should be most careful in the first half of 2004, and if you were born July 8-July 19 you should be most careful in the second half of 2004. (July 6 and 7 birthdays feel Saturn most in June, July, and August 2004.)

If your birthday falls from July 19 to July 22, Saturn will come close to the degrees of your birthday Sun, but will actually visit your birthday Sun in the first half of 2005. You have plenty of time to get yourself in top shape before then.

Losing Weight Will Be Easier Than Usual; This Year Start a Fitness Routine in June, July, or December

If you are interested in losing weight, Saturn's visit to your sign will make it possible to lose those stubborn pounds.

Design your weight-loss plan to shave off those pounds in a slow and steady way. What will be tricky is that your vitality during this time will be at an all-time low, and your responsibilities will be at an all-time high. If you want to lose weight, it is absolutely critical that you find time to exercise to offset stress.

Always begin an exercise and fitness plan on a favorable new moon. Concentrate on your level of physical output, but do not cut back on calories at the onset of your program. After you have been working out for a while, begin your sensible diet a few days after the full moon.

Here are your three best new moons of the year to begin a fitness program:

○ **July 17, 2004**, is a new moon in Cancer that falls in your solar first house of vitality and looks. The full moon will occur July 31, so wait until August 3 to cut calories.

○ **September 14, 2004**, is a new moon in Virgo, a sign ruling fitness. The full moon will occur September 28, so wait until October 1 to cut calories.

○ **December 11, 2004**, is a new moon in Sagittarius, in your sixth house of fitness. The full moon occurs on December 26, so wait until December 28 to start dieting. I realize it's difficult to begin a fitness routine at holiday time, but if you wait until January you will lose your window of opportunity.

FOREIGN TRAVEL, HIGHER EDUCATION PROVIDE ELECTRIC STIMULATION

With idiosyncratic Uranus fueling your thirst to learn, you'll be a virtual sponge in your effort to soak up as much as you can from your environment. And best of all, to help things along, your environment is likely to change—so strong is the possibility that you will begin to travel more—often at the drop of a hat. You may have enjoyed this trend last year, especially starting in June 2003. Some periods will be more pronounced for travel than others, but the trend will last through this decade. Unusual experiences will mark your travels, as nothing about a Uranus visit is normal or usual in any sense.

A relocation overseas may appeal to you now, whether for work, study, or to start over, perhaps due to the end of a relationship.

Uranus teaches us to think for ourselves, so your family may not understand your views. This won't faze you; you will be on a mission to understand what you believe now, not what you were taught when you were younger.

To understand why this trend is so important, we need to go back to March 2003, when Uranus, the planet of revolutionary change, innovation, and sudden insights, moved into your intellectual ninth house when it entered Pisces and where it will remain for the balance of the decade. Uranus hasn't occupied Pisces in 84 years—the time it takes to revolve around the Sun—so this is new for you.

Uranus' job is to set up trends that shape your experience over many years. For the past fourteen years, you haven't had a particularly friendly Uranus, so now that you have powerful help coming your way, you will find it hard to believe how much better things are!

Like the third house (the area of your chart that Jupiter will be visiting for the main part of this year), your ninth house deals with ideas, methods, opinions, learning, and insight you gain by reading, taking classes, debating ideas, doing research, or simply observing the world. While the third house rules learning, it is in the ninth house where we integrate all we've learned to build our philosophy of life. This is precisely what you will be doing from 2004 through 2011.

Uranus wants to open you up, so the changes that take place in the ninth house happen internally. This is an important point—sometimes the world presses down on us and we change because of these outside forces. But this will not be the case for you this year. You will go through a process of reassessment and may become more interested in politics, art, culture, books, the sciences, the legal system, philosophy, ethics, morals, theology, languages, or graduate-level study and research—all ruled by the ninth house. Uranus is in the spiritual sign of Pisces, so you may feel a longing to make religion or spirituality a larger part of your life. Some Cancers will convert to another religion.

No matter what, your goals will become larger and more complex, and later you might say, "In the past I used to focus too much on the small details. Now I paint life on mural-size canvases." That's the effect of Uranus in the ninth house.

The ninth house also rules international endeavors, but you may not have to leave home to experience a global influence. For example, you may launch a website that becomes very popular around the world, providing much more interaction with people from other countries. You might open an import/export business, work in the international division of your company, or if you're an agent, represent talent based abroad. If you are the talent, you could do very well by being represented in foreign countries.

As another part of this trend, you may decide to go back to college or graduate school and may even be awarded a scholarship to help you pay for your tuition. The legal field glows brightly for you, so if you were deliberating about law school, go for it. Don't assume you won't be accepted by a certain prestigious institution—with Uranus in your ninth house, anything is possible!

Publishing also falls under the ninth house, because it entails both the dissemination and preservation of information. If you are interested in writing, editing, or designing books or websites, you could do well, for Uranus is well angled to your Sun. If you write a book, it could become a best seller, as Uranus has the power to make you famous. This dovetails beautifully with Jupiter's visit to your third house, and when two major planets say the same thing, their influence is particularly strong. You will have to reach out to the world to make this happen, but if you do, you should see solid results.

CANCERS BORN JUNE 21–27
BENEFIT MOST FROM URANUS IN PISCES
DURING 2004

If you were born in the early part of Cancer, from June 21 to June 27, you will enjoy the positive vibrations of Uranus this year, despite feeling the most pressure from Saturn. In astrology, when there are two conflicting messages—one helpful, one challenging—the aspects of the slower-moving planet override the others, and Uranus in this case is the slower-moving planet. Uranus' job is to sweep out the old elements in your life and bring in the new, while Saturn quickly stabilizes them.

Every Cancer, even those whose birthdays are not mentioned above, will eventually receive the direct vibrations of Uranus between now and 2011 and, in the meantime, will feel some upbeat spillover.

YOUR LUCKIEST DAY OF THE YEAR:
SEPTEMBER 21 JUPITER AND THE SUN CONJOIN:
AGREEMENTS SHINE BRIGHTLY

September 21 is everyone's favorite day in 2004, for that's the day Jupiter will walk arm in arm with the Sun. Optimism, expansion, and opportunity will rain down on us. Use this day to sign a contract, schedule an interview or presentation, or accept a job offer. You may speak to a group that day or even appear on TV or radio. It is also an outstanding date to take a short trip or make plans with a sibling or close relative.

If you were born on or within five days of July 21 (the closer, the better), you will be doubly lucky, for the mathematical degrees of this conjunction will directly reach out to the degrees at your birth.

September 21 falls just after the powerful new moon on September 14, and that new moon will set much of your luck in motion. Circle these dates! With Mars, Mercury, Jupiter, the Sun, and new moon in your third house of communication and travel, something is sure to turn up!

Take Control of Your Career in January and at the New Moon March 20 and Full Moon September 28

2004 starts out with a bang insofar as your career is concerned, with your longest and most sustained period of career progress to happen in January. (To be more precise, this window of opportunity will begin a bit earlier, on December 16, 2003, and remain open until February 3, 2004.) This is when Mars, the energy planet, will enter Aries and your tenth house of fame and promotion for the first time in two years. Mars will make you assertive and will give you to the courage to go out there and take what you feel is yours.

If you want a promotion or new position, your best chance of the year to do so is in January. Don't underestimate this vital period; Mars has the ability to move mountains. If you don't want to leave your job, schedule a performance review to find out what growth opportunities are available. If you want to run your own business, January is an ideal time to open your doors.

Whatever changes occur will be because you initiate them, not because you are forced to or because opportunities land in your lap. Be proactive. The next big opportunity will fall on either the new moon in Aries on March 20 or the eclipse in Aries on April 19 (also a new moon). The latter, a new moon solar eclipse, will be in perfect angle to Uranus, so any news that develops could be thrillingly positive and come up suddenly.

If you were born early in your sign, near June 20, you will feel the March new moon more powerfully. If you were born late in the sign, near July 21, you will feel the eclipse on April 19 more powerfully. (When I say "near" a certain date, I mean within five days on either side of that date.) If not, you will still feel a push, and with two new moons to fall in your house of career this year, you have two chances to make an important career move that suits you.

For the April 19 eclipse, Mars will be at a tough angle to Pluto, so a co-worker may be jealous of you and not want to see you advance. If this person spreads untruths about you, be ready to present your case. Honestly, dear Cancer, I don't think anything can stop you from moving ahead.

The aforementioned eclipse in Aries (April 19) and another in Libra (October 14) highlight both your career and home life, and suggest that you may be working at a brand-new job before the year is out. There is a strong chance you will need to relocate to take that new job. If you do, finding a new place to live won't be a problem during the last three months of 2004 (or in most of 2005, for that matter), for as previously discussed in the section on Jupiter, your fourth house of home will be the most blessed part of your chart later in the year.

Should you experience any setbacks during these eclipses, take it as a sign that your old job is over and the universe has bigger plans for you.

Later in the year may also bring big career news. Watch for news on September 28, 2004, plus or minus four days. On that day, a full moon will fall in your tenth house of honors and promotion. This date happens within another golden period for improving your residential situation. All the preparations for your move to your job—and possibly into your new home—could fall into place.

Late September could bring a breakthrough for another reason, because just two days earlier, on September 26, Mars, the ruler of your tenth house, will receive a visit from Jupiter, the planet of happiness and good fortune. This happens only once a year, and this aspect is simply spectacular.

YOUR FINANCIAL OUTLOOK BRIGHTENS IN 2004
THANKS TO URANUS
LEAVING YOUR SOLAR EIGHTH HOUSE

Last year was a study in contrasts. You had one of the best possible aspects to make money (Jupiter in the second house) and one of the hardest (Uranus in the eighth house).

Uranus' position may have given you a rocky ride with credit card bills, student loans, taxes, and other financial obligations. Uranus also brings disruption, surprise, and unpredictable events to the house it touches, so having this planet in a financial house was not fun. While Uranus can be stimulating (especially in your mind-expanding ninth house), it caused trouble during its tour of your financial house, spanning 1998-2003. These years will not be repeated.

If you had planned to receive money from a certain person or company, those funds may have never materialized. For example, you may not have gotten child support that was expected, a scholarship on which you depended, or a pension due to your company going bankrupt.

Things looked bright when Uranus left this house in March 2003, but Uranus retrograded back into your eighth house in mid-September 2003 and remained there until December 30, 2003. Hence, January, February, and mid-September through December 2003 brought more of the same uncertain financial conditions that you were trying so hard to leave behind. Happily, as of December 30, 2003, Uranus left this area of your chart for the next 84 years, which allows you to put this period behind you forever. In 2003, you also had Jupiter in your second house of income, so certain Cancers did very well financially in 2003, at least until the end of August. Even if you didn't make a killing, you were protected from the harsher reversals of financial life. However, you were at the mercy of clashing forces last year, so it was probably hard to hold onto the money you did make.

This year, you will no longer have Jupiter's financial protection, but you also won't have the difficulties wrought by Uranus. Your financial life will normalize, and you will move to higher ground, dear Cancer.

ASK FOR A RAISE
AFTER THE NEW MOON APPEARS ON AUGUST 16

Neptune, the planet of inspiration, creativity, and also confusion, remains in your solar eighth house for several more years. This means that you can make good money from creative and artistic endeavors, but that you should show all contracts and deals to a lawyer who can examine them for you.

With Neptune in your house of money—a planet known to make things invisible or, at the very least, confusing—you do need to be conscious of the fine print!

This year, your best time to ask for a raise will be at the new moon on Monday, August 16 and the two weeks that follow. Try to time it as close to August 16 as possible.

GOOD MONEY CAN BE EARNED FROM CREATIVE PROJECTS ON OR NEAR NOVEMBER 29

If you are creative or work with creative people, November 29, 2004, is a day likely to bring outstanding financial news concerning a creative project. On this gorgeous day, Jupiter and inspirational Neptune will be magnificently aligned (the week leading up to November 29 is also strong), and this exceedingly rare and jewel-like aspect is truly a gift from the universe. Use this day to present ideas to influential people or begin a creative endeavor. If you do, the Muses will help you every step of the way.

A FEW FINANCIAL TROUBLE SPOT DATES TO WATCH

The full moons of February 6 and July 31, 2004 (plus or minus four days), are danger periods. You may enter into a financial relationship without paying proper attention to the terms of the deal.

The new moon on August 15 is also a time when long-term problems could emerge from a new project not completely thought through.

Also watch your spending when Mars tours your solar second house from June 23 to August 10, 2004. Mars could burn a hole in your pocket!

Your Romantic Life
to Be Strongly Influenced By Two Eclipses
and the Orbits of Mars and Venus in Late '04

The Moon rules your sign, so lunar eclipses are Cancer's big cosmic events of the year, more powerful and important than any other event in the chart. All lunar eclipses are full moon eclipses, which means that they tend to make everyone more emotional, but especially you because the Moon is your ruler. Lunar eclipses have the power to stir up old memories and long-forgotten dreams. Eclipses seem to move up the timetable on events so they happen much sooner than anticipated.

In 2004, there will be four eclipses: two new moon solar eclipses and two full moon lunar eclipses. Both lunar eclipses will fall on your love/friendship axis. Full moons denote endings or culmination points. The other two eclipses will fall on your home/career axis. For career and residence, a new chapter is forming, and with love and friendship, you are reaching a culmination or finish.

Before you react, let me add something of a twist here. The eclipses that affect your home and career will be in Aries and Libra, signs that don't blend easily with your water sign element, which suggests the fresh start will require an adjustment. They will pull you out of your comfort zone, which will ultimately be good for you.

The two lunar eclipses—the ones that will affect your love life—will be in Scorpio and Taurus, signs that blend wonderfully with your sign. The changes in your love life will be good ones—perhaps triggering decisions or actions that are long overdue—and you will adjust well to them. These eclipses are blessings in disguise.

May 4 Eclipse in Scorpio
to Bring Romantic News

The most important eclipse for your romantic relationship will fall on May 4. That eclipse will touch all Cancers, but especially those whose birthdays fall on or within five days of July 6. It's a full moon eclipse and it's in Scorpio, so certain conditions in your relationship will reach a culmination point. You will no longer feel your relationship is in limbo. If you're single, this eclipse could introduce you to the love of your life—possibly dramatically altering your single status sooner than you think. If you have been dating for a while, you may suddenly want to get engaged or married. Or if it is evident that you are incompatible, the relationship could end.

If your relationship is in a rut, you will see what the problems are and be able to fix them. Luckily, the May 4 eclipse is beautifully angled to many of the other planets, forming a grand trine, one of the happiest and most harmonious aspects possible in any chart. With such supportive planets, if you do break up, it is because the relationship was flawed and a better one is waiting for you.

With Saturn in Cancer, you are more serious about your actions and will want your time to count. If you are dating, you will probably want marriage. If you are married, you will want to work toward bigger goals together. Saturn will also give you a greater ability to see things as they really are. An eclipse in Scorpio suggests that a subtle power struggle could exist within the relationship. This can be draining for both parties, so if this is true for you, this eclipse will allow you to talk openly about this struggle and decide how to handle it.

In addition to romance, the fifth house rules children and pregnancy, so a discussion about having children may come up. Or if you already have children, one of them may be leaving for college or may announce they're getting their own apartment. A few Cancers won't experience these eclipses in terms of romance, but will channel their sexual energy into creative endeavors, whether consciously or unconsciously. If this describes you, on the May 4 eclipse you may begin a creative project or receive a response from a client about a previously presented idea. Watch May 4 plus or minus one week. Also watch for news one month to the day earlier or later, plus or minus four days.

Eclipses fall in certain series of signs. Last year brought a lunar eclipse on May 15, falling in the same house of your horoscope, your fifth house of love. That eclipse had the most powerful effect on those born July 16. The May 4 and October 28 eclipses will follow this year, and 2005 will bring two others. After that, your eclipses in the house of true love and friendship will be over.

FRIENDSHIP IS THE FOCUS OF THE OCTOBER 28 ECLIPSE

Your lifestyle and interests have changed, and so will your friendships—and this will be most evident near the October 28 eclipse. A friend may leave your environment or change their status—by getting married, for example—and suddenly your relationship will feel very different.

It appears that you and this particular friend have grown in different ways, perhaps without either of you noticing. You may stay in touch, but it will be evident that your friendship relates to a life you used to live, but not your new one. You may feel a little sad when this eclipse highlights the amount of time you have spent together. (All eclipses play with our sense of time, which is what makes them so dramatic.) Happily, new faces will arrive to fill any emptiness you may feel when your friend departs. Be patient.

The October 28 eclipse will touch those whose birthdays fall on June 26, plus or minus five days. This eclipse falls in your house of friendship, but because love and friendship are on the same 180-degree axis, ecliptic energy may bounce back and forth between the two houses, affecting them both.

A STEADY RELATIONSHIP IS CLARIFIED IN EARLY JANUARY

On January 7, there will be a full moon in your house of committed partners. Some Cancers will get engaged, while others will wed. However, this full moon will bring certain truths into the open, so if there have been subtle problems or resentments that have not been addressed between you and a partner, you will probably get an earful. Mars is in a belligerent mood, so the time you spend at work may be a source of your partner's anger.

AVOID A TEMPTING CLANDESTINE TRYST APRIL THROUGH JUNE

With sexy Mars and Venus in your twelfth house of secrets, it will be easy to fall for someone you feel is completely irresistible. However, while you are under Venus and Mars' spell in April, you may be tempted to have a clandestine relationship with someone who is married. Don't do it. By mid-May your affair may come out in the open, possibly in an explosive way, much to your dismay. Don't forget there is an eclipse in April, which means you'll need to allow for few unexpected developments. If you begin a secret relationship you will cut your-self off from truly good aspects coming from elsewhere in your chart.

The twelfth house also covers blind dates, and those would be positive for you in April. If you are single, get your friends to make introductions and arrange dates at this time of the year.

Venus Retrograde May 19 to June 30: Love and Beauty Dims; Avoid Engagement, Marriage; Plastic Surgery Not Advised

Venus retrogrades in Gemini (meaning Venus will still be in your twelfth house) from May 19 to June 30, suggesting that you may change your mind about a romantic relationship. When Venus retrogrades, we tend not to think logically when it comes to matters of love. This would not be a good time to get married, engaged, or to go on a first date.

Venus rules beauty, adornment, and the power of attraction, so its retrograde periods are not a good time to buy new clothes, have any sort of grooming or beauty treatments, or purchase expensive fragrances or cosmetics. Venus retrograde is also a terrible time to schedule plastic surgery.

Mid-November Through December Brings Exciting Love

Your very best time for enchanting romantic prospects will be from November 11 to December 25, 2004. During this time, assertive Mars will be touring your house of true love, always an indication that something's about to come up!

Happily, the new moon on November 12 will help you by falling in your fifth house of true love. In the two weeks that follow this new moon, you could meet new people or more fully enjoy your current relationship. It would also be a great time for a vacation. If you are attached and want a baby, this would be an ideal time to get pregnant.

The most passionate and exciting time for you arrives on or near December 5, when Venus and her cosmic lover, Mars, meet in Scorpio, one of your best placements to see the spark of passionate love, dear Cancer.

You may meet someone new or hear a confession of love from someone you know. Scorpio is possessive, so you may move toward a more committed arrangement. At the very least, it's an ideal day for a romantic dinner or a festive party. Put a big gold star on this day!

Summary

This is sure to be a significant year for you, dear Cancer. Saturn, the planet that teaches the value of hard work and dedication to long-range goals, is in Cancer and will bring structure to your life. Saturn will remain in this sign until July 2005. This planet first entered your sign in June 2003, so as you read this, you may have gotten used to your new and growing responsibilities.

Saturn will help you use your time and other resources more wisely. Saturn periods usually coincide with major decisions and actions that affect us long into the future. You may choose to get married, have a baby, start a business, buy a house, or make another fateful decision. You will make the commitment by choice and grow enormously as a result.

The two areas of your chart ruling thinking, perception, ideas, communication, travel, and other mind-expanding experiences will be ruled brilliantly by both Jupiter, the planet of luck and happiness (in the third house), and Uranus, the planet of surprises and revelations (in the ninth house). In the year to come, you will reassess your opinions and beliefs, and come up with a new view that is entirely your own, not influenced by your family, friends, or anyone else. You will also learn to voice your views in a compelling way, a powerful skill that will take you far and earn you much respect.

In your career, January is a key time to look for a new position. There are two other points that are favorable for getting that big promotion or switching jobs: the new moon on March 20 and the full moon on September 28. There may also be opportunities for advancement as a result of the April 19 eclipse and the October 14 eclipse. Your best time to ask for a raise would be at the new moon August 15.

Your home is likely to be a big source of pride and joy in the last quarter of the year, a trend that will continue into 2005. This would be the time to buy, sell, or lease a new space. October appears to be the month you may move, renovate, or improve the décor. Family support for your goals should be strong as well.

The eclipses of 2004 may also bring opportunities to improve your living situation, a romantic relationship, or a decision about a pregnancy or child. You will see this in action in April, May, and October, when they are scheduled to come by.

In love, there will be plenty of opportunities to meet new people and to resolve a present relationship. The eclipses will show that you can discuss hurtful things without fear. Saturn in

Cancer, at the same time, will be coaxing you to make your time count or move on.

Two points in the year will be extra special for romance if you are single: the early part of May, not only because of the eclipse then, but because Mars will glide into Cancer and put you in the spotlight, and near December 5. On that day, Venus and Mars will send out a beautiful vibration. It is the first conjunction of these two passionate lovers in a long time, making this a special day for a first date or a holiday party—you could meet someone special! Venus and Mars will meet in the constellation of Scorpio, a placement that is wildly compatible with your Sun sign, dear Cancer.

In all, you have an active, positive year ahead! You will have a sense of urgency to build roots and more security, and to settle old, lingering problems. Cancer has suddenly become a sign on a mission. By this time next year you will have plenty to show for your efforts.

Leo

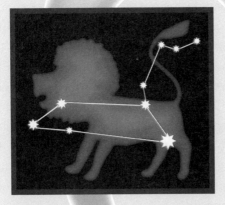

July 23-August 22

The Big Picture

You enter 2004 after having completed an exceptionally strong year. Jupiter, the planet of good fortune and happiness, crowned you celestial favorite last year when it toured Leo, a period that extended from August 2002 to August 2003. You may wonder how 2004 could ever compare to 2003, for last year was filled with much excitement and several memorable beginnings. However, 2004 has the potential to be an even more vivid and prosperous year for you.

When you are at the start of a new 12-year Jupiter cycle, you're lucky enough to have Jupiter's protection and support, and that first year is best for germinating seeds and choosing overall direction. This is what you concentrated on last year for Jupiter's presence in Leo coaxed you to paint your goals boldly on a large canvas. Doors opened for you and influential people went out of their way to help you. You began thinking big, and were exposed to new ideas through trips to distant cities or through college-level classes or lectures.

During that first year it wasn't possible to see results from your efforts—it was still too early. Now that you've entered the second phase of your cycle (in 2004), a cycle associated with financial abundance, those seedlings are starting to grow.

When Jupiter was in Leo last year, you may have felt a bit undisciplined or even lazy. With so much coming your way, you didn't have to exert much effort. Jupiter creates a lovely comfort zone. This year you'll be back to your energetic self and will want to take advantage of this new cycle with potential for much reward.

With Jupiter in analytical Virgo, you will be more intent on putting your time and money where it counts. Jupiter becomes

practical when it tours Virgo, a sign that stresses tough decisions so that resources are not wasted. You'll be able to build
a sturdy foundation to support the dreams you began spinning
last year, in order to bring them to a more advanced level. If
last year was about the promise of a bright future, this year is
about getting results. Rather than start new projects, continue
developing what you have under way.

The financial bonanza that this year holds will arrive just
in time. In 2003 several unwelcome financial surprises
appeared from nowhere. Part of this was Uranus' doing, but
Mars' extended visit to your eighth house of joint finances
turned out to be an even larger headache for you. Mars finally
moved from your eighth house shortly before 2004 began, so
this financial rollercoaster will stabilize substantially. Uranus
will remain in your eighth house for six more years, so you will
have to remain fiscally conservative, although you will experience some outrageously lucky periods.

Although your year ahead is mostly about money, there
are favorable periods for travel in April, thanks to an
eclipse, and during the last three months of 2004, particularly in October.

Your love life will become more secure and less given
to extremes as in the past seven years. Your still wildly idealistic side is still very much alive. There's no doubt you are
still are in love with love—Neptune, the planet of idealism
is still touring your solar seventh house of partners—but
don't dive head-first into any new relationship, no matter
how vibrant it appears at the start. If you're careful, you'll
enjoy Neptune's positive energy (inspiration) while avoiding
its pitfalls (confusion).

If you are single and met someone interesting in 2003 or
the latter part of 2002, this person could well be your soul

mate. Jupiter in Leo brought a wide variety of people to your life, and some have a vital role to play in your future. You may have a new good friend, mentor, or lover. If you met your current sweetheart last year there is a good chance you will grow closer. If you married last year, you chose an outstanding time to do so.

If you are single and met no one, June, July, and early August will be best for romance. December also promises to be festive. During those times you will be quite irresistible.

Socially, you should start to feel released from recent bonds and obligations that prevented you from socializing as much as you would have liked over the past two years. Saturn, the planet that dampened your carefree lifestyle, has departed from your eleventh house, so fun, friends, and leisure activities should be returning in 2004.

Two of the year's four eclipses will highlight your career and home, where you'll see the biggest changes in 2004. You may be switching jobs and moving, the latter possibly in response to the former. If you don't move, there will be other projects and activities related to home or family. Late October through early November is your most likely time to move, renovate, or change roommates.

You will probably need to change jobs in early May, but you may wait until October or November of 2004. If you stay in your job, it will be because you've been promoted. In May, you may hear a sudden announcement—for example, a boss may leave, your company may merge with another, or you may get an intriguing offer from a headhunter.

As a fixed sign, you don't like radical changes, but once you make them, you're always glad you did. Embrace change and you will be all the better for it.

The Year in Detail

FINANCIALLY, THIS COULD BE YOUR MOST PROFITABLE YEAR IN THE DECADE

You are now in a classic cycle for making money, a trend that will last until September 24, 2004. Perhaps you've already seen evidence of this, for Jupiter has been sending golden beams to your solar second house of earned income since August 2003. If not, start looking at your options, because the market is interested in paying quite a bit for your services.

The second house doesn't rule prize winnings (that's another house), so you probably won't win the lottery. Instead you'll earn your money the old-fashioned way by relying on skill, not luck. Much of this year's profit will be directly tied to discussions and actions that you made while Jupiter was still in Leo (August 2002-August 2003).

Jupiter's tour of your second house will allow you to reassess your most basic values and decide where you'd like to put your best efforts and resources in coming years. For example, travel was a priority, so a large portion of your budget went for airline tickets and hotels. Now you feel it's time to start a family, so a large portion of your money will go toward taking care of that new baby.

ASK FOR A RAISE ON OR JUST AFTER SEPTEMBER 14

Your very best time to ask for a raise would be on or in the days that follow the new moon on September 14, 2004, because five out of ten planets, including the Sun and the Moon, will support your efforts to increase your cash flow.

This new moon will be exerting a strong influence for two weeks following September 14. Rather than wait for the phone to ring, take action. When you have vibrations as strong and powerful as these, you'll get the answer you want.

You may hear good news about your salary on March 6, 2004, when there is a full moon in your second house of money. On this day, the moon will dance with Jupiter. A creative idea could be approved or your boss could reward you with a raise. Be proactive to best benefit from this very positive full moon.

YOUR LUCKIEST DAY OF THE YEAR: SEPTEMBER 21
YOUR LUCK WILL BE PURELY FINANCIAL

Every year Jupiter, the giver of gifts and luck, meets with the mighty Sun and brings us the potential to enjoy one of the best days of the year.

A financial offer or deal could come through on or near September 21, 2004, so you'll want to stay alert for opportunities. This day comes just after the new moon on September 14, which is significant because it will help you locate lucrative sources of gain.

Sometimes we don't know a day's importance until much later, so if September 21 doesn't initially seem that special, you may be surprised when you look back!

ANOTHER FABULOUS FINANCIAL DAY: SEPTEMBER 28

Put a gold star next to September 28, 2004, because Mercury, the planet that rules your house of salary, will meet with benefic Jupiter. It's a superb day to schedule an interview, presentation or negotiation. It's also a perfect day to sign a contract.

Two Dates That Will Stand Out
for Financial Planning and Negotiating:
May 1 and August 17

There are two "stand-alone" dates to enter into your datebook: May 1, 2004, and August 17, 2004. On these days, Jupiter, planet of profit and lucrative financial opportunities, and Saturn, planet of stability, will help you make a wise long-term financial decision. Either date would be ideal for a financial planner to assess your portfolio and make changes. May 1 would be an ideal date to close on a house or sell a possession. Be more circumspect on August 17, as Mercury will be retrograde, which is a good time to plan, but never good to make big moves.

Saturn to Tour Your Twelfth House
Until July 2005
Get Set for High Productivity
While in Quiet Solitude

In August 2003, Saturn, the taskmaster planet that teaches us to aim high and work hard, moved into a much gentler house of your horoscope than it's occupied in a long time. If your life has been too focused on work over the past few years, that situation will now gradually improve in 2004.

Saturn has since moved into your twelfth house—a so-called "cadent" house—meaning Saturn emits a weaker beam. That is good news, because this harsh "teacher planet" is less likely to cause you day-to-day difficulties. In many ways, Saturn's move out of your eleventh house is more noteworthy than Saturn's move into your twelfth house, because it's less troublesome now. This year, you'll have an opportunity to reassess and readjust your compass.

Ancient astrologers used to write that "secret enemies" were located in this twelfth house, so in 2004 you may have a detractor or competitor who is jealous of your successes and who would like to steal some of your thunder. With Saturn due to remain in this house until July 2005, you might have to be a bit more circumspect about those you allow into your inner circle. Leo has a big heart and a warm, winning way, so this behavior may seem a bit odd at first. Don't make a mountain of this, however. It's better to use your energy toward positive ends!

The twelfth house rules confinement of any kind, so between now and July 2005, you may learn that a relative or friend is in a hospital, nursing home, rehabilitation center, or even prison. This person needs your help, so be there for them. Alternatively, you might check into a health care facility for a minor medical procedure.

During Saturn's two-year visit to your twelfth house, you will be highly productive when in solitude. If you plan to write or conduct research, you can make enormous progress by working in a place where you won't be disturbed. Leo is a gregarious sign, not used to spending time alone, but you may enjoy being by yourself to think.

Saturn is the ruler of your sixth house of everyday projects, so its new position in the twelfth house suggests that you may start to take work home, where you won't have as many interruptions. Don't underestimate the power of this aspect—this could be a big factor in your success.

In preparation for Saturn's visit to your own sign, Leo, in July 2005—a much more important trend—let go of certain obligations that have cluttered your life. If your heart is no longer in certain optional duties, disassociate yourself from them. New projects will come once Saturn enters Leo, from

July 2005 to September 2007, so if you don't untangle yourself from more marginal projects, you'll find yourself overworked.

For the same reason, don't initiate big projects in 2004. These would be best left for July 2005 and beyond. Now is ideal to follow up on things you started last year.

A SHARPENED ABILITY TO COMMUNICATE CLEARLY IS THE GIFT OF JUPITER STARTING SEPTEMBER 24

When Jupiter beams its good fortune to your third house from September 24, 2004, through October 25, 2005, you will enter a very busy time, with lots of meetings, phone calls, and travel. If you work in sales, marketing, public relations, writing or editing, teaching, research, or politics, you'll be in luck, as those fields will do exceptionally well.

Jupiter will be the only major outer planet to change signs in 2004, which will happen in late September. The other planets we've discussed changed signs last year or in prior years, but you're still feeling their energies.

Thanks to Jupiter in Libra, a very social sign, your list of contacts should expand exponentially, and you will be in hot demand. You're a fire sign, so the blending of the Sun and Jupiter in Libra, an air sign, is a hot, bright, and highly compatible combination. Air makes fire burn brighter, so for a year beginning at the end of September you will enter a very stimulating period, dear Leo.

Libra is also a partnership sign, so with Jupiter in that sign in your third house, you could be signing a major contract. This will most likely happen on or near October 14, when Jupiter will be joined by a new moon eclipse. At the same time, the Sun, Mercury, Mars, and Jupiter will be in squeezed into that same house of your chart. That's a lot of cosmic action.

Jupiter in Libra will bless your partnership, so if you feel you have the right partner, there's no reason to hold back. You may start a business or buy real estate with a partner, or sign with a high-powered agent, manager, or publicist in late 2004. If you're an aspiring writer, the last quarter of the year would be the best time to publish a book you've been working on. With the sterling twosome quality inherent in Jupiter in Libra, you may consider making your book a collaborative effort.

You could also see a breakthrough in magazine, Internet, or newspaper publishing—you may write for these media, or writers may be interviewing you! Publicity could be quite delicious in 2004. Also, late 2004 would be an ideal time to launch a new website, online store, magazine, or other publishing venture.

Education is under the third house, too, so consider taking classes in public speaking. If your boss wants to give you training to become a better spokesperson for the company, say yes. It would also be a terrific time to take a writing course, learn a language or a computer code.

This year, you may be asked to teach even if you aren't a professional teacher. Perhaps at the urging of your boss you will be asked to share certain skills with other company personnel.

If you want to buy a new computer, car, or any telecommunications or electronics device, do so in October or November 2004. December brings Mercury retrograde, so avoid making any big purchases then.

WATCH FOR SPECIAL NEWS ABOUT A SIBLING, PARTICULARLY IN OCTOBER

Your solar third house, so brilliantly lit for you by Jupiter beginning on September 24, 2004, also rules siblings. Watch for an idea or introduction your sister or brother has for you. If you have no siblings, it could be from a cousin, aunt, or uncle. In fact, you may even benefit financially from this person, so don't assume their ideas won't suit you, even if they have offered only fairly daffy ideas in the past.

Mid-October brings an eclipse in this section of your chart, so a close relative could be a focus. Or the eclipse will bring travel or increased activity at work, concerning Jupiter in Libra in your third house.

BRACE FOR SUDDEN DOMESTIC CHANGES NEAR MAY 5 LUNAR ECLIPSE NOVEMBER 11 TO DECEMBER 25 ALSO BRINGS GOOD HOME-RELATED OPTIONS

There are two points during the year that may send you packing to a new address, put you in a sudden mood to fix up your present home, or make you want to rearrange the things—or the people—in your space.

May 5, the date of a total eclipse in Scorpio, will highlight your fourth house of home and family. This eclipse may be felt on this day or be one month to the day earlier or later, plus or minus five days. Eclipses have a wide field of influence, which is why I have to qualify these dates.

If you are in the market to buy a house or apartment, you will find options. Check for water damage in your new or present home, especially if you are moving or doing structural work near May 5. With Neptune in harsh angle to the Sun at eclipse time, it would be a good idea to have homeowners' or renters' insurance that covers water damage. Also make sure there aren't any unclear clauses in a contract, as Neptune is famous for causing confusion.

This eclipse is a powerful one. The reason for your move could be to take advantage of a job that requires you relocate—possibly cross-country or even to another continent. If this happens, the job would start two weeks later, near May 18. The May 5 eclipse is a full moon. Something is about to come to finality, with a new phase to begin sometime after that.

If you were born on within five days of August 7, you will feel the effects of the May 5 eclipse more strongly than any other Leos.

If you can remember back nineteen years ago, to May 5, 1985, you may get clues to what may come up now. On that date, there was a very similar eclipse to the one that is coming this year. (That eclipse fell at the same mathematical degree.)

Later, from November 11 to December 25, 2004, you will get a wider, stronger, and more sustained window of opportunity to effect home or family-related changes. If you need to move, paint, or reorganize, this phase will allow enormous progress. You won't have a phase like this again for two years.

Some readers will not move or renovate at all this year but rather focus on their mom or dad, as the fourth house also governs family members, particularly parents. You might want to clear your schedule near these dates.

TRAVEL MAY BE A FUN OPTION IN JANUARY AND NEAR THE APRIL 19 AND OCTOBER 14 SOLAR ECLIPSES

Ancient astrologers grouped intellectual growth with travel, for travel was considered one of the most mind-broadening experiences we have. This year holds lots of promise for exciting travel for you, dear Leo, especially during certain months.

January brings your first solid opportunity to fly away. You may be ready for a vacation to recover from the hustle and bustle of the holidays. Mars will tour your ninth house of foreign travel for about seven weeks, making it an ideal time to go. This window is open starting December 16, 2003, to February 3, 2004.

If your trip is for business, plan it for early January. Your mind will be focused on work projects then and you'll be highly productive.

If your trip is for pleasure, consider leaving on Friday, January 21, the date of the new moon in your house of marriage and partners. Doing so will allow you to reignite your closest romantic relationship by spending quality time together. However, if you try to leave any earlier than January 21, pulling yourself away from your desk may be quite hard. You may have to put in a few all-night sessions to make it possible.

There will be four eclipses this year, and two of them will be especially positive and supportive. The first one, to arrive April 19, will fall in Aries, which is an adventurous fire sign like yours. The other travel-related eclipse will arrive on October 14 in Libra, a highly compatible air sign that is known to advance friendship and social interaction, including romance. Both eclipses fall in houses that are associated with travel, your solar ninth and third houses, respectively.

Eclipses are important to everyone, because they are nodal points that point to vast change in a chart. Solar eclipses are doubly important for you, dear Leo, because your sign is ruled by the Sun. The ones we are discussing in this section are solar eclipses, which is why you will travel more than usual. (The other two eclipses will be lunar and will create changes in your home or family situation, discussed in other sections of this chapter.)

The April 19 and October 14 eclipses will fall in your cere-bral third and ninth houses. This suggests that some of the biggest shifts in the year will stem from a basic change in your world view. This year you will also open your mind to new concepts and seek intellectual refreshment from different sources. This change reflects your growing maturity and is considered a very positive, mind-expanding development.

Of the two eclipses, you will probably find the April 19 eclipse more exciting. It could take you overseas or, at the very least, to a city quite far from home. In fact, this eclipse is likely to trigger many trips, for up to twelve months.

With the ruler of your house of travel based in your eleventh house of friends and contacts on April 19, you will travel for pleasure, and your destination will be to places you've never visited, which only adds to the fun.

If near April 19 you take a business trip instead (possible but a little less likely), you could attend a networking event, such as an international trade show or a week of professional seminars. You'd be busy, but the trip will be turn out to be highly productive. Sometimes eclipses assert their messages a month later, so see what develops near May 19 as well.

Another reason to travel on or near the April 19 eclipse may be to visit a college or graduate school, for the ninth house is also strongly associated with higher education. Later in the year, you may decide to study abroad or live at a university or boarding school. Alternatively, if you are out of college, you may need to do research in a far-away city for a book you are writing, as the ninth house is also linked to publishing. There are opportunities to import or export products, too.

Leos born on August 21, or within five days of this date, will be the ones most likely to feel—and benefit from—the April 19 eclipse.

The October 14 eclipse may cause you to travel much closer to home. Siblings will factor strongly into this eclipse, so you may be expecting a visit from a sister or brother (or you may travel to see them) at mid-month. At the very least you should hear news from this individual, or a cousin, aunt, or uncle.

The October 14 eclipse will touch those Leos born August 13 more strongly than other members of the sign.

PREPARE FOR SPARKLING CAREER KUDOS FROM FEBRUARY 3 TO MARCH 21 SUDDEN CAREER CHANGES POSSIBLE IN LATE OCTOBER

The period from February 3 through March 21, 2004, will be your most important period to seek a promotion or new job. Mars will be touring the pinnacle of your chart at that time, lighting your house of honors and achievement, so you should be able to find a job that's worthy of your talents.

If you work as a freelancer or have your own business, this period will be just as outstanding for you.

On or near the full moon lunar eclipse on October 28, there may be professional upheaval for you. A top boss may announce a surprise departure at the end of October or early November, making you a fearful of not having your boss to protect you.

Your company may also lay off some employees. Your income should not be negatively affected by this eclipse, so you'll be safe from any cost-cutting measures that may be announced in late October (or a month later).

Certain political factors seem to swirl around this October lunar event, so remain circumspect, especially of co-workers who may blame you in an effort to deflect attention from their own work. With Saturn in difficult aspect to the Sun, you could feel betrayed by a co-worker whom you'd considered to be an ally. These demands will likely make you feel strung out at October's end. Along with Neptune's difficult angle to the moon, you'll find it hard to separate fact from fiction. Give yourself time to sort things out, and refuse to be rushed.

This eclipse isn't all gloom and doom. On the upside, Uranus, the planet of unexpected events, will be positive, so you may find yourself at the right place at the right time. Jupiter will also help you communicate your thoughts in a particularly articulate way, and may help you negotiate a new contract at that time.

If you were born on July 27, you will be most affected by this October 28 eclipse.

On October 28, 1985, there was a similar eclipse, at the same mathematical degree. You may not be old enough to remember 19 years ago (or perhaps you weren't even born yet), but if you can, that eclipse may offer you some clues of what to expect. The other planets are now in vastly different positions, so there is never an exact re-run of past eclipses, but you can get an idea of certain themes that may emerge now.

BE CONSERVATIVE WITH FINANCES
URANUS WILL FILL YOUR JOINT-RESOURCES SECTOR FOR SIX MORE YEARS

This should be one of your best years for earned income in over a decade. However, something is going on in your eighth house that requires extra attention and care.

In March 2003, Uranus, the planet of unexpected developments, entered your solar eighth house of joint financial resources, a difficult location for this erratic planet. Uranus will remain in this house until 2011. Don't be too concerned, however, because by taking some reasonable steps you can keep your finances safe and secure.

Before I go any further, let me say this. You may get a huge windfall—after all, Uranus rules all things unexpected. You could receive a trip around the world, win a large chunk of cash, inherit money, or a large lawsuit may be settled in your favor.

If that happens, it's great news. However, while you could also suffer a loss, as Uranus is the planet of extremes. Avoid being impulsive about any financial or other eighth-house matter, and you will be glad you did.

As a Leo you love to take risks. You tend to make your decisions intuitively rather than analytically. For the next several years, however, you must learn to carefully look at the downside of each endeavor that you enter into and consider for the elusive "what if."

If you depend on others financially, you will need to develop a few contingency plans. What if your ex loses his or her job and can't send child-support payments for several months? What if your company chooses not to give out a bonus this year? What if your best friend doesn't repay that loan you gave him or her?

It would be a good idea to check your insurance policies to find out exactly what is covered. Your broker can help you sift through the fine print. After doing so, you can decide if you want to strengthen coverage in any areas.

As a fire sign, you tend to fall in love with ideas fairly rapidly, but now you need to have the necessary paperwork in place before you begin work on any speculative creative projects. Your time and energy are your most precious resources—don't let anyone take advantage of you!

If you are not aware of the ins and outs of tax law and how it relates to your personal tax return, a family estate, or your business, you need to learn as much as possible. Taxes are an eighth-house concern. You need to know what the law allows so that you can take advantage of all legal deductions. Ask your accountant lots of questions.

Some of the problems that may come up may have nothing to do with anything you did wrong. For example, you could become a victim of identity theft. If someone is using your name, you need to know about it, for the longer you don't, the harder it will be to clean up your record. Be vigilant about such matters by viewing your credit report every four months.

I am so very sorry to have to point out these concerns to you, dear Leo. You of all people dislike being constrained, especially financially. It might be wise to put a bit of cash aside in case something comes up. I hope you never need this rainy-day fund, and if you don't, at the very least, having that nest egg would be nice!

2004 IS THE YEAR TO LOSE WEIGHT AND GET FIT

June 23 Through August 10
Is Your Ideal Time to Spring into Action

Last year, while Jupiter visited your Sun from August 2002 to August 2003, life was glorious, but there was one possible drawback. While you were busy socializing and traveling, you may have not noticed that your waistline was expanding. Jupiter is an expansive planet, and while we love its goodies and opportunities, many of us leave a Jupiter period a size or two bigger than when we entered it.

Now that Jupiter has left Leo, not to be back until 2014, you will not be in danger of gaining weight quite as easily. You should try to lose the weight that you recently gained, however, and now you will have a chance.

Astrology teaches us to begin exercising on a new moon, and then, only later, to cut back on calories several days after the full moon. (A full moon always arrives two weeks after the new moon. Check your newspaper or my website, *www.astrologyzone.com*.) You also have the option of beginning a sensible diet in the following month, six weeks (plus a few extra days) after you begin your workout program.

One of your best periods to start a new or refined workout plan would be from June 23 through August 10, 2004.

At that time, Mars will make its first visit to your sign in two years and help you kick off a terrific two-year cycle. Mars will see to it that you are filled with vim and vigor, which will make you feel sexier, too. During this phase, you might want to take up weight lifting (Mars rules iron) or book a few lessons with a professional trainer or sports instructor. Or you may want to try out a new class at the gym.

Just after this ideal period to begin a fitness program ends, you will have a helpful new moon on August 15, 2004. At that time you can expand your workout repertoire, perhaps by investigating a new sport or by stepping up your level of proficiency.

Don't begin dieting until three days after any full moon— in August the full moon falls on August 29, so begin your reasonable diet on September 1. (Or wait until the following month's full moon, plus three days.)

If you don't want to wait until mid-year to begin your fitness plan, another ideal date falls in late 2003, just days before the start of 2004. If you are reading this in December 2003 or earlier, you have the option of starting your fitness routine on the new moon of December 23, 2003.

All new moons give you two weeks of excellent energy to make your first decisive action, although the best, strongest part of that two-week period is closest to the appearance of the new moon. Remember the plan: begin exercising as your first step; then after you have eased into your routine, cut back on calories several days after the appearance of the full moon. If you begin your exercise program near December 23, 2003, you should start your new eating plan on January 10, 2004.

You must think I am insane to tell you to begin a major workout and diet plan in the midst of the holidays. Yet the universe sends us these ideal dates so rarely, so when they do show up, even if they are inconvenient, we must use them!

A second new moon won't appear in your sixth house of health and fitness again until January 10, 2005. (Yes, that's 2005!) Strike while you can!

A More Stable Love Life
Is in Your Future at Long Last
Uranus Has Left Your Marriage/
Commitment Sector for Good!

For years, your romantic life has had more twists and turns than a "whodunit" novel, but you are tired of it. After seven years of being in Aquarius, a sign that doesn't always blend well with your own, Uranus moved into Pisces on March 2003. That was a hopeful indication that your love life would finally settle down. However, Uranus made a brief trip back into Aquarius in mid-September 2003 and remained there until December 30, 2003. Suddenly all the relationship chaos and angst that you were trying so hard to avoid was back. If you were born at the end of your sign, near August 20-23, life was doubly hard, for Uranus was moving through late degrees of Aquarius, setting up a tough, 180-degree opposition to your Sun.

If you began to lose hope that you would ever enjoy a settled romantic life, it would have been understandable. But relief is finally here! You won't have to wrestle with Uranus in your house of relationships again in your lifetime!

The area that was so stressed was your seventh house of committed relationships and partnerships, which includes marriage. However, not all Leos felt stress in their personal life, but rather in a business partnership, which is also a seventh-house matter.

Perhaps, unpredictable, bizarre behavior of someone close kept you up at night. Or you were trying to settle funds in the split of a business or in a divorce. In either case, there were probably many arguments. At times you must have wondered if you had wandered into a horror movie because the relationship suddenly seemed so horribly wrong.

If a partner was not the problem, competitors may have been quite ruthless in their tactics. You had to marshal all your strength to fight them. Uranus opposed to the Sun—which every Leo has felt over the last seven years—is considered a serious, slow-moving aspect that has the power to make anyone very stressed out. Indeed, it would have been remarkable if you were able to keep your composure all of the time.

Some Leos may have even found that their health suffered. Because it takes Uranus 84 years to circle the Sun, you won't have this planet in this difficult spot in your chart again during your lifetime. You are done!

IS YOUR RELATIONSHIP
MORE ABOUT LOVE OR MONEY?

During the first nine months of 2004, you will put a great deal of emphasis on money in your closest relationship. I say this because the planet that rules your fifth house of love will spend a lot of time—nine consecutive months—in your second house of money and possessions. If you are married, the ruler of your marriage house is posited in your eighth house of joint resources. No matter what your marital status, money will play a major role in your relationship this year, and in some respect this echoes the strong financial emphasis of 2004.

Single Leos will want to see that new romantic interests are prosperous, and married Leos may suddenly discover that their partner has very different values and spending habits, which they will have to work out together. You could be tempted to overemphasize the role that finances play in a new or established relationship. (There could be factors that explain this unusual emphasis. For example, you may start to date someone that you met in a financial way, such as someone who is a supplier to your business or who is your mortgage broker. There are many possible scenarios, but the most obvious one is that money will become a large factor in your relationship, which is why I bring it up.)

Interestingly, by the end of September, Jupiter will move into your third house of communication and this focus on money will decrease. At that time, rather than money being a criteria for future happiness, the emphasis will be on having a strong intellectual rapport. Married Leos will still feel a financial emphasis due to the placement of Uranus in your financial eighth house, but Jupiter's move into your third house, which pertains to the mind and intellect, helps soften the focus on money. Just as we all need money to live, we also need someone with whom we can share our deepest thoughts and dreams.

YOUR BEST LOVE PERIOD: JUNE 25 TO AUGUST 11
CUPID AND HIS FLEET OF ANGELS
WILL BE WORKING FOR YOU!
DECEMBER BRINGS GLITTERING ROMANCE

Did you meet someone from August 2002 to late August 2003? If you did, or if you became more serious about a partner during that period, there seems to be something quite magical about that relationship. You met while Jupiter, the planet of good fortune, was in Leo, and this person could be a soul mate and you have an outstanding chance for romantic success.

To make things even better, Saturn is no longer creating obstacles in the fun/people/pleasure area of your chart, which it had been doing since April 2001, so you should be able to get out, socialize, and enjoy yourself.

If you didn't meet anyone, there will be many periods during the year conducive for meeting that special someone. You have every reason to believe that true love can happen in 2004!

One of your best periods will be when sexy Mars tours Leo, from June 25 to August 11, 2004. Your confidence will be high, and you're sure to be a people magnet, irresistible and even a little hard to get. Play it up!

Mercury will be retrograde starting on August 9, so try to circulate in late June and July, before that period.

December will be special for many reasons. First, Venus and Mars, the mythological lovers of your horoscope, will meet in conjunction on December 5, 2004, the only time this year this will happen. (These two planets never actually touched in 2003.) They will come together in your house of home, a perfect time to throw a party or to invite that special someone for a home-cooked dinner for two!

You will also have a gorgeous new moon for love on December 11, just in time for the holidays. New moons are not just special for a day, but for two weeks! Admittedly, the energy will be strongest near December 11. If you are single, be sure to circulate starting on that date. Even if you aren't single, parties you will be invited to as a couple will surely energize your relationship.

Finally, another dazzling period for love will arrive in the final days of the year, specifically on December 29, through the first week of February 2005. It looks like you have a truly memorable New Year's Eve coming up, so start making plans now, dear Leo!

VENUS TO RETROGRADE IN GEMINI FROM MAY 17 TO JUNE 29

When Venus snoozes, she withholds some of her brightest and best energies from us. Venus retrograde periods are not considered a good time to schedule an engagement, wedding, or to throw an important party or benefit. It is also not a good time to try out a new hair stylist, lay out large sums for clothes or jewelry, or have plastic surgery, as Venus also rules beauty and adornment.

Venus will retrograde in the friendship-oriented eleventh house, so you may reconnect with many old friends. In your romantic life, if you've been dating and feel the relationship has advanced rather rapidly, you may put on the brakes during that time, just to give yourself some time to catch your breath. There is no harm in that! Finally, you could hear from an old lover or someone who is "just a friend" but who may want to be much more than that.

Summary

2004 has the potential for enormous financial gain for you, dear Leo. With Jupiter in your second house of earned income, you will be rewarded for your hard work, dedication, and fine performance of past years. In many ways you can consider this payback time. Also, the projects and schemes that you planted last year will now take root. September particularly should be glorious.

Elsewhere in your chart, Uranus is touring your eighth house of joint financial income and obligations. Last year, when Uranus first entered this area, it began creating shock waves. Last year, Mars spent an unusually long time in this area of your chart, six months, and increased your expenses. Arguments over money may have at times been rather explosive, and unpleasant news about money may have kept your nerves on edge.

Your picture will be so much brighter as you begin 2004, as Mars left its difficult position on December 16, 2003. This year, the move of Jupiter into your second house of money will see to it that you get paid what you deserve, at long last.

However, you could receive a financial windfall, too. A relative may leave you money, or you could win a fortune on the TV game show. You will have three points in 2004 when Mars will actually help your joint financial situation, specifically in early February, mid-May, and mid-November.

Yet don't let your guard down when it comes to joint financial resources, since Uranus won't leave your financial eighth house until 2011. Avoid big risks, and be present in all monetary decisions. You will want to retain full control and not leave financial decisions to others.

Romantically, several periods in the year will allow you to enjoy yourself to the fullest or, if you are unattached, meet someone special. Saturn is no longer setting up obstacles in the fun/people/pleasure sector of your chart (it had since April 2001), so you should be able to get out and enjoy life. In late June, all of July, and early August, you will be at your charismatic best! December is also due to be a sparkling month, with many reasons to kick up your heels.

If you are married or about to be married, your relationship should become much more settled and less given to the wild emotional fluctuations of the past. Uranus was the culprit; this unstable planet filled your seventh house of committed partners for seven years, and left only recently. Partners were the source of your excitement in life, but they were also the source of nerve-shattering unpredictability, and you felt this either in a personal or business way. If you were born near August 21, life probably felt grueling at times. All Leos underwent cosmic tests, however, starting with July-born Leos from 1996 to 1998. Leos with birthdays that fall from August 1-10 felt this hard aspect from 1998 to 2000, and the rest of Leo from 2000 to 2003.

Neptune is still visiting the marriage and commitment-oriented seventh house, suggesting you have retained your rosy view of romance. That's what makes you so very lovable, dear Leo. However, Neptune may cause you to idealize your partner a little too much, which could leave you open to disillusionment. Be sure you know the person you are dating quite well before you jump into a more serious arrangement. Try to see things as they are, not as they might be!

In September, Jupiter will move into your third house for a thirteen-month stay, and will open your mind to many new concepts and ideas. You will reassess old opinions, attitudes, and principals and re-evaluate your stance. What will emerge is a stronger, more confident sense of self. You will start to think more critically, too.

Jupiter will also help you communicate in a much more articulate way, and thereby will allow you to get your ideas across more powerfully. You may begin to write and publish books or articles, work on a new magazine or web site, or get your own radio or TV show. Late 2004 would be an ideal time to initiate any publishing or broadcasting project.

It would also be an ideal time to take classes or seminars on subjects ranging from creative writing to public speaking, from learning a new language to writing computer code. If you need to buy a new car, computer, or other electronic or telecommunications device, October and November are sensational months to do so.

Jupiter in Libra will help you negotiate a good deal for yourself, and you could sign important papers later in the year. Partnerships glow for you starting in late September, so you may start a successful business with a friend.

All year, Saturn in your twelfth house will help you increase your productivity when you work alone. Leo is not a sign that generally is known to spend much time away from friends, but this year you may begin to show a new more reclusive side.

From now until July 2005, decide if there are any obligations that you can gradually offload. When Saturn enters Leo in July 2005, you will want to have room in your schedule to take advantage of new responsibilities coming your way.

In matters of health, the most dramatic change is that you will be able to lose weight more easily this year, if that is a goal for you. While Jupiter was in Leo, it was hard to avoid gaining weight, as Jupiter expands all that it touches!

The most dramatic changes in 2004 will relate to your career and in terms of living arrangements and family decisions. Watch the eclipses on May 4 and October 28.

You may take a new job in another city, or your new position—which may come by way of a promotion or by switching jobs—may enable you to trade up to a better standard of living. Eclipses bring news out of the blue, so you will need to roll with whatever they bring.

If you were born near July 29, you will feel the eclipses more strongly in career terms, and if born on near August 7, you will feel the shifts in regard to home- or family-related matters. Leos born at other times of the month may hear news too, but it will be less dramatic.

Finally, travel is likely to be a big theme this year, and may allow you to jet off to a locale you've always dreamed of visiting. This comes to you as a result of two other eclipses, due on April 19 and October 14. Your trips won't be limited to just those times of the year—you appear to be moving about much more than usual in 2004. Even business trips will have more zing to them. Get your suitcase ready!

In all, it's an action-packed year, dear Leo!

Virgo

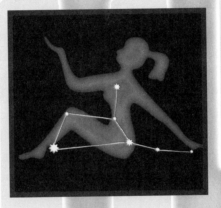

August 23-September 22

The Big Picture

You will enter 2004 at the very top of your game. After several difficult years, you will sense a lightness in the air that you haven't felt in ages. The tide has turned in your favor, dear Virgo, which you will be able to experience in almost every area of your life. You will become increasingly self-assured, confident, and ready to take on the world. 2004 will be a simply glorious year.

You will be in such high spirits this year due, in major part, to the presence of Jupiter, the planet of happiness and good fortune, touring Virgo for the first time in twelve years. Wow! Jupiter will remain in your sign from the start of this year until the end of September, a total of nine months, making this your wonder year. You should have already sensed the warming effects of this configuration because Jupiter entered this position in August 2003.

Virgos born early in their sign were the first to see these interesting developments, although this trend will expand to include all Virgos. Your strongest period will be between May and late September.

With the arrival of Jupiter in your sign, you will begin a new personal cycle in 2004. In the months to come, you'll align yourself with people and projects of special significance, and those alliances will set you on a path that will continue for more than a decade—until 2015. This year, while you have so much luck on your side, map your course and don't be shy about telling others your goals.

Jupiter will teach you to think in wider, more panoramic terms than you have in the past. After you've been exposed to the "think big" coaxing of Jupiter, you may feel you've missed the full potential of some endeavors because you focused too long on the small pieces of the mosaic. That's a potential hazard of your sign, dear Virgo, for you often spend a great deal of your time on the details, when you should step back to see the whole picture. Now you will want to envision your endeavors in their largest possible way.

You will also learn not to jump into anything too quickly. Your energy, organizational ability, and talent with detail can work against you because you easily see what needs to be done and you do it. Your recent experience with Saturn in your career sector made you choosier about the projects you take on. With Jupiter in your sign, you will see just how far you will be able to take an idea.

If you're single, with Jupiter now conjunct the Sun, you could very well meet your soul mate. All kinds of new people will be entering your life, and one or two appear to have a large role to play in your future. Many people report that when Jupiter was at their side, they met the person they married.

To meet a new romantic partner, you will have to show the universe your true intent. Jupiter will help you meet someone if you circulate during this glorious, glamorous cycle! If you stay home, not much will happen. If you are already attached, Jupiter will bring your union to the next stage, by encouraging you to marry, have children, or devise new goals as a couple.

However, one close and possibly troublesome relationship that caused you quite a bit of concern in 2003 will continue to occupy your thinking in 2004. That person may be your spouse, steady sweetheart, or even a business partner. Uranus and Mars in your seventh house of committed relationships are at the root of the tension, so this person may have caused you a number of sleepless nights. This was especially true for

August-born Virgos, although all Virgos felt this pressure from June to December of last year (at its strongest), and it is likely to subside in 2004. Although things are not yet resolved, the relationship seems far less inflammatory as you enter the new year. Deciding what to do about this relationship may take all of 2004, as this appears to be a complex problem. If this is your situation, Jupiter's presence in your sign will be a soothing influence and will provide special protection and help this year.

If this is not the case, there are two other ways this tension-filled aspect—Uranus and Mars opposed to your Sun—may have manifested itself. In business, you may have discovered that a competitor acted ruthlessly in the second part of 2003, or you may have found yourself in the middle of a stressful political situation. In either case, things will be a little better this year, although you'll still need to keep your guard up. Jupiter will help you this year, where you had no such help last year.

You may have also felt unwell physically. Some Virgos may have been tired or drained, while others may have gone through a medical ordeal. (Virgos with birthdays on August 23-29 know what I am speaking about.) In matters of health, Uranus opposed to the Sun is known to lower resistance to disease or sickness. If you are ailing, you will feel better, but you still have to take proactive steps to keep yourself well: good diet, enough sleep, and plenty of exercise to offset stress. If you are under a doctor's care, you have every reason to believe he or she can help you, so follow the treatment to the letter and be optimistic.

With your career, your ideas will have strong sticking power this year, and you will be able to rally several influential people to your cause, particularly from January through

September. You can also expect to make faster professional progress now that Saturn, the taskmaster planet, has finally moved out of your tenth house of career, a position it held from April 2001 to June 2002. Armed with the maturity and strength you obtained from meeting many of Saturn's recent tests, you should be unstoppable.

Friendships may take on a larger-than-usual focus. Saturn will tour your eleventh house, ruling platonic relationships and charitable or humanitarian efforts, and will remain there until July 2005. This is an easier location for this teacher planet than has been the case in the past. For past two and a half years, Saturn was in harsh angle to your Sun, but now that it's touring water sign Cancer, it will be in a highly supportive angle to your earth sign Sun in Virgo.

Saturn will show you the benefits of forging solid bonds with both new and old friends. You may be elected to a post in an organization you belong to and experience a great deal of personal growth as a result. This part of your chart is all about giving back to society—this year you may make your mark. You can easily apply the managerial and leadership skills you learn here to your job, so it's a win/win situation.

Most people say, "Who has time to volunteer?" This year you prove the old axiom, "Give a busy person something to do and it gets done on time." You achieve twice as much as most people simply because you're organized.

The universe plans to help you succeed through these new friendships. This year you may find an older person to act as a mentor or sounding board. This person will help you make new and valuable contacts, and will lend savvy advice when you need it most. This person may appear at any time this year or in early 2005! You'll either already know this person or will soon meet them.

There will be four eclipses in 2004. These events are key indicators of sudden shifts and opportunities that are due in the coming year. The first two will fall in mid-April and early May (eclipses always come as new and full moons, falling two weeks apart). The second set of eclipses will arrive in October. Judging by the houses in which they will fall, expect changes in your finances, travel, publishing, legal matters, and plans for higher education.

Financially, it appears that one large source of income is about to end near the time of one of the two eclipses due April 19 and October 14. Later, a new source will replace it. If you receive revenue from any source for longer than two and a half years, you are over the average and should look for new sources of income as a precaution. (I have always found that rule of thumb helpful, and perhaps you will, too.) Not to worry!

Luckily, you have some sensational financial aspects in the last quarter of 2004, thanks to the actions of happy-go-lucky Jupiter. Toward the end of the year, your services will be highly valued. Should you hear negative news involving your income (e.g., if you lose your job or a major client), your predicament will likely be solved in a pleasing way, so keep your cool. At eclipse time, we often hear sudden news, and you need to have faith that the universe will pull us out of one situation to reward us with a better one.

I'm not necessarily saying anything adverse will happen; it is just as possible that you may choose to change sources of income, or your company may merge with another firm, so the name on your paycheck will change (your income will emanate from a new source!). Both these eclipses are new moon eclipses, suggesting fresh starts, not endings.

The other two eclipses should bring positive results, as they both relate well to your Sun sign. Arriving on May 4 and October 28 as full moons, each of these eclipses, in Taurus and Scorpio, will open your mind to new learning experiences. You could travel more than usual this year or work with people in international settings.

This same house also rules education, so you may decide to go back to school and obtain a graduate degree. If you are already in school, you may complete an important research paper, take a certifying exam, or complete your graduation. If you are hoping to change careers, these eclipses may make it possible to go back to school.

Dear Virgo, you are in the process of rebuilding your life to reflect the new person you are. You have matured and grown quite a bit over the past few years, and your lifestyle, friendships, and other areas have shifted accordingly. Rather than dread change, embrace it. You are very lucky to be crowned the celestial favorite in 2004!

The Details of Your Year Ahead

JUPITER, PLANET OF GIFTS AND LUCK,
WILL GRACE VIRGO UNTIL SEPTEMBER 24

You are embarking on a new twelve-year cycle that will take you in an exciting direction, straight into the next decade.

In 2004, you are ready for something new. You may take on a new look, a new job, make more money, move into a new house or apartment, or fix up your existing digs. (I added the possibility of a home or lifestyle-related upgrade because Jupiter rules your solar fourth house of home.) You could travel much more than usual, possibly to other countries, because Jupiter, one of the quintessential travel planets, will work to open your mind and heart to new experiences. The eclipses will also urge you to fly your magic carpet, so several areas of your chart are singing the same "travel now" tune!

The hard work you put into your career over the past two years under the watchful eye of that difficult-to-please boss or client (indicated by the recent position of Saturn, now finished with its tour in your professional sector) will put you in line for impressive new responsibilities or fabulous press on your fine performance. You will be able to work without the degree of scrutiny you've had to endure. You've finally proven yourself.

If you're single, Jupiter will bring a whole host of people into your life, including friends, mentors, and yes, possibly that special sweetie. Among these faces may be one or two people whose role in your life will seem fated, and they will act as catalysts for bigger and better experiences.

No other aspect will have as powerful an influence on your life as Jupiter's impending visit to your sign. You haven't had this cosmic favor in twelve years, so you'll notice the upbeat effects of Jupiter in your everyday life. Your situation is all the more dramatic because in 2002 and 2003, Virgo was one of four signs hardest hit by angry planetary energy. With personal victories few and far between, you found it hard to keep the faith. That will all change.

Jupiter began touring Virgo on August 27, 2003, so as 2004 dawns, you've had a few months to get used to Jupiter's presence. If your birthday falls between August 23 and September 11, Jupiter passed directly over the mathematical degrees of your Sun last year, so you may have

already seen a breakthrough in one of many areas in
your life.

Jupiter will retrograde from January 3 until May 4, 2004.
This is common—Jupiter retrogrades for four months without
interruption every year, and although you won't feel its
strongest expression, Jupiter will still have the power to help
you. If you are starting any new venture where everything
needs to be "just perfect," do so between May 4 and
September 25, your brightest period of 2004.

Jupiter retrograde is not like Mercury retrograde, the latter
being a far harder aspect because Mercury rules communication. When out of phase, Mercury tends to make everything in
our normal lives go haywire. Mercury is your ruler, too, which
is why you feel the effects of Mercury retrograde much dis-
tinctly than other signs.

From January to early May 2004, Jupiter will travel back
over the degrees of Virgo that it had traveled before, beaming
golden vibrations back on those birthdays it already visited
last year. That's like getting a double dip of pleasure!

Jupiter will remain in Virgo until September 24, 2004.
Between now and then, enlist as many influential people
as will listen. One person will turn out to be quite an ally
to you.

As you go through the year, think about what might be
holding you back from larger success. By freeing your
schedule from obligations or people who drag you down,
you will create a space for the universe to fill with new
opportunities. Any change, even enforced ones, will benefit
you because they remove you from outdated situations.
When this happens—we break up with a romantic partner, a
good friend moves away, or we lose a key client—it seems
so sudden and random. It's not. There is wisdom in the

actions of the universe. Don't be quick to judge something as "good" or "bad" until the universe delivers the improvements you so dearly deserve. Sometimes that takes a little time. Have faith!

Jupiter will help your timing, and timing is everything. In 2004, you will be at the right place at the right time, both in your professional and personal life. You aren't used to having special favor or luck—now you will have it coming at you from all sides.

Your first order of business will be to set your priorities. The only way Jupiter can help is if you know what makes you happy. If you are typical of your sign, you have been so focused on nurturing others that you probably haven't focused on what you want. If you can dream it, it can become a reality!

Virgo is not a sign generally associated with taking risks, but this year you'll feel confident enough to take one. Luck will be on your side. Will you take a chance on love? Or will you quit your job and move cross-country? Or will you add parenthood to your responsibilities? This year, whatever you put your mind to has a strong chance of succeeding, so if you want to make a move, do it in 2004. You'll have until the end of September to put your plans into place.

Here is an important point: don't expect any of your seeds to fully blossom during the first three quarters of this year. Think of this first phase as a gestation period. If you work diligently now, you will have quite a harvest by time your second phase, one of financial abundance, begins in the fourth quarter of 2004. This glorious monetary luck will last through the first nine months of 2005. After Jupiter exits your sign at the end of September 2004, it will not return for another year's stay until August 2015. Use this glittering period for all it is worth!

MARS AND MERCURY WILL BE IN YOUR CORNER FROM SEPTEMBER 2 TO SEPTEMBER 25: A PERFECT PERIOD TO INITIATE PLANS

This year, Mars will arch over the eastern part of your chart, suggesting that you will have more control over everyday affairs than you did last year. You won't have to wait for others to come to you with ideas or opportunities—you'll be able to develop your own.

One of your very sweetest periods will span from August 10 through September 25, when Mars will zoom through Virgo, providing extra presence, energy, and drive. Mercury will be retrograde from August 9 to September 2, so the smaller window from September 2-25 will be your best. Jupiter will still be at your side, making this a truly memorable period.

YOU'LL BE HEALTHIER IN 2004 WATCH YOUR WEIGHT AND FIND WAYS TO DE-STRESS

Jupiter, now in Virgo, is known for its potent rejuvenating powers. If your health has not been robust, Jupiter in Virgo can help you get the medical help you need. Your chart suggests that the doctor you choose is likely to be quite esteemed in his or her specialty. Do your homework and research the various medical professionals available to you. If you have a chronic ailment, new technology and recent medical discoveries may bring some long-awaited answers. If you require a medical procedure within the next thirteen months, it could offer you reason for hope. If you just had an operation, you should mend nicely.

The negative side to hosting Jupiter in your Sun is that you're likely to gain weight. This is a well-known result of hosting Jupiter in your sign. To counter this possibility, make regular visits to the gym and be watchful of your waistline.

August-born Virgos have been under some health strain and may continue to be in 2004. Since March of 2003, Uranus has been in harsh angle to these early-in-the-sign Virgos, and they will still need a boost. Most Virgos suffer from overwork or a sensitive central nervous system (causing digestive problems), so these issues may be more pronounced. You tend to work so hard—try to schedule some quiet time this year.

Neptune has been touring your sixth house of health for several years, so a small number of Virgos may have discovered a condition that is hard to diagnose. Alternatively, some Virgos have or will find unexpected side effects from certain medications. All Virgos should ask about possible side effects of their medications.

Keep in mind that Jupiter is a healing planet that ancient texts describe as capable of miracles. Should any medical problem arise (and there is no reason to assume it will), it doesn't mean Jupiter isn't working, but that you're finding this problem at the right time, when treatment is most likely to help.

YOUR CAREER IS COMING UP ROSES IN 2004

After almost three years of challenging career aspects, you may not believe that a new and radically improved situation could ever be yours, but you've paid your dues, dear Virgo! You can now reap the benefits of your hard work.

Over the past three years, there were many new facets of your job to be learned and mastered. For most it meant taking on more responsibility; for others it meant learning the ropes in a brand-new industry. Saturn's journey over the highest point in the chart (the "mid-heaven") almost always coincides with massive career changes. Fortunately, you're done with that vitally important phase.

Much of your past experience was colored by Saturn's visit to your tenth house of career from April 2001 to June 2002 and, prior to that, from August 2000 to October 2000. Saturn comes by only once every three decades, so its presence tends to be memorable. You learned to be patient with career progress— certain steps could not be skipped or rushed. For some, Saturn's visit during those years was a wake-up call to be more practical and less idealistic when it came to work matters.

Some Virgos found obstacles when they tried to solve professional problems. Old solutions would no longer work, and a fresh approach and new attitude were required.

Luckily, you are a Virgo, classified by astrologers as a mutable sign, known to be supremely flexible and versatile. As you coped with challenging career conditions over the past few years, you became even more resourceful, ingenious, and adaptable. Now the traits you honed will stand you in good stead as you take on new responsibilities. You will not go through another similar Saturn period for another twenty-nine years, as remarkable as that sounds. You won't have to prove your mettle in the future, either—you've done that!

YOUR BEST CAREER PERIOD IN 2004
MARCH 21 TO MAY 6

If you want a new job, it will be hard to beat March 21 through May 6, when Mars will throw a spotlight on you from your tenth house of fame and achievement. However, Mercury, your ruler, will be retrograde during part of this period, from April 6 to April 30. This may indicate that someone you used to work with—perhaps now in a new setting—will contact you to explore the possibility of working together again. If that happens, it is the one way in which accepting a job offer under Mercury retrograde is a good idea.

Mercury wants you to find closure with the past, so whether that means reconnecting with friends or an old boss or reigniting a project that was put on a back burner, you should look behind you for clues to what you should be doing.

You have the added advantage of Venus and Mars in close proximity in your house of fame from the middle of April through the first week of May, adding to the buzz surrounding you. Going on an interview during this period? Your natural warmth will help you nab the job.

Generally, it is not a good idea to start a job during a Mercury retrograde period, unless you have a prior association with your boss or the company. If you're offered a new job, try to respond during the first week of May. Mercury will then be out of retrograde, and a full moon total eclipse, due May 4, will fall in your house of communication and agreements.

CIRCLE IN RED
THE JUNE 17 NEW MOON, PLUS TWO WEEKS, FOR DAZZLING CAREER PROGRESS

June 17 to June 30 is a better time to change jobs, with the best energy clustered closer to June 17. At that time, you will have four heavenly bodies lighting your house of fame and achievement, a lovely configuration that includes a very powerful new moon, which is considered the most critical of all.

Pluto opposes the new moon, so you may have to over-come the skepticism of a top executive who is not yet con-vinced you can do the job. (You can do it, so plan to be persuasive.) Alternatively, home-related considerations may weigh on you, such as the possibility of relocation or a schedule that would make it difficult to meet family obliga-tions. Uranus squares Venus at this time, so the salary offered may not meet your expectations. Still, there are ben-efits to this offer, so maybe you can get, in writing, a promise to review your salary in six months. As you'll see, you'll like the results of the full moon that arrives six months later!

POSITIVE CAREER DEVELOPMENTS
SHOULD ARRIVE AT THE FULL MOON NOVEMBER 26

Your other big career moment in 2004 should arrive near the full moon November 26, plus or minus four days. That's a Friday, falling over Thanksgiving weekend in the United States, so this news is more likely to come when you are at work, either just before the holiday weekend or the day or two after you return. It will not come later than that.

On this full moon, you have much going for you. By then, Jupiter will be in an ideal position to help you get the salary you deserve. Better yet, Jupiter will be sending a golden beam to the full moon in your house of promotion and reputation. This is ideal! If you could not get the right new job during the other periods (April, May, and the new moon June 17), you will get one last chance to try with this full moon, and in many ways it's the best.

FINANCIALLY, YOUR SERVICES WILL BE IN HOT DEMAND
SEPTEMBER, OCTOBER, AND NOVEMBER KEY MONTHS

In astrology, the two houses that rule finance are separate from the career sector. This explains why we sometimes change jobs but don't necessarily see an increase in salary, or an increase in salary may occur without changing jobs. However, sometimes our stars are aligned and both come at once.

The seeds you planted during the first nine months of 2004 or in the last four months of 2003 will begin to bear luscious fruit in late 2004. Jupiter, the giver of gifts and luck, will move into your house of possessions and money you earn on September 24, 2004, and will remain there until October 25, 2005—thirteen months!

This means that in late 2004 or 2005, substantial financial growth should be within reach. The second house, in which Jupiter will be based beginning in late September, rules money earned, not money won. That's great news, for it means that the market will start to pay you handsomely for your skills, and as a result, your confidence will rise. (The ancients always put self-confidence in the same house as earned income. Interesting, eh?)

Before bountiful Jupiter can get to your second house of money, an eclipse will take place in this same sector on April 19, 2004. This eclipse is a new moon, which means a new start, and sends an important missive to Pluto in your fourth house of family. You may get a raise, or you may receive a loan, inheritance, or gift from a relative—most likely a parent. Uranus (surprise) and Saturn (stability) are both friendly to this eclipse, too, suggesting that unexpected funds could be invested or appropriated wisely, and hence add to your overall sense of security.

New Moon September 28:
A Prime Time to Ask for a Raise

Your best dates for seeing a raise in 2004 will occur either at the full moon on September 28 (plus or minus four days) or the new moon eclipse on October 14, which will have a larger sphere of influence.

First, let's look at September 28. Mercury, your ruler (planet of news), will be in exact alignment with Jupiter, something that happens only once a year. These planets will meet in your second house of earned income and possessions. You may get a raise or buy something expensive that you've long wanted (a day at a spa, jewelry, a computer, artwork, or clothing). Of course, you might receive money and spend it!

Someone may surprise you with a gift on this day as well. (A delayed birthday present perhaps?) If a present does show up, it should be something special. This is a day worth four stars, so you will want to plan a key financial talk for this day!

Eclipse on October 14
Brings More Good Financial News

On the new moon eclipse of October 14, five planets will be in your second house of money, including this powerful eclipse, making this a banner time to ask for a raise or interview for a new, better-paying job. You will have two weeks from October 14 to make things happen, although your cosmic energy will be much stronger near the 14th. Some people find that eclipses deliver their messages one month to the day later, so also watch November 14, plus or minus four days.

If you feel you are due for a raise, expect the best! Schedule a meeting with your boss to assess your short-term future at the firm. If your boss says the company can't afford to give you a raise, consider options elsewhere. Contact friends, business associates, and headhunters. Planetary energy in your chart shows your earning power is about to rocket skyward, so leave no stone unturned.

If you don't like the kind of work you are doing, consider a career change. This would be a fine year to make a shift. The eclipse in May could help you get the ball rolling. Be ready for a move to a new job or a pay hike in your present job by October, because by then all systems will be go!

NOVEMBER SHINES BRIGHTLY FOR THOSE WORKING IN THE ARTS

Toward year's end, you will have two more four-star days to increase your cash flow, and both arrive in November.

The first is November 4, the date that Venus, ruler of your second house of income, meets with Jupiter, the planet of bounty and generosity. Give November 4, a Thursday, plus or minus one day. Not only will Venus and Jupiter cooperate on your behalf, but Neptune will send a golden beam into your financial sector as well, which suggests that if you work in the arts or with artistic people, you will do exceptionally well. Do something to increase your salary, dear Virgo! Your efforts will pay off.

Later in the month, Jupiter will signal Neptune, an exceedingly rare aspect, on Monday, November 29. (Give this aspect plus or minus four days.) Again, if you work in the arts, this date is for you, because it is a day on which your creations, ideas and expressions will be lauded. Financial benefit should ensue immediately or shortly after this date. So whether you are an actor, poet, photographer, director, musician, dancer, or other arts professional, on November 29, Neptune, the patron planet of the artist, will inspire and protect you while Jupiter will reward you. Show your work to the world!

NEED TO MOVE OR MAKE HOME-RELATED CHANGES? DECEMBER IS YOUR BEST MONTH

Your best time to move or make any changes in your home—including roommates—will be at the new moon of December 11, 2004. You will be amazed how easily you are able to accomplish your goals from this day forth.

Later, from December 25, 2004, to February 6, 2005, Mars' marvelous energy will be in your fourth house of home to help you move or to effect other changes to your abode. Mars' appearance in this house at holiday time also suggests that if you aren't making changes or improvements to your home, you will be entertaining, for sure.

Another relevant date, but not as critical as the dates listed above, is the full moon on June 2, plus or minus four days. Career news will be happening simultaneously, so you may be considering relocating to take advantage of a job opportunity. Uranus will be in a fussy mood, so this is a tense moon for home and family matters, and a costly problem could suddenly appear. Rather than initiate any decisions on June 2, sit back and respond to outside events. If you are to move or make changes, it will most likely occur at year's end.

Uranus Settles Into Your Seventh House Until 2011
A Close Relationship to Become a Big Focus in Years Ahead

In March 2003, something very monumental happened: Uranus, the planet of surprise, change, creativity, and disruption, moved into your seventh house of close, committed relationships. This planet is set to stay until 2011, and this placement has both positive and negative elements to it.

Last year was unusual, however, and should not be considered a template for what's to come. Mars, the energy planet, made a highly unusual six-month visit from mid-June to mid-December 2003 to this same house. Mars—an assertive, combative planet—can be quite explosive when mixed with unpredictable Uranus, so 2003 could have been a time of great relationship difficulty for you. Mars has since moved on, so the harshest part of this aspect is now over, but because Mars made a complete tour of Pisces—the sign that guards your seventh house—this aspect touched every Virgo, although those with birthdays falling from August 23 to August 29 were under greatest strain.

As 2004 begins, you may be somewhat shaken by the recent activity in this house, which began to calm down only in mid-December 2003. This amounts to an enormous amount of energy concentrated in one area of your chart last year.

Depending on when you are reading this, you may not have had enough distance between you and 2003 to feel the calming effects of Mars' absence quite yet. The benefit you gained from Mars' visit was that it forced you to see certain truths about a particular relationship that you may not have noticed previously—and truth is always valuable.

It's important to note that "close relationship" refers to any committed romantic or business relationship. It may be your steady romantic partner, a spouse, or an important business alliance that is contract-based.

Looking forward, you are likely to experience the more positive qualities of Uranus in your seventh house of partners. If you aren't in a relationship as you read this, you may decide to consciously or unconsciously put yourself in situations that will make this possible. You may start to date more seriously or end a relationship that isn't going anywhere. From now on, you will be less inclined to put up with any sort of relationship that isn't productive (including business), because with Uranus you will feel the need to act. However, watch out for impulsive or hasty decisions—you may be in a whirlwind romance and suddenly decide to wed. This is not like you, dear Virgo, but this is a brand-new planetary influence, so you'll have to wait and see how it affects you. If your friends think your relationship is heating up too quickly, you may want to listen to them and slow down the pace. You and your partner need to be on the same wavelength before making a commitment.

If you feel Uranus' influence in business, you may find that your business partner is unusual in some respect, in the way he or she looks or thinks (Uranus is known to produce genius). This partner may be quite creative, with an erratic work schedule and a tendency towards mood swings. When Uranus tours the seventh house, it often means you can attract an idiosyncratic partner—perhaps delightfully so.

This can also work out romantically. You may date someone highly creative who works in the arts or who is an independent thinker.

Uranus updates whatever house it touches, and this planet has made a rare, once-in-eighty-four-year visit to your seventh house of partners and marriage, meaning you'll want more passion and intensity from the union. You won't accept a dreary status quo any longer—you'll want more!

If you are married but not happy, you'll want to work with your spouse to improve things or you'll leave. This marks a major shift in your attitude, as you'd normally choose to maintain a relationship at all costs than put your needs first. There is nothing wrong with protecting your interests, dear Virgo. I am being very mindful that Virgo almost never leaves a marriage, so conditions must be extremely bad for one to do so. With Uranus in this house, it's clear you aren't going to spend the rest of your life in a very bad situation because your friends or family tell you do to so.

If Uranus affects you in business, you may have been wrangling with a business partner, competitors, or critics, and it may have taken a great deal of energy to maintain the status quo. This trend will continue in 2004, but you will have a better grasp of how to best protect yourself. Remember that Jupiter is on your side, which brings enormous protection.

It is also clear that you will want more freedom. In business, you may need more autonomy to make decisions. In marriage, it may mean a little time alone to pursue personal interests or to take an occasional quick trip alone, to decompress from a busy life, perhaps by visiting a spa.

Even if you've long been dependent on your partner for security, with Uranus in this house, you will see that you are perfectly able to stand on your own two feet. That's a great feeling!

This trend could be felt in a more extreme way for a few Virgos. If you feel social rules are intrusive, you may go your own way, regardless of what others think. You may raise a few eyebrows in the process, but you seem fine with that. For example, you may date or marry a person much younger or much older than you. Or you may choose to have a baby even if you and your partner have no plans to wed. Uranus is a spontaneous planet, so the answers to your needs will spring up from within you, and they will be answers only you—and your partner—will understand. You'll want to do what's right for you and your partner, rather than what society dictates is appropriate.

Finally, Uranus is an exciting and invigorating influence, so you will start to look toward one close relationship as your main source of intellectual stimulation, whereas in the past you viewed your job as the main source of excitement. This marks a major shift of attention.

Don't try to resist an experience brought to you by Uranus—it is simply too big a trend to buck. The only way to approach the coming seven years is with an open mind and a sense of adventure. You are about to go into uncharted territory, and you will grow enormously in the process.

NOT ATTACHED? LOVE GLOWS BEST NEAR MAY 1, JULY 2, AND AUGUST 17

Aside from the fact that you will be the sparkling celestial favorite zodiac sign for the first nine months of 2004 simply by having Jupiter in your sign—an outrageous advantage when it comes to matters of the heart—you also have some other strongly supportive aspects ahead.

Your best moment of the year will occur on July 2, a full moon in your fifth house of true love. That moon will wink at both Jupiter, the planet of happiness, and Uranus, the planet of surprise. Full moons have a range of influence of plus or minus four days, so you will have a whole week to try your luck.

You may also want to mark down two other dates that will stand out. They are May 1 and August 17, when, on both dates, the ruler of your fifth house of love, Saturn, sends a cheery hello to Jupiter.

Of the two, August 17 is the best date of the year for your love life. In addition to the Saturn/Jupiter connection, there will be other positive things going on in the sky at the time: Venus will be in Cancer, touring your house of people, parties, and fun, and Mars will be in your sign, dear Virgo, increasing your sex appeal. August 17 is a red-letter day to watch!

YOUR LUCKIEST DAY OF THE YEAR: SEPTEMBER 21 JUPITER WALKS WITH THE SUN IN VIRGO

Every year features one day (plus or minus three days of influence) that seems more special than all the rest. It usually happens when the mighty Sun and Jupiter walk arm in arm—as it does this year.

If your birthday falls on September 21, then you've just won the jackpot, because not only should this day be quite amazing for you, but your whole year ahead should be, too! (Your "solar return" is falling on this spectacular day.) Mars, Mercury, and the Sun will be in your sign (giving you lots of clout), as will Jupiter in its final days in Virgo.

Your reign as celestial favorite may be coming to a close in September 2004, but Jupiter will depart with a great flourish and leave many gifts for you. It should be an outstanding time for scheduling an action that's very important to you. On this day, take a risk—show that manuscript or screenplay, go out on that blind date, sign a lease on that wonderful new office space for your own business. You name it! On this day your name is written in lights across the sky!

Summary

An amazing year awaits you, dear Virgo! Jupiter will expand your thinking, allowing you to see the possibility in small projects and opportunities that others miss. New faces will enter your life and have an important part to play as catalysts for your new lifestyle, both personally and professionally. Among the new people in your life may be one special romantic partner who changes your perspective—and possibly your destiny.

While Jupiter is in Virgo, from January to September, sow as many seeds as possible to make your dreams come true. See anyone who will see you, and let them know your goals.

By the time Jupiter moves into the second phase of its cycle, in late September, you will begin to see results which will directly relate to conversations you have had when Jupiter first entered Virgo, in late August through December 2003, or in the first nine months of 2004. This is why it's critical you know what you want early in the year, and to take baby steps to get there. You won't have a period like this again for twelve years and there is not a moment to lose.

If single, this could be the year you meet that special someone, as having Jupiter in your sign is a strong indicator for a bewitching first meeting. However, you must circulate! Early May, the first week of July, and mid-August will be especially bright periods.

Many attached Virgos went through a trying period last year with a partner, perhaps a spouse or steady lover. There was no question that last year, your partner had more control over your relationship, but this year you do. While you may not have all the answers quite yet, at least now you will know what you want to do about this alliance, and how to plan accordingly.

If this person was not your mate or lover, but a business collaborator or competitor, the same rules apply. Tensions should subside gradually in 2004 and should be even more improved by 2005.

This year, a friend or colleague—someone older, with a great deal of insight and maturity—may begin to play the role of mentor or sounding board for your greatest plans. This person will help you achieve a vital goal. You may already know this person, or they may show up now or in very late 2004, depending on your birthday, and come as a gift from Saturn.

Saturn's position in your eleventh house of community suggests you may take on a leadership post in a club. The eleventh house is where we grow through giving back to society—if you find a cause that resonates, you can make quite a difference.

In matters of health, the planets are sending conflicting messages. On one hand, Uranus is opposed to your Sun, which can be harsh, but mainly for those born August 23-29. Be sure to continue to treat your body well by eating a lot of fresh foods and by getting enough exercise and rest. Stress-related disorders and digestive problems could become a problem. It would be best go for checkups throughout the year.

With Neptune in your house of health, your doctor could find it hard to make a diagnosis. If this is the case, get a second or third opinion and don't give up. If you have an intuitive feeling of what might be causing your difficulty, share your thoughts with your doctor. Jupiter in your sign is a powerful healing influence—never say never when Jupiter is around!

One downfall of Jupiter's presence is that you could gain weight. Be careful, Virgo!

The difficult career situation you endured for almost three years has finally come to an end. You have proven your abilities; now is the time to nail the promotion you have worked so hard to achieve. Look for a new position just after the new moon in mid-June, your most beneficial moment of the year for professional advancement. If you are artistic, be sure to present your grandest creative ideas to higher-ups in November.

Financially, there could be a sudden shift in April, due to the eclipse on April 19. One source of income could end this year, but if so, not to worry. Your salary should take a dramatic turn for the better in late September and mid-October. At that time, you could also lay down the money for an item you dearly need or feel would be a good investment. It looks like you can afford it!

Travel could be glorious this year. This trend comes thanks to Jupiter in Virgo and two eclipses that will coax you to pack and go. Watch February, March, May, or mid-November.

If travel is not possible, this same mind-expanding cosmic energy will help you with international commerce or encourage you to delve into an exciting publishing project or return to school to get an advanced degree. In that case, February, March, and May hold the greatest potential.

At home, you may decide to move, sell or buy property, or give your surroundings a needed face lift—December 2004 will be your best month to do so. This golden home-related cycle continues straight into early February 2005.

As you see, you have a great year ahead, dear Virgo. Make the most of this glorious year by stretching until you touch the sky!

Libra

September 23-October 22

The Big Picture

2004 has every indication of being a glorious year for you, one that will help you turn a critical corner and set off in a brand-new direction. You have not seen a year like this in over a decade, dear Libra. Considering how hard you worked in 2003, you may question whether a year that promises so much is even possible. It is, and you will see this for yourself very soon.

In many ways 2004 will be two years rolled into one, with the first part being fairly quiet, but with the second phase, near your birthday, busy and brimming with so much opportunity, that at times it will leave you breathless. No one deserves this more than you!

To what planet do you owe all this favor? Thank Jupiter, the planet of good fortune and happiness, in an impending once-in-twelve-year visit to Libra that will last thirteen amazing months. Jupiter will arrive in Libra on September 24, 2004, and remain there until October 25, 2005.

With so many planets on the north/south/east/west points of your chart, you are in the process of building a sturdy foundation for the future. The underpinnings of your life have been in need of some refurbishing, and now the planets will help you get the job done.

What's needed is a new vision and sense of self, and Jupiter will help you in that quest. By the end of next year, you may be surprised by how wide and all-encompassing your thinking has become.

You will learn to see things not as they are, or how they are presented to you, but at their fullest potential. You can do this because your maturity, insight, and imagination are all growing exponentially. Others may still be thinking small, so you will have to lobby them to see the world as you do. That should not be a problem—as an air sign, you know how to debate effectively. Later others will wonder why they didn't see what you did from the very start.

With Jupiter at your side during the last four months of the years, your endeavors will seem to be growing like the beans in *Jack and the Beanstalk*. Naturally, not all projects or relationships could—or should—get that kind of nurturing from you, but the ones that merit it will certainly benefit from your new "think big" attitude.

View the phase that you will enter in September as one of conception. You won't see the fruits of any new endeavors until the last quarter of 2005. The harvest you reap in late 2005 and through 2006 will be a result of conversations and relationships during your earlier gestation phase (September 25, 2004, to October 25, 2005). Throughout this period, Jupiter will see to it that you will have luck on your side, and that is sure to keep your spirits buoyed.

It will soon be evident that you will need to shift your vision to the long term. This is a radical change, for last year you spent a lot of time putting out fires on a day-to-day basis. This won't be the case in 2004, thank goodness. This year you will have all the time you need to plan for the future. Before your golden epoch begins, reflect on what truly makes you happy.

Setting down your priorities will be important, for if you don't, you may run in too many directions. By autumn (in the northern hemisphere) you will be presented with many options—some quite dazzling—and you may be tempted to accept them all. You won't accomplish as much if you spread yourself too thin, so choose the options with the best long-term potential. If you take the time to map out your future in detail, you will be unstoppable.

Your growing confidence and optimism will allow you to take a few risks, whether professionally or in your personal life, or both. For example, if over the last few years you've been wary about falling in love again, this year you may find that you are now ready. Or if you've always wanted to start your own business, but have felt too hesitant to quit your present job, conditions could converge in late 2004 to make you feel the time is finally right. You have the time, the money, the confidence, and the opportunity—and you'll take the plunge. The environment will be conducive to creating the changes you have long wanted to make.

Sure, there will be periods when nothing seems to go right—every year has moments like that. That will be particularly true when Venus, your ruling planet, goes retrograde, from May 17 to June 29. Use this time and Mercury retrograde periods (listed in its own chapter in the back of the book) to revise your blueprints.

In terms of career, Saturn will be beaming energy from your tenth house of honors, achievement, and promotion. Under Saturn's tutelage, you will grow into a position of greater power and control, and, if you deal conscientiously with Saturn's challenges, you will garner more respect from both supporters and competitors in your industry. You may move into a new sphere in your current profession, or you may make a complete career switch. Either way, a period of apprenticeship will be involved, and it will likely last until mid-2005.

Saturn's visit to your career sector is a rare—this demanding teacher planet comes by but once every 29 years—but because it entered your sign in June 2003, you have become accustomed to your added responsibilities. Certainly, you have worked longer hours.

Still, that no-frills and often no-fun existence of last year is not an indicator of what is to come. 2003 was all work and no play because from June to December 2003, Mars was in your day-to-day work area (sixth house). With Mars and Saturn in this house, you probably doubled your workload. With more responsibilities at work and a large number of obligations to juggle at home, you may have teetered on the verge of burnout. Hosting Saturn in your tenth house demands an intense, dedicated effort but with Mars gone, you should find 2004 an improvement over last year.

There was a method to the universe's madness, however. Last year Mars taught you to increase your productivity and to try new work methods. This year you will learn leadership skills and try out a new role that just a few years ago would have been beyond you.

Saturn's job is to help you bring ideas and dreams into reality through focusing and overcoming obstacles. You will be in the process of building a strong, new career direction, and that takes time. These rewards will more than compensate for the time you put into your career until July 2005, when Saturn leaves its critical position.

Saturn rarely brings on responsibility suddenly or without consent. Your new role will be offered rather than thrust upon you. Saturn can turn you into a powerful force to be reckoned with, but only if you are willing to work with this planet's demands.

Now let's turn to your romantic life, which is due to brighten soon! Last year you had almost no time for a personal life, but this year, you more than make up for that. Part of this will be due to the presence of Jupiter in Libra at year's end, a classic sign of meeting one's soul mate if unattached.

The year's solar eclipses, on April 19 and October 14, also point the way to a much-improved personal life. There may be a speed bump to get over initially, but the bottom line is you will gain from these eclipses.

This could easily be the year that you get engaged, married, or begin a serious, close relationship, in the personal or business sense. If it is the latter, you may sign with a business partner or have positive dealings with a middleman, such as a headhunter, broker, lawyer, or agent. Or a matchmaker may be lucky for you. If you are married, you may discover a problem that needs to be addressed at eclipse time, but if you approach it fearlessly, you will gain greater closeness. These eclipses will give you the courage to tackle nearly any issue head-on.

The eclipses will make it clear that it's time for a radical self-reappraisal—to decide who you are, as well as what kind of partner is truly right for you. Both eclipses are new moons, signifying that you will present a new image and attitude to the world.

Changes in your finances are due to the year's other two eclipses, in Scorpio (May 4) and Taurus (October 28). Both of these eclipses are lunar full moon eclipses, suggesting an ending or finish to a financial matter. You may see a certain revenue stream end, an unexpected expense come up, or a settlement to a long-pending matter such as a divorce, insurance claim, or inheritance.

Both these eclipses will mark emotional points in the year, but it is unclear why. Generally, Libra is more intellectual than emotional, and you generally don't have strong emotional reactions, but you might under the eclipses. For example, you may lose a client or quit your job on one of these dates, and find that you miss them even though you never enjoyed either. There are upbeat parts to everything, and it is normal to feel a little wistful at the ending.

Jupiter, Saturn, and the eclipses all are issuing the same message: it's time to reinvent yourself. You seem bored with things as they have been—you want something new and fresh to look forward to. You also want a lifestyle that is more reflective of the person you are now. The time has never been better for you to begin a new chapter.

Details on the Year Ahead

LAY YOUR FOUNDATION FOR A BETTER FUTURE
JUPITER IN VIRGO
FROM JANUARY THROUGH SEPTEMBER 24

Until September 24, Jupiter, the planet of good fortune and happiness, is touring your twelfth house, which is a subtle but powerful placement for you. This cycle is simply fabulous for engendering creativity while spending time in solitude. Libra is not a sign that generally likes to be alone, but sometimes it's worth going against type, dear Libra. You have a wealth of planetary power behind you if you decide to drop out of the social scene to focus on artistic projects.

If you develop your talents during this period—and Neptune in your fifth house will provide all the inspiration you need—by the time Jupiter and Neptune exchange pleasantries at the end of November (something we will talk about later), you will be in a perfect position to realize the benefits.

Taking time for yourself will also be valuable for thinking, dreaming, and generally plotting a new path. Later in the year some fairly influential people could be asking you what you'd like to achieve, and will want to help you. You'll need an answer that you can give with conviction. Once you have set your course, don't be shy about asking for advice or assistance from bigwigs.

You will learn a great deal about yourself during the first nine months of 2004, whether by examining your creative output or by getting to know yourself better through quiet reflection, meditation, or prayer.

This position of Jupiter marks the end of a twelve-year cycle and the preparation for the one that begins in September. What you decide to do in the last four months of 2004 and in 2005 will establish the tone of your next decade; it is that important! In preparation, you will want to clear the decks of projects and people who seem to drain you.

Your sense of compassion and sensitivity to others will be heightened during this period too, and you may decide to help a favorite charity. The twelfth house, ruled by Pisces, teaches the universality of the human experience, and to accept others, no matter what their background. Jupiter, the bountiful planet, will encourage you to give back to others, and to leave your mark. As 2004 begins, your gaze will be outward, toward helping others. If you have very little time, you may simply do good on a one-on-one basis, such as reading to the blind or donating blood regularly.

This period will also help you sharpen your intuition. Libra is an analytical sign that often feels a bit uncomfortable relying on hunches. During the first nine months of the year you would be wise to do so anyway, because the universe is about to help you navigate new terrain. Jupiter will protect you from going ahead on projects that will waste your talents, or from handing over your trust to romantic partners who aren't worth a tumble. You may wonder why your intuition and your mind are sending you conflicting messages. Still, if you listen to that inner voice, you'll see that your instinct was right all along.

Your Golden Epoch Begins
Jupiter Is in Libra
September 25, 2004, to October 25, 2005

As we discussed, the first nine months of the year are for planning, but the last three months of 2004 are for action, which will continue into 2005. Wait until this glittering period begins to initiate your biggest and grandest plans!

From the moment Jupiter enters Libra on September 25, you will begin a new twelve-year cycle that will take you into the next decade. Projects and relationships that you put in place now could easily provide you with benefits for years to come.

Over the coming twelve months, you may take on a new look, start a new job, meet a romantic interest, make an important new friend, or move across town—or halfway across the world. You could travel much more than usual too, for Jupiter will want you to take the shutters off your eyes, and its favorite method is by encouraging you to take long journeys. The path you choose and the people you align with during this phase will have greater-than-usual importance. One or two of these new people could become catalysts for setting you on a new path.

Jupiter's role in the horoscope is to effect personal growth and expansion, and this planet will bring in elements to your life that you feel have been missing. Luck will finally be on your side, and you will find your timing remarkably on target. Others will open doors for you, which is new—you've not had much help in the past. Opportunities that you would have never dared to consider will come your way now. Adopt an open and experimental attitude, for you will learn much about yourself by easing into one of these roles.

You will be more curious, more probing, and more experimental than usual and you will push the walls of your life back. Confidence will return, and that's a sexy quality that could help you attract a soul mate if you are single. If you are attached, your optimistic attitude may rub off on your partner.

These cycles are not framed by events, but rather by attitudes, goals, and intentions. While not everything will pan out during your wonder period, many will. Think of this period as time to lay the groundwork for even greater abundance.

Your Love Life Improves
Near Eclipses on April 19 and October 13

Last year you hardly had time for a personal life. This year is different, and improves on so many levels. Two solar eclipses, both in your relationship sector, on April 19 (in Aries) and October 14 (in Libra), indicate a better personal life. The last set of eclipses that were similar to these occurred back in 1995-1996, although the ones in 1985-1986 were more similar to this year's.

There will be two more eclipses in your opposite sign of Aries in 2005 (spotlighting partners), and one in Aries in March 2006. This represents the beginning of a major theme that will echo in your life for some time. These eclipses will create a climate of enormous self-discovery and transformation. Eclipses open as many doors as they shut. We often have to make hard choices at eclipse time, but the universe does this so that you keep moving forward. (It hates stagnation.)

There is no doubt that these two eclipses will begin a new chapter in your life. Luckily, both these eclipses are new moons, signifying starts, not endings. If you are not dating anyone, they could spark an intriguing relationship. If you are in an established relationship, you could also see changes, most likely for the better.

For example, your partner could suddenly be pressing for a commitment. If you aren't ready, or aren't sure you will ever be ready to commit to this person, you may leave (even if you had no plans to do so), so that you can open yourself up to new possibilities.

The April 19 eclipse falls in your partnering and marriage sector, so it's likely to be the most critical one for relationships. At the time of this eclipse, your ruler, Venus, will be within kissing distance of Mars, a sexy aspect, but Uranus is cranky and could set off an argument with your sweetheart. Uranus rules your solar house of love, so try to keep your relationship as steady as possible. Listen, but don't respond just yet—there could be some jarring news.

Luckily, Uranus will be chummy with Mercury, so you can talk your way through any flap that emerges. As said, however, other planetary energy will be quite positive. That new moon will get along well with Mars (sexuality) and Pluto (more sexuality). Pluto and Mars are both in intellectual houses, so again, being able to communicate clearly is the key at this time, for it will lead to either greater love or the realization it's not going to work.

Your partner may be the dominant half in April, but you have firm control by October. With five planets piling up in Libra—and two of them close enough to wink at Uranus— you'll enjoy this time. You are ready to make your decisions and move in the direction you please. Your very appearance may change—you may lose an appreciable amount of weight, radically change your hairstyle, or wear more stylish clothing. (Libra is very trend conscious, and with so many planets in your sign, you'll look ultra-up-to-date, for sure.)

If you're looking for love, be sure to circulate at the new moon on January 21. A new moon in your house of true love could point to an intriguing meeting or a long-awaited pregnancy. New moons set up a ribbon on energy that last two weeks, but your strongest days are clustered at the appearance of that new moon, January 21.

VENUS AND MARS IN DAZZLING MUTUAL RECEPTION PLAN FOR ZESTY ROMANCE FEBRUARY 8–MARCH 5

Very rarely are two planets in mutual reception. What does that mean? A mutual reception occurs when two planets each tour the sign that the other planet rules at precisely the same time. Specifically, Mars rules Aries, while Venus rules your sign, Libra (as well as Taurus; as there are not enough planets to go around, some signs share planets). You will be more favored than most, because Venus is your guardian planet.

In February, Venus and Mars will swap home bases. Mars will be in Taurus, and Venus will be in Aries—that's a mutual reception. Together these planets buddy up and act as one, and that will help you, as a Libra, enormously. It's just the opposite of a sleepy, ineffective period like the one mentioned below, when Venus will retrograde.

A mutual reception is great for romance, especially if you are single and hoping to find someone new to love. Put a gold star on the period that extends from February 8 to March 5.

VENUS IS IN A WEAKENED STATE FROM MAY 17 TO JUNE 29: LIE LOW

Venus does not go retrograde very often, but when it does, projects either go haywire or go on hold. It would not be an ideal time to launch new endeavors or to seal deals. I doubt if you would even get to the signing stage.

Venus rules beauty, pampering, the decorative arts and adornment, and certain monetary transactions. It's not a time to get engaged or married, throw a party or fund-raiser, or redecorate your apartment or house. It's also not a time to buy new clothes, jewelry, or schedule spa treatments. If you want your hair done by a new hair stylist, wait until Venus is out of retrograde. It would also be an adverse time to schedule plastic surgery.

VENUS IN LIBRA FAVORS YOU
FROM OCTOBER 28, 2003 TO NOVEMBER 22, 2004

Circle October 28 through November 22, when your ruling planet, Venus, will kiss your sign. You'll be a standout, and sparks of love should be evident. It's also a perfect time to give your looks a boost.

TWO EXTRAORDINARY DATES:
NOVEMBER 29 AND DECEMBER 4

2004 will finish on an exciting note, with two highly romantic dates toward the end of the year.

○ **November 28, when Jupiter contacts romantic Neptune.** This is certain to be one enchanted evening! These two planets take years to align properly, but Jupiter will be in your sign, while Neptune will be positioned in your fifth house of true love! This is a Sunday, but you will feel the glow in the days leading to this date. If you were born on or within five days of

October 5, the mathematical degrees of these planets will shower you with a double dose of glitter.

○ **December 4, when Mars and Venus finally meet.** Mars has been chasing his mythological lover Venus around the zodiac for more than a year, but has not been able to catch her. Incredibly, Venus and Mars did not meet at all in 2003 and in 2004, not until December 4—just in time for the holidays! Venus and Mars will embrace in the ultra-sexy sign of Scorpio. This should be a red-letter day for you! If you get invited to a holiday party, say yes, especially if you are single and hope to meet someone new. Established? You'll still have plenty of flirtatious fun with your partner.

YOUR LUCKIEST DAYS OF THE YEAR? YOU HAVE THREE! SEPTEMBER 21, OCTOBER 13, AND NOVEMBER 4

For most of us, Jupiter in conjunction with the Sun is the best day of the year. This year these two happy-go-lucky heavenly bodies will link on September 21 in Virgo, in the very last degrees. This will be an extraordinary day if you were born at the very beginning of Libra, near September 22. (The closer to that date, the stronger your luck.) On this day, a friend or person in authority could go out of their way to help you.

September 21 would be a golden day to launch a new endeavor, begin a relationship, sign any kind of paper, ask for a favor, make a presentation, send an application, take a test, negotiate a deal, or do anything else important to you.

The new moon solar eclipse on October 14 could be even more fortunate, especially if you were born on or near this day. With five heavenly bodies in Libra (out of a possible ten), you will have plenty of cosmic clout. This eclipse should help you gain a new appreciation of yourself and your talents, and may even coincide with a brand-new change in your looks. Make the most of it!

One more day that might sparkle brightly is on the date that Venus and Jupiter waltz together, an annual event that this year occurs on November 4. If you were born on or near September 30, it will be doubly important. Not only are all the areas of life that we've been discussing light up for you, but financial matters should go exceptionally well, too. (This is something you will see either immediately or in the long term, from the plans you set into place on that day.)

NEED TO MOVE OR MAKE DOMESTIC CHANGES? JANUARY, MAY, JULY, AUGUST PROVIDE OPPORTUNITIES FOR ACTION

This is not a big year for home-related changes. If you need to find a new place to live, you will have to be very decisive because you won't have any wide windows of opportunity. You will have some small but highly effective moments to find solutions, so be ready!

One of your best moments will come at the new moon on January 21, which will provide you with two weeks of solid planetary support to find a workable answer.

Jupiter will send exceptionally comforting vibrations on May 1 and August 17. A decision made on or near either date would certainly add to your sense of security. If you need to sell or buy property, these days may bring you a good bargain or, at the very least, happy news.

You may also be able to make a real estate or domestic decision near July 2, which brings a full moon in your home sector.

Your Career Is Booming: Keep Your Eye on the Corner Office Saturn Grooms You to Fit the Bill

As you begin 2004, you will be filled with drive and ambition. This is all the more remarkable because you have just come through a hard, sometimes thankless career year that offered lots of busy work but frustratingly little in the way of promotion or accolades. No matter—you did impress a number of higher-ups in your organization, you just weren't aware that you did. This year is different, because the feedback will be stronger and you'll have more opportunities to show your mettle.

In June 2003, Saturn, the planet ruling maturity and responsibility, moved into your tenth house of career honors and achievement for a two-year stay. This is the first time Saturn has visited this part of your chart in 29 years. Saturn will test, stretch, and challenge you to become stronger and wiser until July 2005, when your cosmic tour of duty will be over. During that period you could be rewarded with a much bigger position, one that's likely to have real power and authority. Congratulations!

Saturn crossing over the top portion of your chart, as is happening now, often indicates a new promotion, but it also brings the possibility of a career switch too, whether you had planned it or not.

Keep your resume updated at all times. You might want to keep one on hand whenever you think of an accomplishment you'd like to add. Writing a strong, persuasive resume takes weeks, sometimes even months. Allow yourself the luxury of asking yourself what job you'd really like to have, for this year you may find your true vocation. If it means going back to school, Jupiter will help you find the funds to make your studies possible.

You might be wondering, "How can every Libra be in line for a promotion or better job? This doesn't make sense!" Well, you are right. If you have not worked hard and done certain things wrong—showed up late, turned in sloppy work, talked back to your boss—then Saturn will have different lessons to teach you. I don't consider these possibilities because I know you would never work at less than one hundred percent. However, you may see some Libras who are having a hard time with this transition. Saturn will give you just what you need—no more, no less.

Saturn's presence suggests that you will need to learn many new things—new jargon, new procedures, new standards, and a new cast of characters. You get the picture—there will be lots to learn.

Saturn comes by in a given house only two or three times in a lifetime, so Saturn will make sure that what it teaches you will be unforgettable enough to carry with you for decades into the future.

CAREER WILL BE A BIGGER-THAN-USUAL FOCUS FOR LIBRAS BORN FROM SEPTEMBER 29 TO OCTOBER 20

Last year, Libras with birthdays from September 23 through October 6 felt the most direct challenges from Saturn.

Libras with birthdays from September 23 to September 28 will not experience the full force of Saturn this year. If your birthday is listed above, you are finished with Saturn's tour of duty. However, at the start of 2004, Saturn will still be moving within the fairly early degrees of Cancer, close enough to annoy you a little bit. If you feel that life has not yet become easier, things will soon. With each successive month, you should like the year better and better.

If you were born on or near September 30, you may feel that you have little choice but to take a new job. Occasionally, the universe will push us, and if this is the case for you, even enforced changes can have a very positive and upbeat result now. Keep pressing forward.

This year Libras with birthdays that fall from September 29 to October 20 will feel Saturn's influence most in 2004. Yes, there is some overlap of birthdays from last year to this year because Saturn went retrograde, but everyone gets about the same amount of time with Saturn's tutoring—about six months.

If your birthday falls within the range just listed, don't worry—our biggest and proudest accomplishments almost always coincide with a Saturn visit. I published my first book and started my website (*www.astrologyzone.com*) when Saturn made a two-year visit to my tenth house. Those years changed my life's direction. This could be the case for you, too.

If you were born in early October, from October 1 to October 7, you will notice pressures mounting, but not until the end of September.

If your birthday falls after October 7, you will feel the main part of this trend in 2004 and early 2005.

In 2005, Saturn will move forward through all remaining degrees, highlighting Libra birthdays that fall from October 13 to October 23.

Saturn will leave Cancer on July 5, 2005, at which time all Libras will have finished with Saturn. Saturn will not be back for 29 years, and you will carry these lessons for another three decades, if not the rest of your life.

These Dates Are Also Best for a Career Boost

You won't be done with Saturn's tutoring until July 2005—your "graduation date"—but in the meantime you can still make impressive progress. You may want to circle these key career dates on your calendar. Try not to be on vacation during the following dates, because if you do, you will miss some of your best opportunities to grow.

- **May 7–June 23** is a superb seven-week period to search for a better job or to angle for a promotion in your present company. This will be your best, most sustained planetary energy for career advancement in 2004.

- **The new moon on July 17**, which falls in your tenth house of achievement, will bring on two weeks of bright energy, perfect for interviews, lunches, and career talks.

- **The full moon on December 26** will be simply fabulous for career, too. The full moon will be in perfect angle to Uranus, the planet of surprise, so look sharp! You may be called into the big boss' office or asked to give a statement to the press. If you are self-employed, you may bring in a big, new client before the year is out.

Expect Financial Shifts as a Result of Eclipses on May 4 and October 28

Financial reorganization is almost a given this year, because these eclipses will light up your financial sectors on two occasions. Both are full moon eclipses, so you will close the door on a certain monetary situation.

The first eclipse, May 4, will fall in your house of earned income and possessions, so a financial matter (for example, a raise or the purchase of a house, car, or furniture) will quickly come to conclusion.

This full moon and the Sun are both in tough aspect to Neptune, so be careful about any deal you strike. There could be confusing clauses or, worse, missing clauses. If things are not clarified, you may be sorry later.

Even so, there are good parts to this eclipse too, in that Uranus is perfectly angled to the Sun—news you receive unexpectedly should put a smile on your face. The Moon and Uranus are also in a superb angle to Saturn, meaning that whatever decisions you make at this eclipse will stick, and presumably, that is exactly what you want! The Sun is also in perfect angle to Jupiter; confidential financial talks should go exceptionally well. Should anything happen that seems adverse, look closer—in time this eclipse is going to benefit you quite a bit.

October 28 brings a full moon eclipse. This will have to do with money other people will give you or money you owe them. It could involve a credit card account, loan, inheritance, settlement from a divorce or insurance company, child support, sales commission or royalty, funding from venture capital, or the like. It may relate to an earlier financial decision you made in 2003, near May 15 or November 8.

That full moon and the Sun are in tough angle to Neptune, which could cause confusion. If you are signing a document, have your attorney read it carefully. Not only are there likely to be problematic clauses, but missing clauses (about issues neither side even considered) may come back to bite you.

Still, the October 28 eclipse is not without positive aspects. One of the best is Uranus' perfect angle to the Sun—this could bring profits and checks that you never expected! Neptune is not only behaving, this time it's a model planet by sending Jupiter a lovely missive. If you are creative, artistic, or have a special talent, this eclipse could allow you to seal an outstanding deal, commission, or licensing deal. Watch October 28, plus or minus four days, as well as one month to the day later, November 28, plus or minus four days.

Your Daily Routine
Has Become Highly Changeable Due to
Unpredictable Uranus, in Pisces until 2011

Last year, you got a glimpse of your future when Uranus made a historic move into Pisces, into your house of work and health on March 10. Uranus will remain in this house until 2011. For clarification, Uranus did not move into your tenth house of achievement and fame—the house we discussed above—but rather your day-to-day work assignment house, which also rules your general well being.

This is big news, dear Libra. You have probably not hosted this planet in your solar sixth house in your lifetime. The last time Uranus had this placement was from 1919 to 1927.

This area of your chart rules routines, so your normal schedule will change dramatically in the months and years to come. Between now and 2011, you may undergo a very radical shift in day-to-day workflow, which could be caused by a number of factors. For example, you could move out of a very predictable industry (like insurance or banking) to one that has lots of change from week to week (advertising, public relations, or publishing).

Alternatively, you may choose to work on a freelance basis or work from home a few days a week, so that you can cut down on daily commutes to your office.

New technology will play an even larger role in your everyday life than it has in the past, if that's possible! You may get a new computer or new software designed to make your work easier and more productive. There may be new procedures in your department, too. The number of people who work alongside you may change—there may be much fewer co-workers or many more than usual.

With this creative planet in your house of day-to-day duties, you may be assigned a new plum project. Do a good job, and a promotion could well be in the cards.

CREATIVE EXPRESSION
REACHES NEW HEIGHTS IN 2004
INSPIRATIONAL NEPTUNE
WILL BE YOUR STEADY GUIDE

Neptune, the planet ruling the arts, is now touring one of the most superb placements possible for Libra, the fifth house of creative expression. It takes Neptune 214 years to rotate through all twelve signs, remaining in each sign many years. This is an outstanding, once-in-a-lifetime opportunity for you. If you are an actor, photographer, musician, dancer, art director, graphic artist, film director, stylist, makeup artist, painter, writer, or work in any other area of the arts, you could reach levels rarely achieved before.

Even if you aren't in a traditional artistic field, Neptune can still enlarge your imagination, whether professionally (in any field) or when spending time on personal interests.

If your birthday falls from October 3 to October 9, Neptune will be working overtime to help you make artistic expressions of outstanding value. This is your year. Make time for creativity!

A rare date to watch is November 29, when Jupiter will send an exceedingly rare missive to Neptune. This day could produce a breakthrough in artistic expression or help you get funding for a project. It's a great day to audition or present ideas to those with the power to help you advance.

In Matters of Health, You Are Radiant However, Jupiter in Libra May Add Pounds

Jupiter will spend the first nine months of 2004 in your twelfth house, ruling your subconscious mind. If you have been troubled with a long-standing problem, this year would be an ideal time to have counseling. You don't have to suffer in silence!

The twelfth house also rules efforts we make to rehabilitate our physical body, including substance-abuse detoxification and physical therapy. If you need help to feel your best, this is the year to do it!

When Jupiter enters Libra in late September, your transformation may become very apparent, as Jupiter is considered a planet of healing, but will be boosted by doing some of your homework during the first nine months of 2004.

The twelfth house also rules places of confinement, such as hospitals and other medical facilities. Should you need an operation or any sort of medical procedure, you will have the very best medical practitioners at your side. It would also be an ideal time to schedule any operation you have been putting off, including a dental procedure.

If you have been grappling with a serious, fairly new health problem or have dealt with a chronic problem, Jupiter's arrival in Libra in late September might bring hope. Don't assume that your problem can't be helped—it might. Make an appointment with a specialist to find out if there is a new treatment, technology, or discovery that could make a difference in your life.

It's known in astrological circles that when Jupiter tours your sign, there is always one downside to this otherwise glorious phase, which is that Jupiter makes it quite easy to gain weight. Jupiter, the biggest planet in our solar system, will work to expand all your opportunities, but unfortunately this same planet will also try to expand you physically.

On top of that, Jupiter in Libra is considered a placement that promotes socializing, with food readily available (especially gourmet foods, laden with fat and sugar). Not only will you be busy, you will be eating all kinds of foods, and that may add up to pounds that you may not even notice initially.

The good news is that you can outsmart this planet by exercising regularly during your golden Jupiter period, which will last from September 25, 2004, to October 25, 2005.

URANUS, BEAMING RAYS TO YOUR WORK SECTOR, MAY CAUSE STRESS-RELATED DISORDERS—FIND WAYS TO CHILL

Looking at your chart, nervous tension is apt to be your most pressing problem. Uranus is the planet of electricity, so you'll certainly feel the buzz from time to time, and it is likely to stem mainly from office pressures. Cutting out or curbing consumption of caffeine is certainly a good idea. In your case, regular spa visits would not be an indulgence but a necessity.

Pick up some scented candles to burn at the end of the day, and do what you can to feed and revitalize your body and soul in a healthy way.

BEST TIME TO KICK OFF A FITNESS EFFORT: FEBRUARY 20
THE OCTOBER 13 ECLIPSE IN LIBRA IS IDEAL, TOO

The best date for you to begin a fitness plan or new sport would be on February 20, a new moon that falls in your house of fitness. This moon will send a cheery signal to Saturn, the planet of stability and self-discipline. If you start then, you will begin a routine that you could follow for a very long time. Saturn's job is to get results, and if you start on or just a few days following February 20, you will.

Always begin exercising on a favorable new moon, but don't cut back on calories just yet. Allow your body to get used to the new activity. Then just after the full moon (which always occurs two weeks later, in this case, March 6), switch to your lower-calorie healthy diet. Don't cut calories on a new moon, only just after a full moon—allow three days or so. So if the full moon is March 6, wait until March 9 or 10 to begin your diet.

If you cannot begin your new regime in late February, wait until the new moon solar eclipse in Libra on October 13. This is another fabulous point in the year, as five heavenly bodies— Jupiter, Mars, Mercury, the Sun, and new moon eclipse—will be in Libra. That's impressive planetary power behind you! With Mars included in the group, you will be brimming with energy! It is often said that endeavors started when Mars is at your side have a greater-than-usual chance for success. In your wonder year, nothing is impossible!

Summary

2004 is going to be a big year, and next year promises to be even bigger. All the excitement revolves around the arrival of Jupiter, the planet of happiness and growth, to the sign of Libra on September 24, 2004, to remain there until October 25, 2005.

In the months leading up to September 2004, review your long-held dreams. If you've outgrown your old aspirations, or if they no longer excite you, it's time to draw up some new ones. Aim for a short list of one to three big, grand ideas, ones that fill you with passion and excitement.

If even thinking about one of your dreams wears you out, it's the wrong idea. If it's the right one, it will energize you in a way nothing else ever could. The right dreams have staying power, so that on those occasional days when you may be feeling discouraged (we all experience setbacks), you will still be willing to work on your goal. That's the acid test: if you feel compelled to stay with your idea, no matter how many rejections you receive or obstacles you encounter, you will ultimately succeed.

You will have nine months in 2004 to make your wish list and to deliberate deeply on your aims. In the meantime, try to offload unnecessary obligations or responsibilities that no longer seem to serve the purpose they once did. You'll want to make space for some new options that will be coming your way. Luck will be on your side, and influential people will want to help you, but you will have to be the one to take the first step.

Saturn, now in your tenth house, is grooming you for a big career role. This tough teacher planet entered this house in June 2003 and will remain there until July 2005.

Saturn will show you your shortcomings and help you fix them. New standards of excellence will be presented to you, too, and you will have to come up to speed on them. This year, you may undergo a complete career switch, a common occurrence when Saturn crosses the tiptop of the solar chart, as is happening now. Or you may go to work for a new company or new division of your present company, and that may be the reason you have so many new things to learn. Keep in mind that Saturn never forces you to accept new responsibility—you opt for it because it's a good opportunity.

If, during the course of the year, you are tempted to go back to the "good old days," remember that moving forward is right, going backward is not. Nothing about your past has revitalized energy—the future is where it's at.

Now that Mars is no longer locked in your sixth house of work, as it was for six months last year, in 2004 you will have more time and a more balanced lifestyle. Freer from the constraints of work, you can make progress on personal goals, and have more time for love and romance. Last year was your hard-driving, high-productivity year—this year you have much to learn, but the process won't be as dreary or as intense. Travel, family, home, hobbies, friends—all will get more time in 2004.

Your health should improve noticeably this year, too. If you need surgery or a certain medical procedure, do so early in the year, and be sure to avoid Mercury retrograde periods for best results (see the back of the book). Venus retrograde is to be avoided for cosmetic surgery.

If you want to devise a new exercise routine and diet, late February or mid-October would be ideal starting points. Although Jupiter will try to make you gain weight (the only downside of a glorious visit by this planet to your sign), the eclipse in Libra on October 14 may help you lose weight and get started on a healthier, more active lifestyle to help you keep the weight off.

Relationships appear to be a steady source of joy this year. The eclipse on April 19 will almost certainly be an important moment for Libras who are in established relationships and want to grow closer. With Jupiter in Libra, the sign of marriage, during the last part of the year, many Libras will choose September through December 2004 to wed or set the date in 2005—prior to October 25, that is. Either way, you could not wish for a better time to marry— this bodes very well for long-range happiness! If you are not dating anyone, this is the year you could meet your soul mate and find lasting happiness.

Mid-October is particularly vital because it finds you setting off in an exciting new direction. By then you will be firmly ensconced at the helm of your ship, and navigating into uncharted but welcoming waters. With five out of ten heavenly bodies stacking up in Libra, you will have plenty of control, which is new, as you have not had much cosmic help in recent years. Rarely will a month be as divine as this! If you drew up your wish list early in 2004, now is the time to work hard on it! The tide will be clearly moving in your direction.

Libra, 2004 will be the start of a whole new personal cycle, your wonder year. Take this year seriously! After Jupiter leaves your sign in October 2005, it won't be back for another 12 years. Yet this glitter period won't end in October 2005. The people and projects that are with you now may carry you far into the future, providing you with happiness and profits for years to come. Plant your seeds—soon you will have a bountiful harvest!

Scorpio

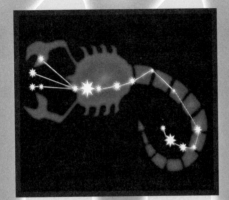

October 23-November 21

The Big Picture

This will be a watermark year for you because the eclipses are back in your sign and in your opposite sign of Taurus. This is major, headline news, because eclipses are the main tools the universe uses to move us from one phase to another, packing a great deal of wisdom into a very short time span. When an eclipse series is over, we often feel like many years have been compressed into one. Fasten your seat belt, dear Scorpio, an adventurous ride is ahead.

Eclipses uproot us, shake us out of complacency, and push us forward with a great force. They also have the power to dismantle the irrelevant elements of our lives and jettison them by creating unexpected outside circumstances that help us view a situation or relationship in a brand-new way. But that's not all. Eclipses allow us to strengthen and stabilize the parts of our lives that are valuable. (To learn more about eclipses, see the chapter on eclipses at the end of this book.)

You already experienced two eclipses in Scorpio/Taurus last year; there will be two more this year, and one more eclipse in Scorpio in 2005. After that the transition will be complete. Before last year, it had been ten years since you experienced these cosmic lightning rods of change.

Last year, you experienced the first two eclipses on May 15 and November 8, 2003. Perhaps those dates stand out. The eclipses of 2004 will build on themes established last year and push them to a higher level of development. It's best not to view the eclipses as separate from one another, but as necessary parts of a larger whole that work in unison and are capable of producing a profound transformation. Some eclipses may be subtler or more dramatic than others, but they all have direction and purpose.

Readers born on November 8 and 24, plus or minus five days, almost certainly had a dramatic 2003 as a result of these eclipses. If you remember nothing dramatic from last year, chances are that this will be your key year.

In 2004, the two eclipses in Scorpio/Taurus will arrive on May 4 and October 28. One more eclipse will be due in April 2005. We need to focus on 2004, which is when you will make decisions that set the tone and direction of your life for many years to come.

Scorpios whose birthdays fall on October 28 and November 7, plus or minus five days, will feel the eclipses of 2004 the most, but all Scorpios will see some seismic shifts. Parts of your life are disappearing into the history books, with or without your compliance, but new parts are springing up just as quickly.

There is one caveat: if you are to gain from these eclipses, you will need to give up certain parts of your old life to make room for what will be added. The universe cannot replace these worn-out parts with something better if you cling to all things familiar to you. In a jumbled and chaotic environment, you could trip over a golden opportunity and never notice it. Think of this as shedding a skin, a concept Scorpio understands, for the snake, one of your sign's symbols, does precisely that.

As a creature of habit, dear Scorpio, you often choose "the devil you know" rather than the one you don't, which explains why you so often stay in bad situations long after you should have bailed out.

Undoubtedly, a close relationship will be under the microscope this year—whether it is a romantic or business-oriented one—for alliances will be one of the focuses of the eclipses. This is not to say you will break up. You might, but you could also draw closer to your partner. Eclipses bring a change of status, that's all. This year's eclipses will also raise issues concerning money, namely in terms of joint resources and financial obligations, and those questions will have to be worked out.

In a larger sense, these eclipses will also ask you to make a profound reassessment of your life, and to consider what would make you truly happy. While eclipses are known to sweep away old debris, they also blow open new doors. These two events—taking things away, bringing in the new—rarely dovetail, but rather occur within a few months of each other. The tricky part is deciding which to replace, with what. You will play a part in making this happen when these cosmic events come by in May and October. (I should add that eclipses can be felt one month to the day before or after they arrive, plus or minus five days.)

After the eclipses, should you find yourself pining over a loss (I am not saying you will, but in case you do), have faith in the wisdom of the universe. You won't see the full picture immediately, because eclipses rarely deliver their messages all at once. Don't be too quick to judge an eclipse as favorable or unfavorable, because they often produce an unanticipated twist later. In the end, these eclipses are your friends and they will protect your interests.

When you begin to experience these changes, especially in a close relationship, you may think only your partner has changed, but the truth is that both of you have changed. You've grown and matured, and so has your partner—the trick is to get on the same wavelength or give up and go your separate ways. Don't be tempted to long for the "good old days," because you can't go back, only forward. We cannot manipulate a project's lifecycle or a partner's interest in the relationship to suit our needs. When something is done, it's done. We can try to revive things, but sometimes we can't, and we should realize that not all things are within our control.

All this questioning and probing in 2004 is coming at the perfect time. Jupiter, the planet of happiness and good fortune, will journey through Scorpio from late 2005 through almost all of 2006, and at that time, Jupiter will shower you with luck during an extraordinary, once-in-twelve-year visit. That will be your wonder period, unlike any you have experienced before. The eclipses in 2004 will help you clear out the unnecessary clutter in your life, and help you regain balance and clarity. When your extraordinary year does arrive, you will be in perfect position to take full advantage of it.

It's been said that typical Scorpios have three chapters in their lives, and they can arrive at any time. They might be evenly spaced in life or come in rapid succession, bunched within a very short time span, say, in childhood or in old age. Each stage offers a completely new view of life. Remarkably, no other sign is said to have this remarkable ability to regenerate in quite the same way. 2004 could be one of those years, when you start an exciting new chapter.

Now, let's touch briefly on other parts of your life, specifically money, career, and residential or family conditions.

Managing your money over the past few years has not been fun. Scorpios are good with finances—you know how to make money multiply while you sleep—but your chart suggests it's been in short supply. More cash should come your way this year, and best of all, you will also have a chance to put past money woes to rest.

Saturn was mainly to blame, for this tough taskmaster planet had been challenging you from your eighth house of joint resources. This house rules taxes, loans, credit cards, child support, scholarships, mortgages, inheritance, severance, and other areas of income that come to you in ways other than salary. One area has been a source of concern. Saturn has since moved on (after a long, thirty-month visit) and won't be back to that sensitive financial position in your chart for several decades. You enter 2004 with a greatly improved financial picture.

At the same time, Pluto, your ruler, will continue its long journey through your second house of earned income. This tells me how much you value financial security these days, and shows me just how determined you are to transform your life by creating new sources of income. Pluto won't leave this house until 2008.

In terms of your career, if you played your cards right, 2003 could have represented a landmark year for promotion, success, and professional reward. Jupiter beamed radiant vibrations to your career house in a once-in-twelve-year opportunity. If you changed jobs from August 2002 to August 2003, you probably made a savvy move, for it established you on a whole new level.

In 2004, you will want to set new career goals. It appears as though you have come as far as you can in your current position, so in 2004, you need to choose a new mountain to climb. You may contemplate taking a new job this year, or you may decide to undergo a total career switch.

If you do change your job or vocation, you will get powerful help from friends, business contacts, or even casual acquaintances in 2004. Friends will make introductions, provide tips, and offer references. In 2004, it's not what you know, but who you know—and apparently you have an amazing Rolodex of names to make career progress happen.

Neptune is still completing a long trek through your fourth sector, ruling home and family. Neptune has given you a vision of what kind of home you want for yourself, but it seems to still be a dream you'll have to work toward.

Last year, Uranus, the planet of innovation, moved into the sign that Neptune rules, Pisces, while Neptune has remained in the sign that Uranus rules, Aquarius. This means that both planets will work together in what astrologers call a rare "mutual reception." (Mankind has waited centuries for this mutual reception!) You may get an impressive home-and-property-related breakthrough, or there may be good news concerning a family member. Now that Uranus and Neptune are finally working together, they will remain that way until 2011.

This has been a quick snapshot of your year ahead, but there are more details to cover, such as when to ask for a raise, when to begin a fitness program, when to fall in love, among many other intriguing dates. I will help you take full advantage of 2004, dear Scorpio.

The Details of 2004

THERE WILL BE FOUR ECLIPSES IN 2004
TWO—POSSIBLY THREE—WILL TOUCH YOU

This year will bring a total of four eclipses. Two will arrive on the new moon, as solar eclipses, signifying fresh starts. This year, the new moon eclipses are in Aries and Libra, falling in your sixth and twelfth houses of health, fitness, and mental well-being, as well as co-workers, work assignments, and work environment. These eclipses are very positive.

The other two eclipses will come as full moons, and those are lunar eclipses, signifying a culmination or catalyst point. Full moon eclipses generally cause us to become more emotional than solar ones, because they bring up dreams and memories. Lunar eclipses can crystallize events that you have worked on a long time. Occasionally they are difficult when they mark endings.

As we discussed, the ones that are most important to you are the full moon eclipses on May 4 and October 28 (or five days plus or minus those dates, as well as a month to the day earlier or a month to the day later; full moons have a wide area of influence). Another may affect you, on April 19, but only if you were born at the end of your sign, on the cusp of Scorpio/Sagittarius.

The other new moon solar eclipse, on October 14, may bring you in contact with someone in the hospital, or you may decide to get a medical or dental checkup. You will feel this eclipse the least.

A serious romantic or business relationship is due for the greatest and most dramatic development in 2004.

If you are unattached, you may not feel this part of the eclipse. However, relationships are only part of the message of these lunar events—your own self-image is also due for a massive revision, and how you view yourself is by far the biggest change an eclipse can bring. You will also try to change how others view you, and you will probably be quite successful. The eclipses will affect all Scorpios, regardless of marital status.

If you are attached or in a business alliance, you might decide that you and your partner need to synchronize your lives and goals. The eclipse may mark a turning point, and in May or October, you may decide to seek counseling.

Or you may have grown too far apart, but because you dread the idea of being alone, you remain in the relationship. If this is the case, the cosmos doesn't want to hear that you are too shy, busy, or frightened to leave. Pressures will build and if you decide there are irreconcilable differences, you may break up.

The very best way this eclipse may work out is if you are single and dating someone special. Since eclipses change the status of a relationship, you and your partner may decide that it's time to exchange rings and promises. There would be no reason to wait any longer. (In a business sense, you may sign papers to make your working relationship legal.)

As you see, a radical change in status will occur no matter where your relationship happens to be.

Single? Your section follows the discussions of the eclipses, in the section on Uranus in Pisces.

Specifics on the May 4 Eclipse: Money Is an Issue With a Partner; Expect a Dispute

The aspects of the May 4 eclipse are mixed. Beyond what we have been discussing, there will also be talks on money and how best to share, split, or appropriate joint funds with a partner. The amount being discussed may be sizable, and the talks could put you on edge, for there is certain finality about the decisions to be made. If you're getting a divorce, this could be the date of the final settlement.

Alternatively, your discussions may have to do with a financial obligation. With Pluto in harsh angle to Mars (both planets rule Scorpio), you appear to be in a tug-of-war about this issue with your partner, so prepare to enter into some very delicate negotiations.

Neptune will be at a hard angle to the Sun, so something you don't understand or was never told in a past contract could come back to haunt you. Ask questions, be present, and take nothing at face value. Allow some time to pass before you sign any agreement, as Neptune could veil the very questions that need to be asked.

If you were born on November 7, plus or minus five days, you will feel the effects of the May 4 eclipse more than any of your other Scorpio friends.

THE OCTOBER 28 ECLIPSE IS EASIER
A SOLUTION IS THERE IF YOU SEARCH FOR IT

On the October 28 eclipse, your personal or business partner is once again highlighted. Neptune will be exerting the same kind of influence it did on the May 4 eclipse, so be careful about any deal you agree to. The clauses that are missing may be more problematic than the ones that are there.

This eclipse seems less stressful than the May 4 eclipse— Mars will be well behaved, and that alone will make a difference. The Moon will be in hard angle to Saturn, however, so your partner will be under stress or upset about something and will be more vocal than usual.

Also at the eclipse October 28, your boss seems to be overworked and pressured—and therefore quite critical and cranky. If you need a favor, wait to ask. Legal issues won't go smoothly at this time, either—if you're asked to give a deposition or negotiate a settlement, prepare for a conflict. Have all pertinent facts ready and develop a battle-proof presentation.

Still, despite these problems, you can reach a suitable solution. Mars is acting downright conciliatory to powerhouse Pluto, and Uranus, planet of surprise, will be sending a warm signal to the Sun. Luck is on your side, so even though things may initially look glum, keep plugging to find a workable solution. One will show up.

If you were born on October 28, plus or minus five days, you will feel the effects of the October 28 eclipse more than other Scorpios, and a relationship will be the focus.

APRIL 19 ECLIPSE TO FAVOR SCORPIOS BORN ON OR NEAR NOVEMBER 21

One other eclipse may affect you quite powerfully this year, that falls in the very last degree of Aries on April 19, which will highlight those Scorpios born November 21, plus or minus five days.

An eclipse in late degrees of Aries would touch you directly because it will make an "out of sign conjunction" to your Sun, meaning it will rub shoulders with the mathematical degrees of your Sun, within one degree, but only if you were born near November 21.

The April 19 eclipse is not a full moon like the other two we've discussed. It is a friendly new moon, and should bring a number of exciting new developments in your career or with regard to a partner, or both. If it involves your partner, this person may have good news to share, or you may be planning something together. If you have no partner, you may meet someone new.

Sometimes we have more than one person who might be considered a partner, such as a marriage partner, a manager, and an agent. That person has three partners. If they also have a major client or sponsor, that makes four!

Even if you were not born near November 21, this eclipse could signal the purchase of computer equipment or other changes at work. There may be a change of personnel or news of clients leaving or joining the firm.

Your health should improve impressively, too. You can start a fitness routine, or if you've suffered an illness or chronic disorder, you may be able to find a doctor who understands your condition and can treat it effectively.

I want to reiterate that even though certain developments will come out of the blue this year, in the end you will be in control of the overall direction of your life. You have free will and have a big say in how things turn out.

Never underestimate the power of your personality. It is reflected in your first house, and is the locomotive that drives every part of your chart. I can't predict what you will do—that is in your hands—but I can show you both the pressures and rewarding energies that will be operating on you, dear Scorpio. What you make of it all will be up to you!

SINGLE? YOUR LOVE LIFE SHINES

If you are single, you will have new reason to hope you'll find someone special in 2004. While the eclipses will not affect you in terms of a partner (not unless you have a business partner), you will benefit from fresh perspective this year.

Uranus, the planet of surprise, is touring your fifth house of true love and is in a position to help single Scorpios experience exciting, surprise meetings. Uranus may also create a few just-as-sudden partings, so to avoid those, grow your relationship slowly to keep it from heating up too fast and then burning out. When Uranus first entered this part of your chart in March 2003 it was the first time in your lifetime that you'd experienced its influence, so it may take time to get used to.

Uranus moves slowly; it takes 84 years for this planet to revolve though the entire zodiac. If you divide 84 by the number of signs, 12, you will see that this planet stays in each house for approximately seven years.

Now in your solar fifth house of love, creativity, and children, Uranus will send enormous cosmic favor because it will be perfectly aligned with your natal Sun. Until March 2011 Uranus will be in Pisces, a fellow water sign that blends perfectly with yours.

Scorpios who will enjoy a double dip of luck from Uranus are those born October 23-29, as the mathematical degrees of Uranus will single out them for special favor. In the years that Uranus remains in your house of love, this planet will send direct beams to every Scorpio birthday eventually. Uranus will still help you this year!

While you never can predict what Uranus will bring, it certainly has the power to make your social life sparkle. Uranus is in Pisces, so while your new relationships may seem volatile, the total effect should please you.

Many single Scorpios met someone special in 2003. If you did, there's a good chance that the relationship will continue. Saturn, the planet of stability and long-term gain, was in a supportive, rare angle to Uranus in early to mid-2003. Mars, your secondary ruler, was also working overtime last year to bring new romantic interests. Perhaps something intriguing did develop in the second half of 2003, and it bodes well for the future.

Uranus is known to bring extremes wherever it is located in a chart. Your emotions may find themselves bouncing back and forth in an unpredictable fashion. Your aim will be to manage those extremes.

You may become more impulsive when it comes to romance, which may have a positive influence. It could be a drawback if you act too hastily in matters of the heart, like getting married too quickly. Be sure to look before you leap.

Uranus encourages independent thinking, sometimes to the extent that it shocks others. Over the next few years, when it comes to love, you might decide to follow your own drummer. Should you feel it is necessary, you will flaunt society's rules about love and marriage. For example, you could form an attachment with someone much younger or much older than yourself, or you could adopt a child on your own, even if your family does not approve.

Another benefit of Uranus in the fifth house is that you'll likely experience the full depths of love. As a Scorpio, even though you are a feeling water sign, you tend to tightly control your emotions. Now you may experience a sense of abandon when you fall head over heels for someone special. Under this influence, you won't always be in full control of the relationship—you will have to acknowledge that it takes two to tango. Relinquishing full control may feel liberating, so enjoy this without becoming too analytical.

Starting this month, for the next seven years, Uranus will stimulate your love life, children, and your creative expressions. Uranus will push you, prod you, and open you up to a host of new experiences.

FANTASTIC TIMES OF THE YEAR TO FALL IN LOVE: LATE FEBRUARY THROUGH EARLY MARCH

The Weekend of December 4–5 Is a Dazzler, Too

Your most exciting moment for new love will arrive on the new moon on Friday, February 20. Uranus, the Sun, and new moon will usher in a most enchanting trend for matters of the heart. Surprises are sure to happen, so be sure to circulate not only on this day, but in the two weeks that follow. The full moon on March 6 should be pretty special, too; there is also a strong indication you'll have fun with friends.

The year ends on a magnificent note! Mars and Venus are the solar system's cosmic lovers, but last year they never got a chance to embrace. Mars and Venus adore being together—when they are, they almost always kindle new love, but last year both planets were busy elsewhere. This year, they have planned a passionate rendezvous in time for the holidays. Circle December 4–5 as a five-star weekend for love! (This won't happen again until October 2006.)

DREAMING OF HAVING A BABY? THE STORK MAY ARRIVE SOON!

If you're not ready to have a baby, be careful. Uranus in the fifth house, which rules love and pregnancy, is an indication that you may be knitting baby booties sooner than expected. Uranus is setting up a long, seven-year trend, so if you use contraception, it might be a good time to review your various choices with your doctor.

Some people may have had difficulty conceiving a child. If that describes your situation, the following dates might be worth jotting down. Conception is most favored on the following four points of the year.

- The new moon on **February 20**, in the fertile sign of Pisces.
- The new moon on **May 19**, in Taurus.
- The new moon on **September 14**, in Virgo (Jupiter's presence makes this extraordinarily positive).
- The new moon on **November 12**, in your sign, Scorpio.

In all cases, a new moon sets up two weeks of energy, so hopefully you can time things to nature's cycles. Uranus is trying to help things along as well. Good luck!

Also, for couples that have not been able to conceive, new medical technology may give you new reason to hope. Uranus rules inventions and high-tech discoveries, and this planet will be in a highly supportive position to your Sun. Ask your doctor about any new developments.

Finally, if you already have children (and feel you have all you want), you could see certain talent emerge in one child. Watch closely—if you can identify a special interest, try to help your child develop his or her natural gifts.

CAN A DEARLY HELD WISH COME TRUE? YES!

Jupiter in Virgo Will Brighten Your House of Hopes and Wishes January Through September

Jupiter, the planet of happiness and good fortune, made a rare and monumental move into Virgo in late August 2003. For the first time in twelve years, Jupiter is sparkling in your eleventh house of friendship and social groups, a trend that will last through the first nine months of 2004. But that's not all. The eleventh house also rules your deepest wishes, so a spiritual or material wish may come to fruition. Jupiter in this house can have many delicious manifestations, and we will discuss them all.

Jupiter in Virgo can help you more than this planet was able to in its previous position of Leo. Virgo is an earth sign that blends well with your water sign element. Also, this year Jupiter will travel through almost all degrees of Virgo, so all Scorpios will benefit. Jupiter will be at its most robust in your eleventh house from early May to September 24, 2004. Your largest gains will come through an association with those met in a social setting.

October-born Scorpios already experienced some of Jupiter's influence during the second half of 2003, so if you're one of these Scorpios and were unable to reach your goal last year, Jupiter will retrograde back far enough in 2004 to give you a second chance.

With Jupiter in this position, it is easier to make and keep friends. If you've had a falling out with a friend, this would be an ideal time to mend the friendship.

Since Jupiter naturally rules your solar second house of income, networking will help advance your career and will be more effective than blindly sending resumes. Someone you befriend or a program or seminar you attend will provide life-altering ideas.

At long last, Jupiter is in a position to help you achieve something you've wanted for a long time. It could be a spiritual dream ("I want to help others who are less fortunate") or a material one ("I need a new computer"). Any dream could become a reality between now and September 2004.

Since the eleventh house is also linked to the tenth house of career, everything in your chart indicates that you may begin to see a payoff for all your hard work in 2003. If you are self-employed, this is an especially strong trend.

Yet there are even larger possibilities for Jupiter in this house. The eleventh house rules, among other things, humanitarian efforts and volunteerism. There will be a sterling opportunity to make a difference in the community, your industry, or world at large, so you should think about how to use this awesome energy. You may choose to help battered women, or you may want to roll up your sleeves and help at a soup kitchen.

It's also an ideal year to join a new club, but be sure to attend meetings so you can benefit, and if you want to get a lot of personal growth out of Jupiter's position in your chart, you should consider running for an office or committee. The managerial and other skills that you hone in this club (such as fund-raising, accounting, and communication skills) could be transferred to your career. Best of all, you'll learn them in a low-pressure atmosphere where it's safe to make mistakes!

Romantically, Jupiter in your eleventh house will bring you in contact with many more people than usual. The fifth house of true love is opposite the eleventh house on the horoscope wheel and therefore is on the same axis. Energy in one house often bounces to the other house on that axis and back again. Remain optimistic! You have some of the strongest aspects of any sign for matters of the heart, dear Scorpio.

VENUS TO RETROGRADE
MID-MAY THROUGH JUNE
LOVE, BEAUTY, INVESTMENTS ARE PUT ON HOLD

Venus rarely retrogrades—in 2003, it was at full power all year—but in 2004, Venus will nap from May 17 to June 29. When any planet retrogrades, it rests, meaning its powers are not available to us.

Venus rules love, beauty, adornment, and some financial matters, so its retrograde periods are not good times to get engaged or married; buy jewelry, expensive clothes, perfumes, or cosmetics; or book any luxury spa or salon treatments. Avoid Venus retrograde for plastic surgery procedures, too.

This year Venus will retrograde in your eighth house of joint finances, so this period would not be a good time to invest or launch new profit-oriented endeavors.

CAREER SHINES BRIGHTEST ALMOST ALL SUMMER

If you are looking for a new job or hope to get a promotion, your best period of 2004 to do so will be during Mars' visit to your solar tenth house of profession from June 23 to August 10.

Five days after this period ends, there will be another boost thanks to a brilliant new moon on August 15 bringing you two more weeks of positive energy for job hunting.

If you need a date earlier in the year to find a new job, watch the full moon on February 6, plus or minus four days, for career progress. This date is especially strong if you are involved with creative work or if you work with artists. As a nice bonus, Saturn and Uranus are well angled, so you may be able to find a remarkably stable situation, and Uranus and Mars will be harmonious, too— your breakthrough may arrive unexpectedly. With Pluto so well angled to the full moon, you should like the salary offered. If you want to take advantage of this date, start your search in January so that you can get a final answer by this full moon.

Your Luckiest Day of the Year: September 21

Although one of your luckiest days of the year will be September 21, your luck will start to snowball as soon as the new moon appears on September 14 in your solar eleventh house of hopes and wishes.

Four heavenly bodies will be supporting you: Jupiter (happiness, expansion, and profit), the Sun (favor from influential people), Mars (energy), and the new moon, which will kick everything into motion. You will see the realization of something dearly important to you! If a friend goes out of his or her way to help you, you could profit considerably from that advice, tip, or special favor.

One week after the new moon, on September 21, your luckiest day of the year will arrive thanks to a conjunction between the Sun and Jupiter, an annual event that connotes pure good fortune. After that, Mars will meet with Jupiter on September 26, a perfect day to ask a favor, have a confidential meeting, or to take a risk. This day is worth four gold stars. And finally, on September 29, Mercury will meet with Jupiter, making it a perfect day to sign a contract. Use these days to schedule your biggest, most important actions!

A Personal Power Phase Begins
November 11 Through Christmas

You will end the year with a bang. On November 11, Mars will enter Scorpio, creating a vortex of energy around you. Launch any vital projects during this period. Keep in mind that Mercury will retrograde on November 30, so even though Mars will be behind you until December 25, Mercury will create snags in December.

There are other reasons you should move forward purposefully in mid-November. Just one day after Mars enters Scorpio, you will have the benefit of a "the cosmos loves Scorpio" new moon on November 12, at which time three planets will be in Scorpio, giving you plenty of rocket power. Venus and Mars will beam a galaxy's worth of sex appeal to you, so you cannot fail. What more could you ask for? This period near your birthday is sure to be special.

If you were born on or within five days of November 12, then you are due double the good news!

Do You Want a Raise?
Try at the New Moon December 11
for Outstanding Results

Your very best time of the year to ask for a raise or to get a review that will lead to one is during the December 11 new moon, which falls in your solar second house of earned income. Jupiter will be well angled to Mercury, the Sun, the Moon, and your ruler, Pluto, which, taken together, is outstandingly fortunate and rare. Also, your secondary ruler, Mars, will still be close to Venus in Scorpio, which indicates, among other connotations, a positive chance to make a profit. Remember, new moons are active for two weeks, but the strongest energy is close to the day it appears.

This is a one-in-a-million new moon, so I urge you to speak up for your raise, and if you can't get one, survey your options elsewhere. With Mercury retrograde, you may be able to get an increase that was promised but never delivered. Or you may be offered a job from someone who'd offered you one previously. This time you may accept.

SATURN OPENS YOUR MIND AND HEART TO KNOWLEDGE, HIGHER EDUCATION, AND TRAVEL

Last year, Saturn moved into your ninth house, in Cancer, a fellow water sign that relates well to yours. The ninth house is a house of attitudes and beliefs, so Saturn is urging you to reconsider your guiding philosophies. If you've outgrown any of your old attitudes, you'll soon develop your own independent views, as this is a vibration of intellectual maturity. You'll see the world in much more complex terms.

In addition, the ninth house rules in-laws and relatives. You may become concerned about a family member, or you may find a certain in-law is difficult to get along with over the next 18 months.

Legal matters come under the ninth house, so if you initiate a case between now and July 2005, you may find it dragging on longer than anticipated. You may want to settle out of court rather than embark on a lengthy, costly lawsuit. A lot depends on your specific natal chart. I would advise you consult a good astrologer to make a final decision.

If you are in college or graduate school, Saturn's new position suggests that you could have tough professors who will set very high standards, but you'll learn to like them anyway. Try to meet their expectations. Remember, Saturn is in superb angle to your Sun, so you will gain much from Saturn's presence! Saturn takes 29 years to circle the zodiac, so you haven't had Saturn in this house for many years, if at all.

NEED TO MOVE
OR GIVE YOUR RESIDENCE A NEW LOOK?
YOUR BEST BET IS TO ACT IN LATE JANUARY
FOR GREAT RESULTS

If you need to move, renovate, sell, or buy property, your best moment to do so would be the new moon in Aquarius on January 21 or in the ten days that follow. Mars will be in perfect angle to Pluto, and considering that these are your ruling planets, this is an especially good omen for success.

You will also have a full moon in your house of home on July 31, indicating you may be moving in for an August 1 occupancy (or you may do any number of other home-related initiations, including a home improvement project). Still, there are problems with this moon. If you need to sign a lease, deed, or other contract, Uranus is opposed to Mercury, making it a bad time to do so. Uranus' presence suggests that unforeseen problems could arise. You might want to sign your papers when Saturn conjoins Mercury, one month earlier, on June 26, as a long-term agreement would result.

Your Creativity Will Soar to New Heights in Late 2004
Your Key Date: November 29

You're fortunate to have Uranus, the planet of radical, insightful change, experimentation, and innovation, in your fifth house of creativity from now until 2011. Concentrate on developing your craft, for if you do, you will be surprised at the sophisticated work you turn out. You must take your artistry seriously if you want others to do the same. There is real profit potential in your ideas, dear Scorpio.

Creative self-expression is further underscored by Jupiter, who naturally rules your second house of earned income, and when positioned in the twelfth house, reveals that the more you think about your ideas, the more you'll succeed with them. This period starts in late September. One of the most vital points of the year for creativity will occur on November 29 (and in the weeks leading up to that date). Jupiter is in perfect angle to Neptune on that day, so your creativity could have astounding profit potential.

The April 19 Eclipse Could Help You Get Fit and Slim

When you decide to get fit, it's best to rally all the cosmic support that you can muster. Luckily this year brings a solar eclipse to help push things forward, and all Scorpios will be assisted by this new moon solar eclipse.

Here's your plan: begin your new exercise routine on April 19 or very soon thereafter. Do not diet yet—wait at least two weeks to begin after the full moon, ideally three days, which will bring you to May 4. That happens to be an eclipse, and there may be other things happening in your life that make it hard to cut calories. No problem. Keep exercising, and start your diet on the next full moon, which is June 3, plus three days.

Since this eclipse falls in your house of health, use this new moon to seek advice for a medical ailment. Jupiter is called the planet of healing, medicine, and even miracles, so never give up when you have this kind of help.

If you want to kick a bad habit, you will have most of the solar system at your side on October 14, a new moon solar eclipse. It would also be an ideal time to go on a retreat or solitary vacation.

AT YEAR'S END, LAY THE FOUNDATION FOR YOUR GOLDEN EPOCH TO LAST THROUGH LATE 2006

By the end of 2004—specifically beginning September 24—you will be on the verge of one of the very best, most glittering years of your life. It will begin on October 25, 2005, and will last a full twelve months, until November 26, 2006.

The year that you are anticipating will herald the arrival of Jupiter, the planet of gifts and luck, in your sign, dear Scorpio. The last time you had a year like this was ten years ago, 1994. You are older and wiser now, and if 1994 was good, late 2005-2006 could be great.

A year as special and extraordinary as this merits careful preparation. You will have to show the universe your deepest intentions. Begin the process and choose the one or two areas that would make you happiest.

Luckily, the part of your horoscope that is so lit up by Jupiter is considered the house of solitude. During this period, you should try to sneak in time alone. When you do, you will come up with some very important conclusions for your future. Jupiter in the twelfth house will help you harness your inner powers and break through barriers. Think of the road toward your dream as an adventure, one filled with passion, enlightenment, and much-needed change. Force yourself to take the first step—the subsequent ones will be easier, I promise.

If any part of you believes you won't realize your vision, you will undermine your ability to succeed. You will have to make space in your life for the realization of your new wish, and you may have to alter your behavior in some way once it arrives. You may have to change or give up certain familiar elements, and that takes energy. Let's say you hope to meet a new romantic interest. You may have to give your appearance a once-over, and perhaps ask friends for frank suggestions. True change does not happen without effort.

Your appearance may become different in some way, which may be an outer manifestation of inner change. You may subconsciously attract different types of people to your circle and, in the meantime, become impatient with your old life and want to move quickly toward your new self. For clarity, I will sum up an important point: the period between September 24, 2004, and October 25, 2005, will be your time to plan and to prioritize. On October 25, 2005, Jupiter will be in Scorpio, a phase that will last until November 26, 2006.

In October 2004 you will become more optimistic and confident, and your magnetism may easily attract suitors or encourage current beaus to become more enamored.

Your wonder year will become all the more vital if you have taken the time to meditate about your future. By late 2006, all the pieces of the puzzle will fall into place.

Summary

2004 will allow you to focus on developing your personal side, dear Scorpio. While there will be a strong opportunity to advance your career during the summer months, and a sterling chance to get a salary increase in December, your main focus will be on your own personal development.

The eclipses, in your sign and in your opposite sign of Taurus, in May and October 2004, will give you a moment of truth. You will be offered several new paths to follow, and you will choose the one that is best for you.

You began an evolutionary process toward greater understanding of the world around you last year, when two eclipses arrived in the signs of Scorpio, in May 2003, and in Taurus, in November 2003. It was the first time in a decade that you were experiencing eclipses so directly. In the year ahead, you will experience two more eclipses in Scorpio/Taurus, in early May and in late October.

Each eclipse in a series (or family, such as Scorpio/Taurus) builds on the themes presented by the previous eclipse, pushing events to a higher level of development, encouraging you to move into a more fully evolved, mature state. You will keep growing under these eclipses, sometimes easily, sometimes painfully, until the cosmos feels you have experienced enough change for the time being, and will let you rest. The April 2004 new moon eclipse (an easy one by most standards) will be your last.

A close relationship was under the microscope last year, and the discussions and meditations about this relationship will continue into 2004. The news could be exciting or traumatic—you may take your relationship to the next level or you may break up. Or you may seek counseling to learn to talk to each other more openly and honestly.

No matter what happens, in 2004 your life will come out of limbo and into a more energetic phase. You will change the way you see yourself and also find ways to change the way others view you.

Many new and exciting people will pour into your life, and it behooves you to join clubs and to network more than usual during the first nine months of the year.

Travel and higher education will help you see life in broader terms, and Saturn's position in your ninth house will also encourage you to review and possibly revise some long-standing beliefs and opinions, possibly in regard to politics, ethics, or theology. When this trend is over in July 2005, you will be a truly independent thinker.

When Jupiter enters Libra in late September, you start getting ready for one of the best years of your life. Your golden year is set to begin one year later, in October 2005, when Jupiter in Scorpio will crown you the celestial favorite for twelve months. A year like that is weighty and requires preparation if you are to get the most from it. In 2004, you will begin the review and weeding-out process, deciding what elements should stay and which ones should go. The eclipses will be part of this transition period, to sweep out all that has been cluttering your life and help you embrace the people and projects that are right for you.

Sagittarius

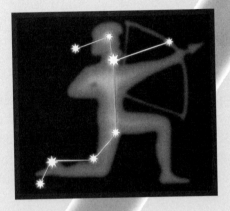

November 22-December 21

The Big Picture

This should be a wonderful year filled with surprise, adventure, discovery, professional recognition, and even romance. For the past three years, you have been sledding through harsh terrain, dear Sagittarius, and probably wondered when—or even if—it would ever end. It officially did end in June 2003, thanks to the departure of Saturn from a difficult angle of your chart. By the beginning of 2004, you should see crystal clear blue skies just ahead. While certain parts of life may still not be perfect—life rarely is—the main sting you felt from mid-2001 to mid-2003 is now gone.

With Mars traveling through all the upper regions of your chart in 2004, you will have a more public role than you did last year. Residential and family concerns kept you out of the limelight last year, but this year is a whole new ballgame. It would be a good idea to get your wardrobe ready, because you will soon assume a new, high-profile role and you'll want to look the part.

One of the most fabulous areas of your chart in 2004 will be your burgeoning career. You are about to experience a heartwarming reward cycle, one meant to pay you back for all your hard work over the past decade, thanks to a rare visit by Jupiter, the planet of good fortune, to your solar tenth house of career advancement during the first nine months of 2004. Mars will play a part in this as well.

If you're not making the best use of your talents in your current job, this year may bring a chance to find your true vocation. If you like your work, you may be promoted. If you want to change jobs, you may find a setting that will truly allow you to shine. You may either start or expand your own business!

This trend began in August 2003, so you may have already received intriguing professional offers. The trend continues and intensifies in 2004, so even if you *did* get a promotion or new position last year, you can expect even more career action and acclaim in 2004. That may surprise you, for your new job may be pretty special. All I can say is stay tuned, dear Sagittarius.

In terms of career offers, late August through September should leave you positively breathless. That period will be special not only because Jupiter is working hard for you, but because several other planets will join in to shower you with luck. There could be other important dates—early March and August hold promise—but late summer will be the finest period of all.

If you have delineated your goals and done your homework, you will be in place to grab the brass ring. Don't let time slip through your fingers, dear Sagittarius! Make September 25, 2004, your deadline to nail down your glamorous new position.

Romantically, things are improving day by day. If you are attached, one of your closest personal relationships seems to have turned a corner. Saturn, which caused many of your recent relationship woes, has moved on and is no longer challenging you as it did between 2001 and mid-2003.

Over the past one to three years, you might have walked away from a debilitating relationship. Or you may have worked hard to improve one you felt was basically sound. Or you and your partner may have related well, but Saturn's presence may have signified that you were concerned about your partner's health or welfare. No matter what you faced, those problems are now behind you.

If you are single and have not yet met a new romantic partner, there will be many sparkling opportunities to do so in 2004. If you met someone in the past year, your forecast is for smooth sailing. There's no reason to believe that adverse news will break the fairy tale spell of new love.

Eclipses represent key areas of powerful change in a horoscope, so it's vital to know where they fall in any coming year. In 2004, two outstandingly positive solar eclipses will occur in your solar fifth and eleventh houses of love, fun, and friendship, on April 19 and October 14.

Solar eclipses are like triple new moons and can affect you for a year or can be permanently life changing. These solar eclipses could bring on events that add just the right amount of spice to your social life, and could mark the start of something big. April should be quite glorious, and October possibly even more so. If you've been alone, you won't be that way much longer!

This remarkable social trend will be magnified even more by the visit of Jupiter to your eleventh house of friendships and groups, set to begin in late September 2004 and last through late October 2005, a period of thirteen months! Expect your Rolodex to explode with new friends and contacts—and at least one romantic attraction if single—in late 2004.

Most of your personal development will occur by associating with others, so the fall and winter would be an ideal time, for example, to volunteer for a charity fund-raiser, join a committee, or help a political candidate get elected. Networking this year will help you get ahead, so join that professional organization. Friends and acquaintances figure so sharply in your chart in late 2004 that they hold the keys to your biggest personal growth.

Take this trend seriously. This is the house in which we give back to society, and in late 2004 you will have an opportunity to make your mark on the world. The eleventh house is a humanitarian house, so you may even organize a group to help those less fortunate.

There will be two additional eclipses—these are lunar eclipses—falling in houses that rule your mental and physical well-being, as well as daily work assignments and relationships with co-workers. These eclipses will occur on May 4 and October 28, and since they are full moons, they suggest culminations or endings to the area of the chart they will visit.

In terms of your health, the May eclipse may make you more determined to turn over a new leaf and kick a bad habit once and for all. Treating yourself with the loving care you so often show others is long overdue! You could also decide to have a procedure or an operation to take care of something you have been meaning to attend to for some time.

The October 28 eclipse seems to underscore work and health. First on your agenda will be developing new working procedures and getting in sync with new co-workers. This may be because you change jobs, or because your company restructures its hierarchy and moves you into a new department.

Also as a result of the October 28 eclipse, a new fitness routine may be part of your plan, for at the end of October you will be capable of developing one you'll stay with, which will bring results. Eclipses mean business!

Of course, not all parts of life are sunny, and one area of your chart that may be problematic concerns joint resources, such as balances you owe on credit cards, student loans, back taxes, a divorce settlement, or child support. Try to have financial contingency plans for any eventuality, as Saturn's presence suggests you may need them.

Your residence or other property that you want to buy, sell, lease, or renovate was a major theme last year, but will be less important in 2004.

Smaller, but no less vital, windows of opportunity to make changes in 2004 will arrive in early March and mid-September, just when your career will be blossoming. If you do move this year, it could be to relocate to take advantage of a job offer.

Sagittarians whose birthdays fall early in the sign, November 22–30, may still feel jarring residential or family-related shifts, and they are the exceptions to the rule stated above. If you were born in November, a stable, settled home life may still be a bit elusive, but it's a goal worth keeping, because you can get there. As soon as you make the necessary living adjustments you will be done with this trend. Tough planetary aspects demand a decision. Once one is made, tension is released.

Keep in mind that Uranus upgrades, modernizes, and revamps whatever house of the chart it visits, and for you that's the fourth house of home. Although you may find it hard to make the necessary changes, in the end you will be glad you did. If your physical home was not the center of your attention, perhaps you were the caretaker for an elderly relative, most likely a parent, last year, a trend that continues into 2004. It is clear by your chart that your relative is grateful for your assistance, even if they have not put their appreciation into words.

If you are a late-born Sagittarius, born near December 19, expect some surprising help from a sibling this year, due to

Uranus being in what astrologers call an "out-of-sign sextile" to your Sagittarius Sun.

Now that you have an overview, let's look at some of the more specific trends and details of your exciting year ahead.

The Details of the Year Ahead

2004 BRINGS YOUR MOST IMPORTANT CAREER YEAR IN A DECADE

Jupiter, the planet of good fortune and expansion, moved into your solar tenth house of fame and honors in August 2003. This is exciting news, because it represents a wonderful new cycle of reward for you which will last until September 24, 2004.

All your work experience, education, hard work, and passions will be tied together in one gorgeous career package, one that will lead to something special. The harder you've worked, the greater your payoff. Higher-ups will go out of their way to open doors, so you'll need to know exactly how they should help. This period is exceptional because you're likely to get a position of true authority, and it will change how others view you.

You have not seen cosmic career help this strong for twelve years, and when this trend begins you will need to be decisive. Once the offers begin to roll in, you won't have time to think or look for counteroffers. A promotion, a new job, or even a total career switch may be in the making, and if you're a recent college graduate, you are entering the work force at the best possible time.

Jupiter will be in Virgo, so your new position may be in book or magazine publishing, library research, public relations, marketing, accounting, computer software, nursing, medicine, hospital technology, nutrition, spa treatments like massage, travel, or any job that prizes detail, organization, grooming, cleanliness, skill with hands, or communicative skill. This placement in Virgo also emphasizes the need to be practical and focused on results in your job.

If you're not working, you can still benefit by doing volunteer work or part-time work in the community, for this trend will develop your leadership style and your ability to inspire others for a common goal. If you are still in college, you may decide to run for student office or become the star quarterback. Or you may be chosen as the lead actor in an upcoming theater production.

THE BEST TIME TO LOOK FOR A NEW POSITION IS MID- TO LATE SEPTEMBER

This will be an amazing year when everything you touch in your career is likely to turn to gold. You might want to look back to late 1991-late 1992, the last time Jupiter toured this same part of your horoscope, for clues of what might come up.

There are several extra-special periods, including late August through September, that you will want to highlight. A full moon on Saturday March 6 could bring surprising, positive news (full moons have an area of influence of plus or minus four days). You may score a major victory or be offered a job. You also could start a new job on the following Monday, March 8, which is a good time to do so.

Jupiter will retrograde from January 3 to May 4, so during that time career progress may be too slow for your taste. If so, be patient. You will be entering a glorious period later in the year!

Once you get to midyear, your window of opportunity will open wide. Mars, the energy planet, will cruise through your tenth house of fame and achievement from August 10 to September 26, and from that point on, things will happen very quickly.

Mercury will be retrograde in the front part of that cycle, from August 9 to September 2, never a good time to take a new job, but a fine time to have meetings and interviews. I know it may be hard, but try to be patient a bit longer—any delays will work in your favor. The only time you should accept a job during Mercury retrograde is if it's offered by a former employer or an old colleague or friend. In these cases, you can do so without fear, as you are going back to the past to advance an idea.

No doubt, September 2004 will be a big career month. Your plans will begin to crystallize once the new moon appears in your house of fame and achievement, September 14, which will usher in a two-week period so incredibly wonderful that it will rate five stars. Hold on to your hat, because just after that glorious new moon, there will be even *more* career goodies in the days that follow!

YOUR LUCKIEST DAY OF THE YEAR: SEPTEMBER 21

Career Success Blossoms Beyond Expectations!

The Sun schedules an annual meeting with Jupiter one day each year, a day that is usually bursting with cosmic luck and happiness. In 2004, the Sun and Jupiter will meet on September 21 in your solar tenth house of professional advancement. Circle that date in red! You may also see luck on the day prior, September 20. The fact that this date falls within the two-week period that is set off by the aforementioned new moon on September 14 is simply fabulous and increases the likelihood of your success.

But wait! There is more!

On September 28, Mercury will also meet with Jupiter, a once-a-year event. Mercury rules your tenth house of career, so the cosmos is determined to reward you for work well done. This is yet another staggeringly good day! On this day, a friend may be very instrumental in helping you.

Mercury also rules your partnership sector (the seventh house), so if you are forming a business partnership or about to hire an agent or manager, you might want to seal the deal on this day for the best luck.

As a Sagittarius, You Live to Travel
Vacation From Late June Through Early August

It's hard to tell a Sagittarius to stay home—as the international travel sign of the zodiac, your bags are always packed, and you're ready to go at a moment's notice. This year strong travel aspects will be at hand when job opportunities are coming your way. I don't want you to be away during this time, so here is how I suggest you handle this energy.

Your best period to travel will be from June 23 to August 10. After August 10, your career will begin to heat up, so you should be home.

If you cannot get away during this time, another opportunity may arise just after the new moon in your house of travel, August 15. Try not to be gone too long, and have that resume ready on your computer before you go. Mercury will be retrograde in mid-August, so if you do go away on August 15, perhaps the destination will be a spot you've always loved but have not seen in years. Bring your cell phone along—someone may need to reach you.

If you get a chance to travel near February 6, you should go. If your February trip is for business, Saturn will be in positive angle to the Sun, so your goals will be met.

TRYING TO GET SLIM, FIT, AND HEALTHY? THERE ARE PLENTY OF PERFECT OPPORTUNITIES IN 2004

There are several perfect dates to begin a new fitness program in 2004. Rather than make a New Year's resolution in January (when no planets will be helping you succeed), start in February, when energetic Mars will support you all the way. This period falls between February 3 and March 21.

During that period, start eating reasonably—reduce or eliminate fat, sugar, and over-the-top starches, without starving yourself. Mars will want you to become more active, so with your doctor's blessing, take up weight lifting during this period, as Mars rules iron and therefore all gym weights.

Begin cutting calories after the full moon on February 6, plus four days. You need some time to allow that full moon to deflate, the best time to lose weight. If you've had a health concern that you've been meaning to check out (assuming it is not serious), schedule your appointment for May 19, the new moon in your sixth house of health. Venus, the ruler of your health sector, will be retrograde at the time (May 17-June 29), so as long as you're not scheduling plastic surgery, this would be a fine period to take care of health matters you've put off for lack of time.

The full moon lunar eclipse on October 28 may bring a health matter to your attention. Your resistance may be running low, so be sure to take good care of yourself at this time. If you need a minor procedure or test, this is a good time to get it done. You may want to get a flu shot in September (it will take a few weeks to start working) so that you are prepared by the time this eclipse comes around.

If you didn't start your fitness routine in February, another opportunity to do so is just *after* the eclipse on October 28. Again, if you are going to start a sensible diet, begin a few days *after* the eclipse—say, on November 1—for best results.

Time to Fall in Love Again!
Many Radiant Dates Dot Your Schedule, Including a Solar Eclipse April 19

After the relationship difficulties you've had over the past two years, you may have needed a break from romance for a little while. However, if you are ready to date, you can begin the moment the year takes off.

Actually, this trend begins on December 16, 2003, and continues through the holidays, and into January 2004, ending on February 3. If you meet anyone during this golden period, things look good for continued happiness.

On Valentine's Day—February 14—the Moon will glide into Sagittarius, favoring you more than any other sign. It will be nice to have a great day for lovers for a change!

If you don't meet anyone during the 2003 holidays or early in the new year, your next big opportunities will arise at both the March and April new moons. These two new moons, falling 28 days apart, will be located in your house of true love. This almost never happens!

The first, March 20, will favor November-born Sagittarians. Appropriately, that new moon falls on the first day of spring. Be out and open to meeting new types.

The second new moon is a positive, radiant solar eclipse—packing the energy of a triple new moon—which will appear on April 19. This eclipse will help all Sagittarians, but especially those born closer to the end of the sign, near December 20.

Venus and Mars are the two lover planets of the zodiac, and whenever they are together, expect exciting results. Through most of April and the first week of May, Mars is pursuing Venus hot and heavy, so you should see some rather remarkable events in your own love life, no matter if you're single or attached.

However, whatever happens during the first week of April could scare you a little, perhaps because things are moving forward so quickly. By mid-May Venus will go retrograde—a rare, once-in-two-year event—and it appears that you will put the brakes on the relationship for a few weeks to give yourself time to think or slow the pace.

Venus rules love, beauty, adornment, and certain financial matters. It is common to stop and reconsider matters of the heart during a Venus retrograde. Venus retrograde is like Mercury retrograde or any out-of-phase planet. Its best powers are withheld, and it affects everyone of every sign in the same way.

While Venus retrogrades, try not to buy any expensive jewelry, clothing, or have spa treatments. It is considered a poor time to get engaged or marry because the "birth" of the marriage (the wedding day) will have a weak, disabled Venus. Also, do not schedule cosmetic surgery during this time.

THE ECLIPSE ON OCTOBER 14
BRINGS A SOCIAL WHIRL

The full moon in your commitment sector could mark a happy time on June 3. However, Venus will be retrograde, so you may have second thoughts about a current relationship or need to slow the pace. Sagittarians prize independence, and you may be grappling with conflicting needs to be alone and to share intimacy. Only you can say which of the two will prevail.

Romance blooms in late September. First, Mars, the ruler of your house of true love, is meeting with good fortune Jupiter on September 25-26, a weekend sure to be filled with wow. Mars meets with Jupiter only once a year, so be sure to be out and about on September 25.

Second, a full moon will be in your fifth house of true love on September 28, when Jupiter will align close to the Sun. On this magical date, Mercury rules your commitment sector, and Jupiter will be aligned with Mercury. All full moons have an area of influence of plus or minus four days, so this whole week should be outstanding.

Many Sagittarians will receive or make a marriage proposal at some point between the end of September and the middle of October. Jupiter will have just entered Libra, the sign of partnerships and marriage, and will be sending splendid vibrations to your Sun. This would be a fabulous time to get engaged or married.

A solar eclipse will occur on October 14, adding even more oomph to your social life. Friends, fun, and time to kick back will make you almost giddy with happiness. October is unusual in that a whole crowd of planets will be in this sector, which you'll notice!

At year's end, Mars and Venus will actually touch for the first time in years. This hot rendezvous is coming in your twelfth house of clandestine meetings, the most sexual sign of the zodiac, Scorpio.

I'm not sure what to say about this, as a great deal depends on your circumstances and outlook, dear Sagittarius. I don't know why your new love would need such secrecy, but please don't put yourself in a situation where you'll get hurt. The twelfth house is the area of the chart that reflects "self-undoing," as the ancients used to write. You have some truly exceptional aspects this year, which I hope you'll maximize in a positive way. This new love may be a perfectly sound alliance, and if so, enjoy it.

BE CAREFUL WITH FINANCES
SATURN WILL NOT BE IN CANCER UNTIL JULY 2005

In June 2003, Saturn, the planet that teaches us life lessons, moved into your eighth house of joint finances. This is a rare and important two-year cycle, as Saturn will remain in this house all this year and part of next year, until July 2005. Saturn has not been in the eighth house of the Sagittarius solar horoscope for twenty-nine years.

From now until July 2005, you'll need to get involved in all joint financial decisions. For example, if you're getting married, it will be critical that you know and understand the spending and saving style of your partner, or if your accountant presents you with a tax return, you need to inquire about some of the decisions he or she made on your behalf.

Below I will list many possible scenarios that you may encounter during this Saturn visit, but only one or two of the following contingencies will pertain to you. I am only trying to arm you against any possible problems. However, since this house rules joint resources, you'll need to consider a partner as well.

Taxes may become troublesome. Be sure to file your tax return on time, even if you're unable to pay at that time. If you are separated from your mate, but still file a joint return, you will be liable for your partner's taxes should there be a future problem. File separate returns as a precaution, and discuss ways to protect yourself with an accountant. Many people report they are audited when Saturn is in the eighth house, so be prepared for that eventuality with detailed records.

Saturn warns us that any rule infraction during this time, even if done unwittingly, will bring on difficulties. Martha Stewart's decision to sell her ImClone stock was made when Saturn was in this place.

You will also need to be diligent about your credit. Check your credit report every six months or so to make sure you've not become a victim of fraud. Make sure to pay your bills on time to avoid additional finance charges. If borrowing money this year, try not to borrow more than you need, as Saturn's position suggests it may take longer to repay a loan.

If you are divorcing, financial talks may be slow and complicated. The same is true if you are looking for an insurance settlement. Knowing this, you may want to settle in arbitration, rather than go through a lengthy legal process. Saturn is in Cancer until July 2005, an emotional, feeling sign that rules family. Try not to get too emotional about financial talks. Your lawyer has an objective view of the situation and will protect your interests.

If you're dependent on child support, make sure to have a contingency plan in case your ex can't pay on time. If you pay child support, you may find it hard to come up with the funds at some point in the year, but with Saturn in your eighth house, your ex may take swift legal action if you don't. Try not to let this happen.

In your career, you will find it more attractive to work on a flat salary rather than on commission. Your benefits package may also be less attractive. Keep these points in mind if you apply for a new job and make sure to negotiate a high salary to make up the difference for any loss in benefits.

If you lose your job, the severance package is apt to be skimpy, but it's always worth it to ask for more. However, with your career aspects you should be able to find a new, better position in no time flat!

Finally, if you have your own business, don't depend on only one customer's patronage. Instead, try to balance your income from a wider customer pool. Don't extend credit to any customer without checking their credit record.

A word of encouragement: Saturn is in a much better place now than it was from mid-2000 to mid-2003. What you face ahead will not be nearly as hard as what you already went through!

WHEN TO ASK FOR THAT ALL-IMPORTANT RAISE? BEFORE THE NEW YEAR, ON DECEMBER 23, 2003

If you're not changing jobs, you'll need to choose the perfect time to ask for a raise. Remarkably, there are no new moons in your second house of earned income in 2004, so if you're reading this before the beginning of 2004, note that the new moon on December 23, 2003, is your best time to ask. Otherwise, you will need to wait until January 2005, a full thirteen months away. Try to seize the day in late December 2003—your chart suggests you may be pleasantly surprised with the answer! I know it's holiday time, but the planets deliver beautiful vibrations when they see fit!

Bills will arrive by January 7, 2004, the full moon in your credit card sector. There is also an expensive period coming up that spans May 7 to June 23. Knowing this perhaps will give you the courage to ask for that raise in December.

If you are reading this too late, new job opportunities will be outstandingly strong, particularly in September 2004. You either will be promoted or will obtain an exciting new position, hopefully with a nice raise.

SOCIAL OPPORTUNITIES RADIANT IN OCTOBER WHEN MANY PLANETS, INCLUDING JUPITER, CROWD IN LIBRA

This year, only one major "outer" planet will change signs, and that is jolly Jupiter. Jupiter is the planet that loves you best and brings positive changes.

When Jupiter enters Libra on September 25, 2004, it will remain there over a year—until October 25, 2005. Jupiter will spend the entire time in your solar eleventh house of hopes, wishes, friendships, social groups, and humanitarian interests, a lovely place in your chart for this magnanimous planet to reside for so long! In Libra, Jupiter will work even harder for you than it can when in earth or water signs, which is what you want to hear!

The eleventh house is where something you've wanted for a long time comes to fruition. It can be a spiritual dream ("I want to help others who are suffering") or a material one ("I need a new computer"). From now on, any reasonable dream becomes more possible.

If you've recently moved to a new area, this trend will allow you to meet people you'll want to spend time with. If you haven't moved, you'll still enjoy making new acquaintances. If you've fallen out with a friend, this aspect will help you rebuild the bridge of communication. Networking and exchanging information with other colleagues in your industry will help you advance your career even after Jupiter has left your career sector in September, so attend those mixers!

There are even larger possibilities with Jupiter in this house. You will be able to take what you've learned in your career and apply it to the community, your industry, or the world at large. Astrology teaches us that we can attain an even greater state of enlightenment after experiencing growth in the tenth house of career. You will have a sterling opportunity in the months to come to choose a group in which you could make a major contribution. It might be a professional organization, a club you join for fun (such as a chess club or reading group), or even a tenants' committee in your apartment building.

The eleventh house rules humanitarian efforts, so you may volunteer in a soup kitchen or learn to counsel unwed teen mothers. You might start a group to help a social cause, such as helping battered women.

This is the area of your chart where most of your golden luck will flow during the next thirteen months, and where you will be able to give the most to others. The skills you learn—

such as fund-raising, accounting, and communication—will also be applicable in your day job, and you will be testing them first in a safe, encouraging atmosphere.

Romantically, Jupiter in your eleventh house could provide encouragement, for you will likely come in contact with many more people than usual. The fifth house of true love is found opposite the eleventh house on the horoscope wheel. This is significant because the energy in one house on an axis often bounces to the other house and back again. Hence, there is a very strong chance you will see a boost to your romantic life as a result of Jupiter's new placement. Remain optimistic! Actually, you have some of the best aspects of any sign when it comes to love, dear Sagittarius.

Jupiter will move through all degrees, so every Sagittarius will benefit. (Remember, this vibration will be at play in the last quarter of 2004.) The first Sagittarians to feel the glowing vibrations will be those with birthdays that fall from the start of the sign, November 22, to December 9.

If your birthday falls after December 9, you will enjoy 2005 even more, but that doesn't mean you can't enjoy the party atmosphere in late 2004. You will!

YOUR HOME AND LIFESTYLE TO CHANGE—POSSIBLY RADICALLY—IN 2004

We talked a bit about the unsettling influence of Uranus in your house of home, an aspect that began in March 2003 and continues through 2011, a period of eight years. You will not feel this influence the whole time, but only when Uranus aspects a certain planet or the Sun from time to time.

Those Sagittarians born at the very start of your sign, from November 22 to November 26, are likely to be directly affected by Uranus' new placement in the fourth house of home and family.

You may have decided, or soon will, to move, if not across town, then across country—or even abroad. When it comes to your living situation, it's a time to take risks and to trust your instincts, even if the changes you want seem daunting at first.

You may move to take advantage of an educational opportunity, such as to study abroad or to do research for a grant. Or as we discussed earlier, a rare career opportunity may cause you to relocate. For other Sagittarians, a change of venue could offer a fresh start after a romantic breakup. Uranus always encourages independence, so you may move to show you are able to stand on your own.

Uranus' placement also often indicates greater creativity in the house it tours, so with its influence trained on your house of home, you may start to show a special flare for one of the domestic arts, such as entertaining, cooking, decorating, or gardening.

If you are renovating your home, be a stickler about getting everything in writing. Spending could go over budget— tell your contractor not to spend a penny over the estimate without your approval.

With Uranus in Pisces, a water sign, if you are buying a house this year, be sure to check the plumbing, wells, sewer, and other water-related aspects of the property. Also check the roof and basement for past water damage or possible future problems. You could encounter an unusual situation involving water that you would never have thought to ask about. Have the drinking water tested. A thorough inspection of the property will save you problems later on.

With Uranus in the fourth house of Pisces, ruling the sea, you may want to think twice before moving into an area known to have occasional flooding or that is visited by hurricanes or tornados. I know that sounds obvious, but with Uranus here, I would advise you to be aware of this possibility.

Finally, Uranus rules technology and electricity, and it appears that in the coming years you are going to need good wiring in your house to handle all your new electronic toys. Overloading circuits could cause a fire! If you're buying an old house, you'll probably want to upgrade the wiring.

Finally, batten down the hatches by carrying a solid home-owners' or renters' insurance policy for fire, flood, and other contingencies. You'll need to be ready for anything. Uranus will remain in your house of home until 2011. Everyone should carry insurance, but this is doubly true for those with Uranus in the fourth house. With Saturn in your house of joint resources (which includes insurance), be sure to read the policy thoroughly and ask your insurance broker any questions. Most Sagittarians will never need insurance, thank goodness, but it's worth the peace of mind.

LATE FEBRUARY AND AUGUST ARE BEST IF YOU NEED TO MOVE, RELOCATE, OR RENOVATE

With Uranus in the fourth house of home, you may not know you need to move until the last minute, without much notice. Make sure to note the time on or just after the new moon on February 20, 2004. The two weeks that follow will be splendid for finding new, appealing living quarters. If you find a new job on February 20 or in the two weeks that follow, with Saturn so friendly to the new moon, this position will likely offer quite a bit of stability.

Later in the year, on the full moon August 29, plus or minus four days, you may find a solution unexpectedly—be ready to roll very quickly.

THE YEAR ENDS ON A PERSONAL HIGH
BE READY TO JUMP INTO 2005 IN STYLE

December is due to be an exciting month for you!

The new moon in Sagittarius on December 11 gives you two weeks of amazingly powerful cosmic energy to launch plans. Mercury will be retrograde (again!) from November 30 to December 20, but that won't stop you from planning, talking, and laying the groundwork.

The December 11 new moon will help you in a personal way, so think of it as a cosmic gift certificate to use in any way you please. Plan a wedding, find new love, get a raise, get a plum project assigned to you, or improve your home—you name it. Let others know your deepest plans and wishes at this time. By December, Jupiter will have arrived in your house of hopes and wishes, protecting you in ways you still can't imagine. Speak up, dear Sagittarius!

To make sure December turns out to be one of your favorite months, the cosmos is about to give you another big boost. Mars will enter Sagittarius on Christmas Day and remain in your sign for seven weeks. Wow! This trend will help you enter 2005 like gangbusters. When Mars is in your sign, you get control over life in a way you wouldn't ordinarily have—projects and plans will generally go your way. You'll feel energetic and assertive, and Mars will even make you look more attractive. Venus will also be in Sagittarius, which will only add to your aura and magnetism.

Dear Sagittarius, I am so happy to have this news for you! The past years have been so difficult, but now the cosmos is about to make a correction. Enter 2004 with your face turned to the Sun, for your famous trademark optimism will only attract more good energy. For once, the universe will be firmly on your side.

Summary

The coming year brings you a much improved picture from years past. Not only was Saturn on your tail during the past two years, you also had life-changing eclipses in your sign and your opposite sign of Gemini, which threw you into a vortex of change. All that is over, and your new life looks much prettier and much calmer—relatively speaking—than it did before! That doesn't mean it will be boring by any means. You have too much going on in all four corners of your chart for that to ever happen!

One of the most glittering parts of your chart involves your career, and this lovely trend will last until the end of September. Although the first nine months of 2004 are due to be special, the period while Jupiter is retrograde—from January through April—will proceed slowly, and will be perfect for planning and exploration. By mid-September the right offers will be on your desk and you can make your choice. If you're already in a job you love, you will score a major victory.

To understand the importance of this career cycle for you, keep in mind that another cycle this vital will not come around again until 2015. To make important aspects work, you need to be assertive, for only then can the universe provide you with the assistance you need. Astrology tells us that for every goal there is the proper time to take steps toward achieving it—look into career opportunities this year and you won't be sorry!

In terms of home and family, some changes are still due, as Uranus, the planet of surprise developments, has set up shop in your fourth house for a seven-year stay. (The fourth house rules your residence and property, family relationships, and others with whom you interact with regard to your home, such as roommates or housekeepers.) Last year was such a big year for home and property-related matters that you may have "used up" a big portion of this aspect. If you still need to move, renovate, or simply spiff up your space, March or September 2004 is the ideal month to do so. If buying a house, before you sign on the dotted line, have an engineer check it thoroughly for unusual or rare problems, especially related to—but not limited to—water.

Romantically, there are so many aspects for fun and love that if you want to meet a new romantic partner, you should be able to do so this year. Mars will send Cupid by in January, and when Venus circles close to Mars in April, your social life should heat up in a delightful way. However, it is the year's first eclipse, on April 19, that may have the most noticeable and positive effect on your love life. If you are single and looking, you will have a chance to meet someone new within weeks of this solar eclipse. If you're already attached, this eclipse will help you and your significant other relax and enjoy some of life's pleasures together.

Attached Sagittarians may decide to welcome a baby this year, which would be truly exciting news! If you already have children, one of your offspring—possibly your eldest—may be about to enter a new phase, such as attending a new school or showing signs of having a special talent.

The next eclipse, falling two weeks later, on May 4, will occur in your sixth house of health, fitness, and work projects. This is a full moon, indicating culmination. Watch your health, as you may be feeling a bit less energetic at the time of this eclipse. If any health concern comes up, see a doctor or dentist. The eclipse may be trying to get you to fix a problem you didn't know you had or that you simply ignored. Saturn was opposed to your Sun, a far harsher planetary aspect than this one, and it may have lowered your vitality quite a bit sometime in the past two years (depending on your exact birthday). This eclipse will not present anything you cannot handle. You've had harder in the past!

On May 4 or within days of this date, you could also wrap up a current assignment—this one seems to hold special implications for your future. At work, there could be some surprise announcements, and at least one trusted co-worker could depart. You may move into a new department and, once there, learn entirely new methods or projects. Lunar eclipses like this one are usually more emotional than solar eclipses, but try hard to remain objective.

The October 14 solar eclipse will be a glorious moment for friendship, fun, and socializing. You may make an important new friend at this time, and those who enter your life will seem to have an almost fated purpose. You may be elected to an official position in a club or join an organization that turns out to be very helpful to you. Alternatively, you may go to a trade show or seminar that boosts your career.

This eclipse indicates quite a bit of socializing in the months to come, so it won't all end in October by any means. Jupiter, the planet of good fortune, will move into the social area of your horoscope in late September for a year's stay. During that time you may be touched deeply by how much your friends look out for you. In fact, this part of your chart will become the most glowing area in the last three months of 2004, and will continue to be an important area in 2005.

The last eclipse in 2004, October 28, is a lunar eclipse, and may help you eliminate a bad habit, which would certainly be cause to celebrate. A secret that has been kept from you may come out in the open, much to your surprise. Suddenly something that you've not understood will make sense now. You may need to visit someone close to you who is in the hospital for surgery. Your brand of cheer will be particularly helpful for this person to make a full recovery.

The year ends on a fine personal note. The new moon on December 11 will give you carte blanche to direct your energy in any way you see fit. You can do so, confident that all the cards are stacked in your favor. On Christmas Day, Mars will enter Sagittarius for a glorious seven-week stay. This is terrific news, for the Red Planet will give you energy and drive, as well as a sparkling, celebrity-like presence that can't be denied. Venus will also be in your sign at the time. (Wow, aren't you lucky?) If you want to make over your looks in December, Venus will ensure your resulting appearance pleases you to no end.

If you felt invisible at times before this, you certainly won't at the close of 2004. All eyes will be on you, and you'll be completely irresistible! The stage is set for a grand New Year's Eve. Sagittarius, this is your time! You have come through the tunnel and into the light. You have so much to celebrate!

Capricorn

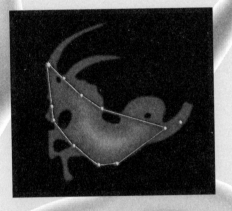

December 22-January 19

The Big Picture

If one word were to sum up 2004 for you, it would be "relationships." You will put all alliances under the microscope this year, but the most obvious one—your close romantic attachment—will get your prime attention. That's not to say you won't make time for old relationships with friends, business colleagues, and even family members. Absolutely you will, as these individuals not only will add to the year's pleasures, they will offer an alternative perspective you'll find helpful.

Capricorn like the stability a close, committed relationship can offer. The concept of building something of value with a committed partner over the course of a lifetime is a very attractive concept. You are romantic and practical enough to realize that when you do partner with someone, you can create a magic that is far greater than the sum of the parts (those parts being the two of you).

Yet when you get into a relationship, it isn't as easy to be in sync as you expected. This year you will meditate about this question a great deal and come to new conclusions about how you'll want to handle your closest relationships.

Part of the reason you are even taking the time to review your emotional history is due to the influence of Saturn, the taskmaster planet that teaches the value of long-range thinking and memory. Saturn moved into your opposite sign of Cancer in June 2003 and currently is filling your seventh house of relationships. Saturn will gauge the depth of your commitment to your relationship, which will force you into being a more mature, insightful person.

Wherever you happen to be emotionally—whether committed to someone or just dating—Saturn's position indicates the relationship is about to move up to the next level. If you don't want to do so, you may leave this relationship altogether, as it will be difficult to keep things in a holding pattern this year. Saturn is on a mission to find cracks and allow you an opportunity to patch them up before they grow larger. Saturn won't be back to this part of your chart for 29 years, and it's trying to help you build a relationship that will stand the test of time or free you to build a better one.

There is no reason to assume that your relationship will break up. If you want it to continue, it could, in fact, become stronger because Saturn will help you create a solid foundation for any alliance you deem valuable.

As 2004 begins, you already have had some experience with Saturn in this sector, as Saturn entered your solar seventh house of serious, committed relationships in June 2003. This is a long trend that will continue through mid-July 2005.

If you had any misconceptions about marriage or relationships in general, Saturn will bring you down to earth and make you more levelheaded and practical, which is necessary for emotional growth. After you have experienced this phase, your attachments will have a better chance of succeeding.

In all relationships we need to find the right balance between dependence and independence, intimacy and freedom. Whatever balance was right for you a few years ago probably won't satisfy you now, because you aren't the same person you were then.

I should note here that the seventh house rules all contractual partnerships. Marriage is considered one example, but a business partner, agent, or manager could be another. Any agreement that is contractually based falls under the seventh house. (And yes, marriage does require a contract, but we tend to forget that we actually sign one on our wedding day.) Although I have focused this discussion mainly in the romantic arena, you could just as well grow through a business partnership experience this year, so do keep that in mind.

While Saturn's move into Cancer last year for the first time since 1973 marked a monumental moment for all signs, it was especially so for you because Saturn is your ruling planet. The sign and house in which your ruling planet is located say a great deal about where your focus will be directed. Indeed, being that you are Saturn's favorite child, its placement indicates your whole being will be centered on this one person who is apparently very important to you.

As you grapple with partnership questions this year, realize that some of these issues may have first shown their faces in July or December 2000 and 2001 or in late June 2002. Those eclipses at those times highlighted the same partnership issues that Saturn will touch on this year. As Saturn moves over the mathematical degrees that those eclipses touched in those years, it will reactivate certain issues. If you did not resolve those relationship questions then, you will have a second chance to do so now.

You tend to do well in years when your ruling planet, Saturn, is in fine angle to Jupiter, the planet of good luck. That is precisely what will happen until the end of September 2004. That is more than enough time for you to cope with new influences operating on your relationship.

Experiencing Saturn in Cancer is perhaps one of the biggest astrological events you have experienced since the

1980's. What you decide now has broad implications for your future, and perhaps the most valuable part is what you'll learn about yourself in the months to come. While it might not always be an easy year, it is one that promises enormous personal growth.

Adding to the general seriousness and weight of the year is the fact that at no time in 2004 will Mars or Venus visit Capricorn, nor will a new moon appear in Capricorn. That is not a misprint, as amazing as this may sound. Mars rules energy and control, Venus rules harmony and magnetism, and the new moon rules fresh starts. Without these planets to side with you for even a brief time in 2004, you may feel alone and that you are carrying much on your shoulders. You will almost certainly be forced to cope with certain personal issues without the authority to change them, suggesting that these events are being caused by forces beyond your control. This rare lack of planetary support in these sectors will necessarily shift more control to your significant other, casting you in a more reactive, compromising, or conciliatory role.

However, there is a good side to this unusual cosmic circumstance. If Venus, Mars, or the Moon were to visit Capricorn, those bodies would find themselves in a tug of war (180-degree angle) to Saturn. Sometimes such an aspect suggests cooperation, at other times stern confrontation. You will be spared that possible emotional turmoil for now. These planets will indeed confront Saturn in early 2005, but by then you will have had the time to reflect on your relationship and sort out the decisions you need to make. Also, by next year, you will have only six months of Saturn left in Cancer, as this planet is due to exit in July 2005. By then, tensions will be gone.

Let us now focus on the four eclipses of 2004, due to fall in Aries, Taurus, and Scorpio. Two of these eclipses, in May and October, will emphasize very social areas of your chart, namely the fifth and eleventh houses, ruling new love, romance, children, and friendships. Your personal life is powerfully accented in 2004.

This suggests that Capricorns will focus on only serious attachments, but if you are single, the eclipse may bring a new person to you, as all eclipses change the status of a relationship. If you are attached, the eclipse in late October may signal the birth of a baby. One way or another, your personal life is about to change and grow.

Another eclipse is due in late April, a fairly friendly one that will highlight your residence or other property you own. You may move, buy a house, or renovate your present home. If you do, there seems to be something pushing you to do so.

If your home is not due for any upgrades or changes, your parents could be up to something big—perhaps they are moving to a new home or they may need you to help them in some other way. The degree that this eclipse is falling, 29 degrees, is the degree of completion, so one chapter is ending while another chapter is clearly beginning. We will talk more about the eclipses later, as some Capricorns will feel certain ones more sharply than others.

Now we get to the most sensational news of all, news that all Capricorns will be overjoyed to hear, for it concerns your career. In late 2004, your career should begin to blossom in astounding ways. Get ready to see your name in lights, thanks to the arrival of Jupiter in your tenth house of career success in late September 2004. Jupiter, the planet of happiness and good fortune, will remain in your house of professional achievement for a full year.

During this blue ribbon professional period you can finally establish yourself head and shoulders above your competition. When things start to happen, they should happen fast. Watch things take off just after the eclipse on October 14. At that time you will have no fewer than five heavenly bodies in your career sector, which is awesome!

Before you get to enjoy your career success, rare action will be happening in another part of your chart, the ninth house, which will have a major, mind-expanding influence. Jupiter will also bring this trend to you at the same time that Virgo, a fellow earth sign, will be in the perfect position to help.

With Jupiter's help you may decide to go back to college or graduate school to finish or start a degree. If you teach, the same influence will also help you get ahead. Some Capricorns will be taking major exams between January and September to gain their credentials. It's an ideal time, so you should do well!

Ever since Jupiter entered your ninth house—the house of the mind and higher learning—in late August 2003, you have become more curious and aware of the world around you. Your opinions are becoming more grounded, and you are approaching other ideas more critically. If you ever blindly accepted an idea because your family or friends embraced it, that is far less likely now. If your opinions stay the same, it's because they've held up under your intense scrutiny. In 2004, the ideas you espouse are the ones that are truly your own.

If you want to go to college but worry about the cost of tuition, with Jupiter in Virgo, there's an excellent chance you'll qualify for a scholarship. Jupiter often brings outstanding financial benefits along with its visit.

Jupiter will remain in your ninth house until September 2004, which also rules international travel. The first nine months of 2004 would be a superb time to take a journey that brings you over a long distance. If you haven't considered taking a trip I urge you to do so this year. Choose a foreign city you have never seen but have always dreamed of visiting. Once Jupiter leaves your ninth house in September, it will be harder to go and Jupiter will not be back to this mind-expanding house for twelve years.

We will talk about the trends I touched on here in much greater detail as we go through your chapter, but hopefully I have already given you something to think about. Read on, dear Capricorn, because what I have to tell you will get only better.

The Details of the Your Year Ahead

SATURN IN CANCER
WILL TEST YOUR COMMITMENT TO A KEY PARTNER

This year, to help you in your quest to solidify and stabilize relationships, Saturn will give you special rhinestone-edged sunglasses that will help you see relationships in an entirely new way.

It is inevitable that everything will change after you gain this new perspective. This includes how you view your partner, but more important, it also includes how you view yourself. Others will begin to treat you differently, for we teach others how to treat us.

Your greater confidence and a new self-image may be the greatest gift the cosmos will give you this year, but neither will arrive quickly or easily. Saturn will make you doubt yourself at certain points. As a Capricorn, you are not averse to putting in a good effort, knowing that there is an upside eventually. You, more than most, know that nothing of value ever comes for free.

During this benchmark year, you will become more adept at expressing your needs to your partner. Capricorns sometimes hold their feelings in, but you will see that it is best not to. Uranus will help you find the words, and since this planet is not leaving your communication house for many years, you can expect to get only better at saying what is in your heart. Uranus is also in superb angle to your Sun, which means you will easily absorb the information Uranus has for you. (December-born Capricorns are especially tuned to this now.) If your relationship is basically sound and you have no major disagreements, Saturn's presence might just reflect a concern for your partner.

Saturn will make you much more resilient and independent. You may have to take on more of the "work" of the relationship than you might like, mainly because your partner is either preoccupied or needy. Or there may be areas where you simply do not see eye to eye, and you'll need to find a way to compromise and communicate so you're on the same wavelength.

Saturn often creates a separation or feeling of isolation for a variety of reasons, but again mainly to build your strength. While most of us hear "separation" and immediately assume that "not getting along" is the reason, other factors may be at play. Your partner may need to travel a great deal for his or her job or may have to temporarily live elsewhere—as when servicemen or women go on a tour of duty—to complete a special work assignment. If you are the spouse that has to leave, Saturn's position in your chart indicates your partner will miss you. Try to be considerate and as attentive as you can be to your mate this year.

If you are single, you will still feel this trend. For example, you will start to look for well-grounded types to date—no more wannabe rock stars living in lofts and eating cereal! Under Saturn's influence, you want a dependable and responsible partner who shares your values.

You have a chance to build a relationship based on cooperation. The best times of year to build a relationship—or to enter into a business alliance—are when Saturn reaches out to Jupiter.

We have been discussing Saturn in your seventh house, but in fact, Saturn is also opposed to your Sun, which raises other considerations, aside from your relationship. I won't sugarcoat this—it is not an easy aspect. You may feel more tired than usual, sad now and then, or overwhelmed by some of the challenges life is presenting.

It is obvious that many people will be depending on you and you will feel pressure to help them. We all have Saturn opposed to the Sun at some point in life, dear Capricorn—you are simply dealing with it now. It is very important that you keep your health up to par and not ask more from your body than it can give.

Saturn comes by every 29 years, so a visit from this planet is rare and quite important. We get only two or three such visits in our lifetime. While it may not visit often, Saturn makes sure that each stay is memorable and productive.

Does Your Birthday
Fall Between December 21 and December 26?
You Are Done with Saturn's Tests!

Luckily, no one ever feels the direct pressures of Saturn during the entire two years Saturn tours a sign, but only when it aligns exactly with the precise mathematical degrees of your Sun. That period lasts six to eight months, but it may not take that long if you resolve the problems you face.

If you are a Capricorn with a birthday that falls between December 21 and December 26, you are finished with Saturn's main emphasis. You felt the strongest vibrations last year between June and December. You will still be dealing with the decisions and revelations of last year, but 2004 should be vastly easier.

Those born between December 26 and January 3 had a short bout with Saturn last year, but will experience more of Saturn's cosmic teachings in 2004. By now you have some experience with this planet and should cope better as a result.

Those born from January 4 to January 16 will feel Saturn's presence in their lives in 2004. You will be dealing directly with this planet, perhaps for the first time in your life. However, if you are old enough, think back to the last time Saturn opposed your sign, from 1973 to June 1976. (Within that window, 1975 into early 1976 was the key period that required your biggest adjustments.) See if you can find any themes of those years that compare to ones you face now.

Those born from January 17 to January 19 will feel some relationship pressures this year, but the strongest influence of this trend will be in the first six months of 2005. You have lots of time to prepare.

WATCH FOR PARTNERSHIP DEVELOPMENTS IN JANUARY, MAY, JUNE, JULY, AUGUST, AND DECEMBER

The best time of the year to form a solid relationship is when Saturn reaches out to Jupiter, on May 1 and on August 17 (and the three days leading up to those dates). Decisions you make during these months should turn out well, and if you decide to form a partnership for business, a profit should result from the union. Please note that August 17 is flawed for signing documents or for getting married, as Mercury will be retrograde. (Please see the chapter on Mercury retrograde for more information.) Use August 17 instead for strategic planning, but not to seal important agreements.

The times of the year when you will see the most tension are in early January, during most of May and June, and the first week of July. Happily, the December holidays bring a softer, sweeter influence, suggesting that things will improve by then.

The full moon in your partnership sector January 7 is when to start watching for possible issues to emerge. Relationship issues will peak early in the year, but luckily, Jupiter will be very friendly. Mars will not, so family opinions or housing problems may add to stress. This full moon will feel very emotional, and its intensity may surprise you.

You will be very focused on your relationship while Mars tours Cancer from May 7 to June 23. If your partner has not been vocal up until now, get ready for an earful. Or if you are getting along well, your partner will bring big news that will affect you, too. This is a time to be cooperative and conciliatory, not controlling or domineering, because that would be nearly impossible. You may also be subject to criticism at work. Listen to the feedback that others will feel compelled to give you, but don't let anyone lower your confidence.

Watch the full moon July 2, when it falls in Capricorn. The Sun and Saturn will be walking arm in arm, and both will oppose the gentle Moon. It may be summer, but it feels like winter. You will have to shoulder a problem alone, but you'll do so with characteristic grace.

On the heels of this full moon comes the new moon July 17. The Sun, Moon, and Saturn will all be closely aligned, suggesting the need to announce a serious decision that has long-range implications. Although the mood is heavy at the time, Jupiter is in a good position, so your decision appears to be one that works well for you.

The year ends on a lovely note. Be sure to mark the meeting of Venus and Mars on December 5. The full moon in Cancer on December 26 will again emphasize your partner, but this time in a graceful, lighter way. Many Capricorns will have worked out any problematic issues and may even get engaged for the holidays. (All full moons have a range of influence of plus or minus four days, so Christmas Day is included in this full moon.) Uranus, the planet of surprise, will be well angled to the Moon, so expect the unexpected—you'll like what develops! The hardest aspect at this time will be Mars in tough angle to Uranus, so a family member—a sister or cousin, for example—may be touchy, but whatever occurs shouldn't ruin your holiday.

VENUS TO RETROGRADE FROM MAY 17 TO JUNE 29
BEAUTY, FUN, FESTIVITIES, OR COSMETIC SURGERY
ALL ON HOLD

Venus rules adornment, fun, love, and beauty, so a retrograde phase means Venus is resting and her strongest powers are withheld from us. It is usually a no-frills time, when life seems more serious than usual.

When Venus goes retrograde in Gemini from May 17 to June 29, it is best not to buy expensive clothing or jewelry, make appointments for spa or salon treatments, or schedule important parties or fund-raisers. It would be a very poor time to get engaged or married and a bad time to schedule cosmetic surgery. For those events you want a strong Venus in the sky!

SINGLE?
LOVE BRINGS REASSESSMENT, REFLECTION

Single Capricorns will feel some of the stresses of Saturn's position, but the long-range effects of these tensions will be positive. You seem more focused and more aware of what you want in a partner, and that will help you attract the right one.

Your best period for fun and love comes early in the year, when Mars tours your fifth house of true love, from February 3 to March 21. The time near February 20 and March 6 would be ideal dates to take a vacation—if you do, you may find love on those trips.

Your chart is fabulously lucky for travel—it appears to be where all your happiness is based in the first nine months of the year. You may also find love on trips during the second half of September.

I want to add that when Mars tours your house of true love from February 3 to March 21, it will move over the very spots that were activated by eclipses last year on May 15 and November 8. Whatever was discussed last year at that time will again become an issue. The dates to watch closely this year are February 28 and March 13, and the few days surrounding those dates. These are invisible mathematical points that will be activated, and they could be quite powerful.

A sweet new moon will be in your house of true love on May 19, but as mentioned above, Venus will be retrograde. Venus rules your solar fifth house of true love, so you may be tempted to rekindle an old romance with a former lover at this time. Or you or your current lover may dive back into an old issue, one that you assumed was done and finalized—but instead is back on the table.

Also at this time, on May 19, Mars will orbit close to Saturn, so you may feel temporarily stuck, not knowing how to resolve things. This new moon may also indicate that you are about to change your mind about a certain relationship, one way or the other.

THE ECLIPSE ON OCTOBER 28 STRESSES LOVE

The big moment of the year for your love life concerns an eclipse on October 28 that will fall in your fifth house of romance and love. This is a full moon lunar eclipse, which suggests it will be more emotional than the ones that arrive on April 19 (causing shifts in home and family) or October 14 (exciting for career developments).

This eclipse brings some sort of romantic issue to culmination. A new chapter is forming in your emotional history, but it is not clear if it is with the same person you have been dating, or if you are moving on. Eclipses come by every six months in pairs, and they remain in one zodiac series for 18 months (such as this one, Taurus/Scorpio). You will have plenty of time to grasp their messages. An eclipse first occurred in this house last year, on November 8. (An earlier one, in Taurus, fell on May 15 in your friendship sector.) There will be only one more in this series next year, falling on April 24, 2005.

The eclipses this year, the one on October 28 and the one discussed below, May 5, fall in the same spectrum, 180 degrees apart. When energy falls in one house, energy often ricochets back into the house directly opposite it. Friendship and love form one axis, from the fifth to eleventh houses.

The October 28 full moon eclipse will make a hard aspect to Neptune, so new, revelatory information could come to you. Saturn is also in good angle to Venus, so there could be good news, for Saturn will add stability and a sense of reality. This eclipse has mixed elements, which is common.

Luckily, the eclipse falls in Taurus, a sign that blends well with yours. If you were born early in your sign, near December 26, you will feel and benefit from this eclipse most.

A pregnancy could come up near the October 28 eclipse, or you may choose to adopt at that time. If you are not ready for a child, be very careful in the weeks leading up to this eclipse. A full moon eclipse in Taurus is considered very fertile.

THE COSMIC LOVER PLANETS MARS AND VENUS MEET DECEMBER 4–5

The year will end on an optimistic note. Venus and Mars, a magical couple that always sets off sparks of new love when together, did not embrace at all in 2003, but will do so on the weekend of December 4-5. This event may signal the arrival of someone new who could become quite dear to you. These two planets will meet in the sexy sign of Scorpio in your solar eleventh house of friends and fun social events.

FRIENDSHIP IS THE TOPIC OF THE FULL MOON LUNAR ECLIPSE MAY 5

A friend or social event may be the topic of this full moon. For example, you may host a charity fund-raiser or be elected to a club position. Alternatively, you may make a new friend—or distance yourself from one. Eclipses change the status in the house in which they fall, so you may have to say goodbye to old friends so that you can make space for new ones.

On this full moon eclipse, the Moon is angry with Neptune, so there could be a misunderstanding or, worse, an outright betrayal. Mars and Pluto are at odds, so this person may not be a friend but a co-worker. You may find yourself unexpectedly in the middle of a political situation at the office. Mars and Venus are close, so near May 5, you may be having an office flirtation with someone at your own level, which may cause problems in the department.

Luckily, this eclipse relates well to your Capricorn Sun, doubly so if you were born on or near January 5. Also, there are many positive aspects—Saturn is good to both Uranus and the Moon, and Jupiter is also friendly with the Sun, Saturn, and the Moon, forming a truly gorgeous formation in your chart. With aspects this mixed, it's hard to say how things will play out. Keep your antenna up, dear Capricorn.

ARE YOU IN THE MOOD FOR ROMANTIC VACATION OR ADVENTURESOME FUN? GO IN LATE FEBRUARY, EARLY MARCH, AUGUST, OR MID-SEPTEMBER

On February 20, you will have a chance for a serendipitous quick trip. With Mars lighting your house of travel and sending cheer to many planets in Virgo, you can journey to places as close or as far as you please. If you travel for work, it may be to present a creative idea which will be successful.

The full moon of March 6 will embrace Jupiter, and Mars will be friendly as well. This is even better for travel, so perhaps your trip will be winding down at this time (full moons bring things to completion). Your next opportunity comes between August 10 and September 26, when Mars will reside in your ninth house. With a plethora of planets gathering in this house, it would be remarkable if you didn't go anywhere. This is also a superb time in your life to start college or to go abroad to study. Watch August 29, when a full moon activates all these planets. Mercury will be retrograde, so you may decide to revisit a place that you haven't seen in years. Good idea!

My very favorite time for you to go away—worthy of five gold stars—is at the new moon on September 14. Mercury will be moving full steam ahead at that time.

Your Luckiest day of the Year:
September 21

Every year the Sun meets up with benefic Jupiter to create the luckiest day of the year for everyone. Each year this meeting takes place in a different part of your chart.

This year, your big day falls on September 21 in your ninth house of travel, so plan a fabulous trip to another country for this week. Were you born on or near January 20? Then you just won the jackpot, because the degrees that Jupiter and the Sun move over will exactly reach out to your Sun. What a wonderful month September will be for you!

For all Capricorns, no matter what their exact birthday, their luck will start to flow at the new moon September 14 and build all week, with wonderful events likely to occur on September 21 or close to it. You won't have a day quite like this one for twelve years. By coincidence, Mercury will also be conjunct with Jupiter on this day, making it doubly special for traveling and for getting good news.

If you are a professor or an instructor at a university, you can expect accolades or a promotion near September 21, and if so, it would be to a position you've always wanted. If you are taking a test on this day, you may pass with flying colors. College students (or prospective college students) may want to meet with a teacher for a conference or interview. If you are presenting a publishing idea for any media (TV, radio, Internet, magazines, or books), your golden day to do so is on or near September 21.

DO YOU WANT A RAISE?
THE NEW MOON JANUARY 21 IS YOUR BEST BET

You need to be ready to ask your boss for a raise by the new moon January 21. Have a list of your accomplishments and contributions ready! If you ask on or within a few days of January 21, you will be working with the very finest new moon of the year.

All new moons have two weeks of influence, but the strongest energy is always closer to the onset of the trend, so try to act soon after the new moon appears on the 21st. This new moon finds Saturn in good angle to Uranus, and Uranus rules your second house of earned income. Excellent!

On February 6, Mars will be in excellent communication with Uranus, ruler of your house of earned income, and so on this day, you may hear some very good news concerning your financials.

Beside February 6, also mark down May 17 and November 15. On all three days Mars will be in superb alignment with Uranus. While you won't have a two-week period similar to the one with the powerful new moon in January, you should have luck on your side on each of these days.

Finally, if you are in an artistic field or work with artists, circle November 29. This day has exceptional aspects because Jupiter, the planet of financial good fortune, is in sublime angle to Neptune, the planet most associated with the arts. In November, Jupiter will be settled in your tenth house of professional promotion and Neptune will stand in your house of salary. This is an exceedingly rare aspect— make the most of it!

Neptune will remain in this same second house of earned income, so when making financial agreements, try to get everything in writing. Neptune will leave this area of your chart in 2008, but until then, be careful.

THINK BIG, SET GOALS
BECAUSE JUPITER IS IN VIRGO UNTIL SEPTEMBER 25

Some of the most positive news of the year concerns Jupiter's monumental move into Virgo, to remain in your ninth house until September 25. Jupiter is the planet of good fortune, and has set up shop in the area of your chart that rules intellectual personal development since late August 2003. In that time you may have already started to see your horizons expand. If not, you will—it will be very obvious in September 2004, just prior to Jupiter's exit.

With Jupiter in an earth sign like yours, it can help you in a more substantial way. It has been years since you've had this cosmic support. Jupiter being in such good angle to your Sun means your health should become more robust and your mood much more optimistic.

Most people travel when Jupiter transits this house, and some even decide to study or work abroad. This sector also rules publishing efforts, which also glow for you. If you are a writer hoping to sell a book idea, get your proposal in shape. If you've already signed a book contract and expect to be published between January and the end of September 2004, this is the very best time of the decade to do so. Your book could be quite a hot seller! The ninth house always demands preparation and a determined effort from you. When we plan to travel, for example, we need to plan an itinerary, apply for a passport, book a hotel, and go to the bank to exchange some foreign currency. You get the idea—nothing about the ninth house is exactly easy—but we make the effort because the payoff is so outstanding.

Are you involved in a lawsuit? You are very lucky. The ninth house, so glittering for you now with Jupiter's presence, means you will have a much easier time defending yourself or prosecuting, as the case may be. You will likely have an excellent lawyer who can provide the right advice and build a solid legal strategy. If you have to be involved in a lawsuit, having Jupiter, the planet of justice and healing, in this house should be a great comfort to you. If you are in law school or if you are a professional working in the justice system, this will be your year to move ahead.

There is a deeper benefit to Jupiter's visit to your ninth house, and it is there for you to investigate. Specifically, the ninth house is a philosophical part of the chart, where we contemplate why we were born, as well as what contribution we might make to the world in the time we are given. Jupiter is comfortable in this ninth house, for it is the house ruled by Sagittarius, and Jupiter is that sign's ruler. You may become very meditative and reflective under this trend. Since the ninth house rules one's intellectual approach to religion (while the twelfth house rules a more deeply felt emotional response), it would be a perfect time to learn more about a religion. Your mind will be very sharp, especially with Jupiter in Virgo, one of the most precise signs in the zodiac.

Jupiter in Libra
Brings Astounding Career Success

Your professional standing will take a huge step forward in late 2004, which is good news. On September 25, Jupiter will rise to a part of your chart it has not visited for twelve years, and remain there until October 25, 2005. Consider this period as your reward for past efforts. It's time for new goals, as you will soon see that you've outgrown your old career ambitions. Of course, if you have not worked hard, if you have continually arrived late or not at all, talked back to your boss, or handed in sloppy work, none of this will happen.

Also at this time of the year, Mars will be at the top of your chart, raising your profile very high. Soon everyone will know your name. Take this period very seriously, dear Capricorn.

STAR THESE DAYS FOR CAREER SUCCESS!

You have the kind of cosmic ammunition that other signs can only dream about, dear Capricorn. The ball starts rolling on September 25, when Jupiter enters Libra and your solar tenth house of professional achievement for a full year's stay. Open the champagne! This is big cause for celebration!

At the very same time, Mars, the planet of red hot energy, will enter your career sector for the first time in two years. Have your resume ready! Mars will spend seven weeks in this house, from September 26 to November 10, your golden period to find a job.

In the middle of this fantastic period a solar eclipse will occur on October 14. Your career should take off like a fire-cracker! In your house of fame and achievement will be five heavenly bodies, all in Libra: Mars, Mercury, Jupiter, the Sun, and new moon. Wow!

Sometimes eclipses are felt one month to the day later plus or minus four days, so keep your eye on the days surrounding November 14 as well. However, I still feel the time around October 14 is your time. Dress for success!

Do You Hope to Lose Weight this Year?
Saturn Opposed to Your Sun
Can Make It Happen

With Saturn in Cancer, opposite your sign, you may lose weight quite easily. If that's you, you should begin your new diet and exercise regime immediately.

If you were born early in the sign, in December, you will feel Saturn's rays before others and will be the first to see weight loss as a result. Be warned, however: Saturn does nothing quickly. Don't expect to lose ten pounds in one week. Saturn will want to see you've done things slowly, steadily, and sensibly. Every Capricorn will benefit from this tour of Saturn from now through mid-July 2005.

There are several optimal times this year to begin a fitness plan. When Mars tours your sixth house of health is an ideal time to start. Your energy level will be high. Mars will visit your health sector from March 21 through May 7.

The new moon in your sixth house of health, June 17, is another superb time to begin your program. When dealing with new moons, always increase physical activity at the new moon, and start to decrease calories two weeks later, *after* the full moon (in this case, July 2) plus three or four days.

You must never start a diet before the full moon, only after its face appears and it is waning. It works! Try it!

In matters of health, you may have dental problems, so go for frequent cleanings. For overall health, schedule a checkup. Put special emphasis on having your eyes examined and cholesterol checked. If you are female, you may want to have a mammogram, as Saturn is in Cancer. More mature readers may want to schedule a baseline bone scan (Saturn rules bones and teeth). Take note of any digestive problems, eating disorders, skin rashes, or unusual moles (Capricorn rules skin; Cancer, the stomach and breasts).

If you take sensible steps to protect your health, there should be no need to be concerned.

Do You Need to Move or Renovate? January Brings Attractive Options

There is a high probability that you will move, buy, or sell property, make extensive repairs, or change roommates. Eclipses usually bring radical shifts, and being that the eclipse April 19 falls in your house of home, something is up.

Your first opportunity to look at solid options will be in January. Mars entered this part of your chart on December 13, 2003, and will remain in your first house through February 3, 2004.

Look to the new moon March 20 if you'd like to make changes. A suitable solution may turn up in the two weeks that follow that new moon, with the best days clustered near March 20-27. The only problem with this new moon is that you may find that your partner doesn't agree with your choice. However, Mars is in ideal angle to the Sun, so you may prevail.

If not much occurs on March 20, then watch the next new moon, an eclipse April 19, and the days that follow, plus or minus two weeks. Options should certainly show up then. If you were born near January 19, you should notice the effects of this eclipse.

You may relocate near the full moon September 28, which occurs during that magical week for your career. If you're not relocating, you may upgrade your living arrangements to correspond to an increase in status in your current job. Either way, you should be excited!

Summary

This year, Saturn will be in direct opposition to your Sun. This is not an easy aspect, and if you were born in December, you already know this to be true, as you have wrestled with it since June 2003. December-born Capricorns are, for the most part, done with the direct demands of Saturn, but January-born Capricorns are about to begin experience them in 2004, and they will show up as soon as the year begins. One important relationship seems to be the whole focus of your thinking, as Saturn will be positioned in your seventh house of contractually based partners.

You instinctively partition life into neat, distinct areas, and this makes you feel organized and focused. It would be easy to think that each part of your life is unrelated to the other parts, but in 2004, they will be far too interrelated for that. In 2004, you will have to move about with more flexibility and mobility. Instead of feeling safety in structure, you will rebuild and find it from friends, associates, and others who will provide the net you need to feel secure.

You won't have full control this year, but at the same time you won't have to be the sole instrument of change, either—others will help you when you need the help.

One main partner may give you tummy aches, yes, but other partners may become the anchors in your storm. Saturn's presence in this house suggests one person may teach you many important lessons of life this year, but other partners may provide the stability you need, too.

In each case, you will get down to the bare bones of the relationship and decide whether your partner enhances your sense of safety and strength or, just the opposite, makes you feel vulnerable or even imprisoned.

If you have been a bit too dependent on your partner, you will become far less so, and perhaps for the first time, realize your inner strength. If you have been quite independent, your partner may need you in such a way that you grow closer and more interdependent. Saturn will help you find the right balance.

In matters of health, keep yourself in top condition, for Saturn's opposition to your Sun is considered very draining to one's health. Luckily, Jupiter, a planet known not only for good fortune but for healing, too, will be in excellent angle to your Sun. Jupiter will provide enormous protection during the first nine months of 2004.

You have much to look forward to, because from January through September, Jupiter will be positioned in your ninth house of intellectual expansion, a fabulous influence that will make you feel as if the shutters of your mind have been flung open. Uranus, the planet of genius and innovation, is positioned in your third house of the mind and will help you communicate in more creative and sophisticated ways.

If you have ever wanted to travel far and wide, you must do so this year, as Jupiter will make your trip memorable and possibly even life-altering. Your opinions will become better shaped as you begin to approach others' ideas with a more questioning, probing manner. In 2004, you will put your ideas through vigorous tests, and the ones you embrace will be completely your own.

Not only will Saturn make you wise, trustworthy, and responsible, this planet is capable of helping you assume a position of leadership at work or in civic, political, or community humanitarian projects. You will live up to your billing as a leader. In late September 2004 you will start to show the world that you have the right stuff to move ahead. This will begin your very finest career period in over a decade. If you are considering changing jobs, you should wait for the end of 2004 to do so. October will be simply astounding—you will be at the right place at the right time, and events will conspire to launch you into a whole new realm.

By this time next year you will have much to celebrate. While in some ways 2004 will be a year of hard work, there will be moments of intense pleasure. You are about to separate the wheat from the chaff in your life, and what remains will be your golden harvest.

Aquarius

January 20-February 18

The Big Picture

Uranus, the planet of innovation and discovery, is your sign's guardian planet, and as its favorite child, Uranus bestows on you a healthy appetite for change. You are also a fixed sign, so you prefer those changes to arrive in measured doses. Over the past seven years, during Uranus' tour of Aquarius, you certainly learned that isn't always possible.

The thought of radical change no longer fazes you, because you realize that change is the cornerstone of progress. What you fear most now is the thought of living a mediocre, predictable existence. Rest assured, in 2004, there is no chance that will happen.

With two major eclipses to touch the pinnacle and base points of your solar horoscope in May and October, expect massive shifts in your career and residential or family life. You are a resourceful soul, so this prospect is exciting. Perhaps you are tired of your old job or feel that where you live no longer fulfills your needs. Some zodiac signs may dread coming shifts, but not you. You say, "Bring it on!"

2004 holds the promise of being your strongest financial year in years, thanks to a visit by good fortune Jupiter in Virgo to your eighth house of "other people's money" from January though September. Mid-to-late September should be simply glorious.

The money you will see could come in one large chunk (or a series of smaller chunks) and will not likely appear in the form of salary. (That is not to say you won't make a good salary—you might—but more cash will probably come to you another way.) It may arrive as a bonus, commission, royalty check, job benefit, court settlement, grant, prize, inheritance, insurance payout, scholarship, loan, or any other source that falls under the umbrella of "other people's money."

You are strongly favored in these areas, so this year if someone (or a whole company) treats you unfairly, be sure to get legal advice, because you stand a good chance of winning if you seek redress through the courts.

If 2004 takes off slowly, have patience. Jupiter will be retrograde during the first four months of the year, and won't turn on full power until May 4. That means some of your biggest deals probably won't click into place until May. Jupiter will remain in strong form for the rest of the year.

Don't let Jupiter's being out of phase hold you up. Uranus, which governs your deepest ambitions, will be in fine form from the moment the year takes off. Uranus will be moving full steam ahead during the first six months of 2004, and it's important to make all your new contacts and present your ideas during that time.

However, Uranus will go retrograde on June 10, and at that time you will be restrained by outside factors. That's fine—you will have extra time to decide on your direction and to set new goals so projects will become stronger when Uranus turns direct on November 11. That's when you will get the green light to roll again.

Jupiter retrograde will simply hold back money temporarily. Try not to launch huge projects, such as incorporating a business, while Jupiter is retrograde. Uranus is the more important planet to watch.

Saturn's presence in your solar sixth house of work this year indicates that you will be very busy and that you won't always have help. Saturn's position also suggests that you will be well paid for your efforts. If you are eligible to be paid for overtime, you may do even better.

The second half of 2004 will be your best. That doesn't mean breakthroughs won't happen before then—it just means that some of your plans and projects will need to be tweaked in the first half.

October is sure to be a magical month, when many planets in air signs will send kisses to your Sun. Those planets will help you untangle any earlier problems and will bring an element of luck. This is no ordinary confluence of planets—it is quite spectacular, and may bring big news. Late November is simply extraordinary for finding a new job. Romance is wonderful in the last quarter of the year, too.

Long-distance travel or interests on foreign shores may provide some of the year's most brilliant razzle-dazzle. Most Aquarians will travel far and wide in late 2004, and this trend comes via Jupiter, which will be in Libra from late September 2004 through October 2005. Business interests in other countries or involving foreign cultures will be outstanding. People who are not citizens of your country but who live in your country will also be lucky for you.

Libra is a partnering sign, so your successes may occur through a business or romantic partner. Libra also rules the industries that cater to brides, parties, catering, flowers, jewelry, spa treatments, and art, and one of these areas might also blossom for you.

This year some Aquarians may decide to go back to college for an advanced degree, and the timing is perfect. Libra rules both the judicial system and the arts, so either area of study would glow doubly bright for you with Jupiter in that sign. If you want to pursue a publishing project, do it late in the year, as Jupiter in Libra will help you. The ninth house rules the dissemination of information, so your book or article could turn out to be quite a lucrative success.

With travel, most Aquarians will have not only Jupiter as encouragement, but two eclipses as well. Those solar eclipses will arrive on April 19 (encouraging short travel) and October 14 (long travel) and will send you on a journey of discovery. There is also evidence that these eclipses could herald a business breakthrough.

Romantically, life will be better than it's been in some time. Saturn, the planet of obstacles, finally left your solar fifth house of true love in June 2003. Having Saturn, a planet that is about power and ambition, in the fifth house for two and a half years was an astrological contradiction. Saturn is not comfortable in this house, for it delays romance and puts more emphasis on duty and responsibility than on carefree fun, which is what this house should be about. You can wave goodbye to Saturn, which won't be back for another twenty-nine years.

Before you can really let go and enjoy yourself romantically, you may still need to iron out some issues. You may be debating whether to rekindle an old romance, or you may still have unresolved issues in a present relationship. You will spend the first part of the year thinking about these areas.

Venus will be retrograde from mid-May through June and will add to that feeling of uncertainty. Perhaps you will pull back in a relationship if you feel it's moved too quickly.

Later, when Mars tours your house of relationships, attached Aquarians may find themselves in a touchy phase.

When summer is over, you will have worked things out and will be in a whole new place, relating to your partner with greater openness.

Mars will not tour your sign at all in 2004, which will take some control out of your hands. You will need to listen more closely to what your romantic partner has to say and be willing to compromise for the sake of the relationship. Jupiter will be in lovely angle to your Sun by October, and that alone will help you feel more optimistic. Jupiter won't be the only planet helping you in October—you'll have a whole constellation of planets behind you (wow!), so there is no reason to worry.

This year, Jupiter will spend a lot of time in your eighth house, a house that rules not only joint finances but also sexuality. You will have a rare opportunity to relate to your partner with an intensity that may have been absent for years. While some people don't have a problem with showing or receiving affection, lack of desire can seem a real concern in the relationships of people—people of all signs. Your focus on money, career, or other life problems may have relegated sex to the bottom of your list, but with Jupiter in this superb position, you have a chance to become calmer, and in the mood to initiate some sexy romance.

Details of the Year Ahead

CHANGES IN YOUR CAREER AND HOME LIFE DUE TO ECLIPSES IN MAY, OCTOBER

The two most important eclipses for you fall on May 4 and October 28, and together they will revitalize your life from the bottom up.

The first eclipse, on May 4, will focus squarely on your professional life. It could bring an end to your current job and the start of a new one. These two events may or may not occur at precisely the same time, but if you do get laid off (and I am not saying you will), the end of the year is perfect for job-hunting.

Alternatively, you may stay at your job, but at the time of the eclipse, you may hear that a top female boss is leaving. This person has been important to you and her departure may make you feel unprotected, so you may want to start looking at your options.

The second eclipse, on October 28, could bring developments with your residence, other property you own, or could focus on a decorating or construction project. The eclipse may also focus on a roommate or your parents, who are included as part of the fourth house. You may relocate to take a new job, as so many planets will be filling your house of professional prestige.

Although it may appear that an eclipse has delivered all its news at once, that is almost never the case. Eclipses come in pairs every six months, and occur in two signs—such as these, which are in Taurus/Scorpio—and they are almost always signs that are on the same axis (that is, 180 degrees apart).

As you experience this year's eclipses, realize that their news is part of a wider message that is being delivered by the universe over an eighteen-month period. You will have plenty of time to make the necessary adjustments. Each eclipse builds on the news delivered by the previous one in the series.

Each eclipse is felt in a different way—some are more potent than others. This year, the full moon lunar eclipse due on May 5 will touch those with birthdays that fall within five days of February 3. Aquarians with birthdays that fall on January 28, plus or minus five days, will feel the October 28 eclipse most powerfully.

The full moon lunar eclipse on November 8, 2003, high-lighted those Aquarians born on February 4, plus or minus five days. Your home, family, and living situation (including any other property you own) were the subjects of discussion, and there may have been some shifts.

Both of the eclipses discussed earlier are full moon lunar eclipses, which suggests it's time to say goodbye to a part of your life so a new phase can begin. These changes are reflective of something deeper. A new attitude and set of values are surfacing, and your renewed passion to make time count will bring a tremendous sense of pur-pose this year.

Finances Will Play a Larger Role While Uranus Is in Pisces, from Now Until 2011

Your finances will again play a very big role in 2004, but they will be far easier to manage.

Your job and home-related changes appear to be driven by financial considerations. Money matters often bore you, as your sign inhabits the ethereal world of ideas and concepts; however, with eclipses in Taurus and Scorpio, signs associated with power and money, they will be hard to ignore.

Last year, Uranus entered Pisces and will remain in the second house of earned income until 2011. To a sign that is known not to be materialistic, this might sound surprising. You won't change—conditions will, and they will bring out a highly creative and entrepreneurial side of you.

The very presence of Uranus in this house suggests that your uniqueness will be prized, and your individuality will be rewarded financially. Admittedly, with this unpredictable planet in your second house of money, you could suffer sudden losses or incredibly large gains, even within the same year. You will have to carefully manage this powerful energy, but if you do, you could be sitting on top of the world.

The shift of Uranus into Pisces may signal a radical switch in the way you make your living. There are certain fields that may grow in importance to you. Uranus rules science, high-tech, and communicative fields, so you may want to investigate a job that allows you to explore those areas. Uranus also rules astrology and new art forms, so you may decide to start a business in one of these fields.

Uranus covers the humanitarian fields, so you may choose to work in animal rights or on behalf of groups that require special assistance, such as the homeless or orphaned children. In fact, you may decide that what you do at work should support your deepest views, and that you don't want to work any longer for companies whose ethics run counter to your beliefs. Nature and environmental protection may become banner issues for you. Uranus will also ask you to re-evaluate your most basic values and decide whether you have placed the right emphasis on tangible things in the scheme of your life.

With Uranus, a planet that prizes independence, now in your house of money, it will become increasingly important that you are not beholden to others for your income and security. To help you make the transition to this new way of thinking, Saturn will be in a superb position to Uranus during the first six months of 2004. Saturn's job is to stabilize things, and to take your ideas into reality.

Last year brought a number of unforeseen financial circumstances that probably translated into heavy-duty expenses that caused much stress. You can close the door on that chapter—nothing remotely like that will happen again this year.

EXPECT TO BE BUSY
AND SUPER-ORGANIZED AT WORK,
SATURN IN CANCER UNTIL JULY 2005

You will be able to master new tasks and juggle many projects at once, stunning others with your self-discipline, organization, and coolness under pressure. All the while, you will be expected to maintain high standards of excellence. With Saturn in Cancer, you can handle these and other challenges that would make others cower under their desks.

Saturn will make you work hard, but if you meet the challenge, you will have a great deal to be proud of. You will learn a new set of skills, and may even decide to take a few classes on work-related topics. Under this tour of Saturn you will streamline your working methods, perhaps by learning new software or designing new methods.

The odd part about this phase is that there will be little fanfare and probably no new job title. This is the drawback to Saturn's visit; reward doesn't come until the end of the cycle, which is July 2005. No one will dispute that you are a linchpin in a project's success, but there will probably not be much praise for your new duties—not just yet. Display a high level of competence and a good attitude, and you'll make the right impression on higher-ups.

Everything you're doing will add up to something big, and you'll see proof of this starting in November 2005 and throughout 2006, a time that will mark one of the best periods in your entire professional timeline.

FRIENDS AND EVEN CASUAL CONTACTS WILL HELP YOU CLIMB THE LADDER OF SUCCESS; JOIN CLUBS AND CIRCULATE

Pluto rules your tenth house of profession, so with Pluto journeying through your friendship house these days, friends and even casual acquaintances will have a strong bearing on your career progress.

This year, you should consider joining a professional organization or social group, as you have much to gain by rubbing shoulders with new people.

If your birthday falls between February 6 and February 10, you will be doubly blessed by those you know socially in 2004, for Pluto will reach out and touch your Sun to exact mathematical degree.

SPECIAL CAREER DATES TO NOTE IN 2004

Your first date to note is May 4, which is an eclipse, so watch the days surrounding it. Your creativity will be very high. Neptune's position suggests it could be a confusing time, so proceed slowly.

A tough period will be while Mars is in Leo, from June 24 to August 9. At that time, competitors and cranky bosses are going to be quite vocal. Listen quietly to criticism, and if you feel it is relevant, you may want to consider it. This would not be the ideal time to unveil your big idea to the boss. There will be improvements after August 9, but since Mercury will be retrograde through August, you may want to wait until September.

You will need to wrap up a freelance project or special assignment by July 2, a full moon in your sixth house. There is an arduous quality with this full moon, so you will be pumping to get the work out. Saturn will walk arm in arm with the Sun and oppose the Moon, so check for accuracy—it's a hard day. This project may run into overtime before it is signed, sealed, and delivered.

For business victories and career and money success, you can look toward the second half of September for a truly golden time.

There is one sterling career date I would like you to watch, September 26, which comes right in the middle of your glorious financial phase in the second two weeks of September. Mars and Jupiter will touch that day, so you should be able to celebrate something big!

Your very best period for career will extend from November 11 to December 25, thanks to Mars' tour of your tenth house of fame and prestige. This is a four-star trend, so you may want to make note of it.

Best of all, the November 12 new moon in Scorpio also falls in the same house. If you did not change jobs in May, you can certainly find a new job now. This new moon is glorious— all the conditions are right for moving ahead, so schedule interviews in the two weeks after this new moon appears. An exciting offer should result.

Finally, when Venus and Mars embrace in your solar tenth house of career success on December 4-5, expect your reputation to rise considerably. VIPs will be looking upon you very favorably, so it would be a good time for an interview or performance review. If you get invited to a holiday party, you might flirt with a highly placed bigwig. I am not even going to comment on that!

Do You Long to Be Healthy, Slim, and Fit? In 2004 Saturn Will Give You All the Determination You Need

This year you will get much more serious about fitness and your overall health. The sixth house, which is so lit up because of Saturn's visit, rules not only work projects, but also your health.

Saturn will act like your personal trainer, making sure you dump the junk food, get your check-ups, and follow the doctor's orders. At first you may complain about Saturn's insistence that you shape up, but you'll look and feel so terrific that you'll embrace your new program with the fervor of an evangelist.

Be sure to take special care of your teeth, skin, bones, stomach and digestive system. If you or an Aquarian friend or relative has an eating disorder, talk to experts who can help. Female Aquarians should be sure to have a mammogram this year (assuming your doctor agrees) simply as a precaution.

The first house of the horoscope rules vitality and overall stamina and energy, while the sixth house—where Saturn will reside through 2004—rules the preventative steps we take to keep ourselves healthy. If any health concern comes up during this year, it will be because Saturn is trying to help you nip it in the bud.

With your fitness routine, you may find that going to the gym on a daily basis helps you get into the swing of things faster than if you go less frequently. Saturn's presence tells me that setting up a daily routine will get you to where you need to be.

HEALTH AND WEIGHT LOSS: FOLLOW A NEW PLAN ON THE NEW MOON JULY 17 AND YOU'LL SEE RESULTS

At the full moon in Cancer on January 7, you appear to be dragging your feathers. Saturn's position so close to the Moon suggests a heavy workload. Keep your diet high in nutrients, and try to get enough sleep.

If you are involved with tense negotiations at the time of that full moon, Jupiter and Saturn will be in cheery positions, so the outcome should please you. Mercury is retrograde only until January 6, the day before—you can sign documents on January 7 or the days that follow.

When Mars tours your sixth house of health and fitness from May 7 to June 23, you will be extremely energetic. This would be a good time to start a weight-lifting plan, perhaps with a trainer. (Mars rules iron and, therefore, weights.) If you want to get fit and sleek, the new moon on July 17 is your very best moment of the year to get started.

To make your diet and fitness plan work, here is what to do. Start to increase activity on the new moon July 17 or the few days that follow that date. Do not cut calories yet—allow your body to get used to the new level of activity.

Then, just after the full moon plus four days, on August 4, begin to lower the number of calories you consume. Do not cut calories before or on the full moon—wait until after it has waned. If you follow this plan, the results will delight you!

At the full moon on December 26, be sure to guard your health (all full moons have a range of influence of plus or minus of four days). The Moon portends lots of social activity for you, but you won't be able to enjoy yourself if you aren't feeling your best. The aspects to that Moon are mixed, with some draining aspects arriving along with the glittering ones. Pace yourself, dear Aquarius.

YOUR FINANCES WILL LIKELY SOAR IN MID-TO-LATE SEPTEMBER FROM OUTSIDE SOURCES, NOT SALARY

The eighth house of "other people's money" is one of the key features of 2004, a place in your chart where some of your most fabulous luck will arrive. First, ask your boss about increasing your benefits package. With Jupiter showering you with favor, you have a good chance of gaining valuable perks.

The eighth house that will glow so brilliantly also rules money others owe you. If you've been waiting a long time to get paid, you could likely receive at least a partial payment—if not the full amount.

You will even have luck in the area of taxes, also ruled by the eighth house. If you owe more taxes than you can pay, you could work out a suitable payment plan with the government. Or, at next tax time, you may receive a generous refund.

Banks will begin to court you, so if you need a loan, you could most likely get one. Just be careful—Jupiter will make you very optimistic (perhaps overly so), and you may have difficulty paying back that loan later. Ask for the amount you need and no more, just to be sure.

I should add here that any astrological trend represents an extension of the way you have conducted your life in the past. For example, if you are not credit-worthy, you won't enjoy the full affects of this trend in the form of a loan. However, if this is the case, you will have a sterling opportunity to repair your credit. This is where your energies should go. Money will come to you, so use it to pay debt.

Jupiter will be retrograde from January 3 to May 5, so during the first four months of the year this mighty planet will be in a weakened state. That doesn't mean you won't see any financial rewards, only that your rewards will be noticeably stronger later.

Undoubtedly, May through September will be your best financial months of 2004. September 14-21 should be so spectacular that any other moment the year will pale by comparison.

ACT ON THESE DATES
IF YOU NEED A RAISE OR WANT TO SCORE
A FINANCIAL OR BUSINESS VICTORY

Your best moment to ask for a raise will come on the new moon of February 20 and in the two weeks that follow. (Try to stay as close to the beginning of the trend as possible.) Saturn will be beautifully angled to this new moon, so it is evident that your hard work will pay off. You may not expect this raise because the Sun and Moon are both conjunct Uranus, the planet of surprise.

Just two weeks later, on March 6, a full moon will highlight money matters, not only salary but also money that comes to you in other ways. This full moon conjoins Jupiter and is friendly to Mars, so the news should be cause for celebration. This would be a good time to settle a court case, an insurance claim, or to hear back about a mortgage or scholarship. For example, if you schedule the final meeting about a divorce settlement for this day, the resulting agreement should be fair.

The period between August 10 and September 26 may find you negotiating or applying for certain funds. During the August portion of this trend, Mercury will be retrograde, so talks will go slowly. It is likely that you will be looking back to a former offer or situation that you thought you'd missed in August. It would not be a good time to put in a first application or to sign key documents until after September 3.

The August 29 full moon brings unexpected financial developments and brings salary talks to a culmination. The Moon is conjunct Uranus, meaning money matters will be highly unstable. Uranus opposes Mercury, so an unexpected expense could require an instant outlay of cash. Uranus also may temporarily destabilize your home situation. Sit tight. See what happens after the new moon on September 14; it should make you jump for joy!

Your Luckiest Day of the Year Is September 21
Money Luck Rains Down on You

Your luckiest day of the year—and everyone else's—is September 21. Your luck is likely to be financial, and this has to be heartwarming news.

The new moon on September 14 opens up two weeks of sparkling energy in your eighth house of other people's money.

At that time five heavenly bodies will be crowded into your eighth house of finances, making this area very fortunate for you! This is rare—you may have to wait decades to see anything this positive again.

Things should really pop once you reach September 21 (or close to it). On that day, fortunate Jupiter will walk with the Sun, a once-a-year event that always portends great promise!

If you need a mortgage, apply for one a bit earlier (it takes about two months to get an answer from many institutions). You will want to time things so that you hear back between September 14 and 21. If you don't like the answer you receive (and I can't imagine that happening), apply to other banks on, or within days after, September 14.

You could also apply for a scholarship, grant, bank loan, or line of credit; receive a hefty royalty or commission check; or win a settlement, as just a few examples.

On September 28, Mars and Jupiter will be perfectly aligned, and being that Mars is the ruler of your sector of fame, you should be able to score a career victory. You've got the touch!

GET SET FOR BRIGHT TRAVEL AND LEARNING OPPORTUNITIES THANKS TO JUPITER IN LIBRA FOR OVER A YEAR

With Jupiter moving into your ninth house—the house that rules ideas and concepts—your take on life will become more open and playful as you become increasingly interested in the world around you. In particular, you may discover an inclination toward law, medicine, or philosophy.

This area of your chart rules, among other things, publishing and broadcasting. You may be offered a book or magazine contract, or given a chance to appear on TV or radio.

If you have felt boxed in and isolated lately, Jupiter's move into Libra will help you bust out. Travel for pleasure seems assured during the thirteen months Jupiter is here. If obligations necessitate that you remain home, there is also a strong possibility that important people based afar will come to you—if so, these visits seem to hold special significance. If you want to go to college, the cosmos will help you get ahead. Do you need a grant or scholarship to attend college or study overseas? Send in your application at year's end. If you are a university professor, you can now grow in status. Do you need to take a test for certification or admission? Study hard and schedule it for October if at all possible. You should do well.

Jupiter will remain in this glorious position until October 24, 2005, more than a year! Jupiter will move through all degrees of Libra, but in 2004 it will move through approximately half the sign. This means that the Aquarians who will benefit most from Jupiter this year are those who were born from January 20 to February 2, although all Aquarians will feel the benefits of Jupiter immediately.

The October 14 eclipse will also bring a plethora of planets together in Libra, and all of them will be beaming fantastic opportunities to *all* Aquarians. This eclipse will affect all the areas we have been talking about. If you were born on or within five days of February 9, you will benefit from this eclipse quite significantly.

FOREIGN OR DISTANT TRAVEL
BLOSSOMS REMARKABLY IN OCTOBER
SHORTER TRIPS POSSIBLE IN JANUARY, MARCH, APRIL

This is going to be your year to travel, dear Aquarius. In addition to your financial luck, which is due in September, travel or study abroad could turn out to be the most dazzling development of the year.

With two merry eclipses in Aries and Libra (different from the ones discussed earlier in regard to your career), plus the appearance of Jupiter in Libra, set to arrive in your ninth house of international and distant travel in late September, things won't be dull! The year starts off with a bang—feisty Mars enters your short-distance travel sector just prior to the start of 2004. (Mars arrives there on December 16, 2003, in time to make your year-end holidays festive.) Mars will remain in your third house of short trips until February 3, 2004, giving you many opportunities to take a weekend breather for a nice change of pace. A business trip taken during this period would likely go well, too.

How about taking a trip to celebrate the first day of spring? March 20 brings a lovely new moon in your house of travel, perfect for a getaway in the two weeks that follow. This is a perfect time for a business initiative—this new moon is zero degrees Aries, which is so special it is called "the Aries point," and is considered highly energetic for all entrepreneurial efforts.

On April 5, a full moon, you may be returning from a long trip or leaving for one. This lovely lunar event has a plethora of good aspects associated with it.

The following month, on April 19, the year's first eclipse, there is more indication that you may travel short distances from this point on all year. After that, look forward to September 28, a full moon in Aries lighting up your third house of short travel. The Sun will be conjunct Jupiter and Mars, so this would be a superb time for another short trip, for business or pleasure. If you anticipate the need to sign a document, this full moon period (plus or minus four days) would be ideal.

Mars will begin perking up your travel house from September 26 to November 11, making this entire seven-week period critically important for relationships with foreigners or for distant travel. Within this period, the best date of the year—and possibly the decade—will fall on the year's other new moon solar eclipse, October 13, and continue for two weeks. At that time, Jupiter will be in your ninth house of travel, and relationships with foreigners will bloom. On October 17, Mercury will be in rare, harmonious angle to Uranus—Mercury rules travel and Uranus rules Aquarius.

With many planets crowded into your ninth house of long-distance travel in October, all in fellow air signs like yours, you will be walking on air! Try to travel for pleasure, but if you can't, go for business. Either would be ideal!

Do You Need to Move or Renovate? Wait Until October Before You Decide

With one of the year's biggest eclipses due on October 28 and set to fall in your house of home, you may want to wait until year's end before making any big decisions, as eclipses always bring up unanticipated factors.

However, if you want to move sooner, look for options from February 3 to March 21, as Mars will see that you will find something good. During this period—from February 8 to

March 5—Venus and Mars will be in mutual reception, which is the best part of this period, so try extra-hard to look at houses or apartments then. It's also an ideal time to redecorate or renovate.

If nothing comes up then, you may find some excellent options at the new moon May 19 and in the two weeks that follow.

ROMANCE GETS BETTER FOR ALL AQUARIANS

Your romantic options will be far improved from last year. Last year you finally said goodbye to Saturn, the planet that was setting up obstacles in matters of the heart.

Attached Aquarians had some radiant vibrations from Jupiter in the house of partnership, which may have translated into marriage or a serious commitment. August 2002 to August 2003 was one of the best periods of the decade to get engaged or married.

If you have children, you probably found parenting hard, and for that, you again have Saturn to blame. Money may have been tight, or you may have had precious little time (or both). Readers with older children may have found it surprisingly difficult to relate to a teen. If you remarried and children were involved, you may have run into problems that proved to be much more of a learning experience for you than for the children. Whatever the cause, you should find that being a mom or dad is much more fun this year—and being a mate should be, too!

Venus Will Retrograde from May 17 to June 29: Cupid Takes a Rest While You Stop, Look, and Listen

In 2004, Venus will retrograde in Gemini, ruling your fifth house of true love, so this year's out-of-phase Venus will be felt more than most times. (Venus goes into napping mode every two years in different signs.)

With Venus retrograde, each meeting appears to reopen old issues or wounds. It may be hard for you to separate from a partner, so there are repeated meetings and partings. Each time you come together, however, it becomes clearer that this relationship is not working, and although you know this to be true intellectually, you finally begin to understand this emotionally. This appears to be a necessary part in the process of letting go. Although this period seems to demand much from you, when you are done with this emotional work at the end of June, you will feel relieved.

On a more mundane level, Venus retrograde would not be a good time to schedule an important hair cut (even for male readers!). It is not a time to spend a great deal of money on clothes or jewelry, either, as Venus also rules beauty and adornment. If you are planning an important party, do so after Venus goes direct on June 29. Try not to marry during this time—you want a good, strong Venus for your nuptials. Also, if you plan elective plastic surgery, it would be best done when Venus is not retrograde.

Your Best Dates for Fun and Love in 2004

The first date to circle on your calendar is the new moon in Aquarius, which will occur on January 21, a Wednesday, but its influence also covers the following weekend. That new moon will appear close to romantic Neptune, and Venus will cuddle up to Uranus, your ruler. If your friends want to make introductions, let them!

The full moon in your relationship house on February 6 will bring a relationship to full boil, which may be good or bad, depending on how you look at it. Neptune may confuse an issue.

March 21 through May 6 will be one of your most sparkling extended periods for love, with Mars lighting up your house of true love at this time. If you are single and hope to meet someone new, luck will be on your side. A quick, short-distance vacation would be a great idea, especially on or near March 21. Mercury, the ruler of your solar fifth house of true love, will be positioned in your third house of short-distance trips. Why not celebrate the first day of spring?

Mars and Venus will be very close in the sky near April 7–17. Although these two cosmic lovers aren't making an exact alignment, they will be close enough. Whenever these two planets are together, they set off the sparks of true love, so you may meet someone at that time. You need not even travel to meet someone—just be out and about.

A major eclipse falls in the area of your chart ruling career gains on May 4, so if possible don't be on a vacation or business trip at that time. Too much will be going on at the office. Rather than take a vacation, you will find prospects for love right in your own city.

On June 17, the new moon is in your house of romance. Four planets in your house of true love make this date a standout, but the outlook is mixed. Venus and

Neptune are beautifully interactive—romance should be divine, almost dreamlike. Venus is still retrograde, so you may reconnect with an old love. The troublesome aspect involves Venus and Uranus in harsh angle—an off-the-cuff comment could trigger a spat!

Mars will be in Leo from June 23 to August 10, and may mark the only tough time for your closest relationship. Your partner may be more skeptical of your ideas and less willing to let you have things your way. If your partner has harbored any complaints, you will hear about them. Compromise and reflection would be your best course during those few weeks, and would clear a path for deeper honesty between you.

September 28, when Mercury and Jupiter conjoin, rates four stars in my book. It's a full moon in compatible Aries in your house of travel, so you may be getting set for a highly anticipated trip.

By this point—the end of September—Jupiter has moved into Libra, so your best part of the year will have begun.

Jupiter and Neptune in Aquarius beam golden, shimmering rays on November 29, which gets my vote for Best Romantic Day of 2004. It falls close to another stunning day, November 26, a full moon in your house of love. Give November 29 a full five days plus or minus the date, for this will be a truly outstandingly romantic time.

On December 11, the new moon in your eleventh house of hopes and wishes will bring you in closer contact with friends, fun, and festivities. With four heavenly bodies in this house, you can't fail. An interesting new person may enter your life through a friend's introduction.

December 26, 2004, through February 6, 2005, finds Mars in this same house of friendship. The year ends with many close pals around you, and possibly a special some-one, too. It looks like you've got a date for New Year's Eve. Happy New Year!

Summary

Now that your ruling planet, Uranus, has permanently departed from the constellation of Aquarius (which it did on December 30, 2003—not to return for eighty-four years), life will start to feel very different for you, dear Aquarius.

Uranus has moved into your solar second house of earned income, meaning you will finally see a financial reward for your experience and hard work. This is a brand-new influence. You have not hosted unpredictable Uranus in your second house so far in your lifetime, as the last time it did so was from 1919 to 1927. You will still have to be conservative about money, but the difference is that in 2004, there is an excellent chance that a solid amount of money will come your way, thanks to a generous Jupiter cycle that will be in place during the first nine months of 2004.

This financial cycle will reach a peak in mid-to-late September. The money will stem from sources outside your usual income, and most likely will arrive as one large chunk. As you get closer to October, when Jupiter moves into your ninth house, you will see enormous benefits from long-distance travel and international interests abroad. This same house rules publishing, legal matters, and pursuits for higher education—all these areas that will glow for you, too. The ninth house is an intellectual one, and with an expansive, growth-inducing planet like Jupiter in this house, you are about to open your mind to the world in a brand-new way. It is a time to set new goals and to let limiting assumptions fall away.

Two of the biggest areas of change in 2004 will be with your career and your living situation, because eclipses on May 4 and October 28 will bring new conditions and require a few sudden adjustments. If you need to move, there will be many opportunities throughout the year to do so, although the best will occur in (you guessed it) October and November.

With changes due on your job in May, you may be seeking new employment. Your most exciting job opportunities will arrive in November and December 2004.

In matters of health, Saturn can help you set up a fitness routine that could prove to be enjoyable enough to make a permanent part of your lifestyle. When Jupiter enters Libra you will feel rejuvenation, and that will continue a full year. If elective surgery is on your list, wait until the later part of the year if possible, for you will be feeling most robust at that time.

Travel should be a glorious, happy option this year, and this trend will continue straight into 2005. You could travel near or far—either would bring refreshment and enlightenment. The solar eclipses on April 19 and October 14 may bring a good reason to pack your bags and go.

Romantically, Saturn has finally departed from your true love sector. If you are single, over the past two to three years, you may have found that everyone you met seemed to be preoccupied, and you probably felt relegated to second place in your sweetheart's life. You can now look forward to a far more positive, bright future.

If you are married or attached, life's obligations may have weighed heavily on you, and it was hard to enjoy yourself with your mate. Life was so no-frills for so long that you began to wonder if you would ever see a change. You will, and it will occur this year.

If your relationship is valuable to you, you will need to clear the air on some old issues. By the fall and winter months, your outlook will be quite optimistic. Your love life should be quite wonderful, and it should continue straight into 2005. Your most festive month of 2004 will be December, because by then you will have a whole crowd of planets in your fun sector.

The last three months of the year will be your best on so many levels: romantically, professionally, physically, and even financially. Dear Aquarius, you have so much to look forward to in 2004! What will make the year ahead special is your new attitude—you will have a bigger gusto for living—that spirit will be positively contagious. Are you are excited about 2004 yet? You should be!

Pisces

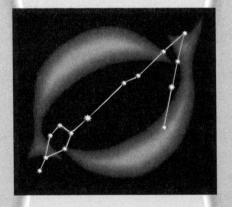

February 19-March 20

The Big Picture

The past three years have certainly been a workout for you, dear Pisces. You had to step up to the plate and meet some fairly daunting challenges on several fronts—home and family, career and money, and close relationships. The planets have finally moved from the difficult spots they occupied during those years, releasing you from the limitations they imposed. You learned a great deal, and armed with that knowledge, you will be able to handle almost anything life throws your way. 2004 brings a brand-new day, and it's brighter than any you've seen in ages.

One of the biggest trends that will affect you in 2004 actually began in 2003 with the arrival of Uranus into Pisces. Uranus will stay in your sign for seven years, so this is significant. Experiencing Uranus on your Sun—as you are now—is like having a permanent buzz. Uranus can help create plenty of change and excitement in your life, as well as a plethora of innovative ideas. Uranus has the power to revolutionize your life from the inside out.

Your personality will take on a new depth and luster, and you'll like the changes that are taking place. Uranus, the planet of individuality, independence, and creativity, will open doors that you never thought possible. You may challenge the status quo or pioneer into uncharted territory, at Uranus' behest. Unusual opportunities will suddenly appear, but it will be up to you to make them happen—you will need to stay on your toes, dear Pisces. Chances are, you will—these offers are too juicy to pass up!

You have never hosted Uranus in your solar first house of personality, as it takes eighty-four years for Uranus to revolve around the Sun and the zodiac. The last time Uranus was in Pisces was 1919 to 1927. This is a once-in-a-lifetime astrological event that some people never get to experience. You are so fortunate to be able to enjoy the fruits of this planet's transit!

Uranus in Pisces will put you front and center and will help you develop your talents on a level you may have never imagined. Uranus is often associated with cultural shifts, so you could play a leading role in the public's changing tastes, whether through the media or through fashion, books, politics, products, dance, or music that you create. Pisces has a sixth sense about what people want next, and you will prove to be uncannily on-target.

Uranus can also bring sudden setbacks, so be pre-pared. It may be helpful to recall that with this planet, things can go either way. When everything does go hay-wire, it probably won't stay that way for long. You can still score a stunning turnaround that can put you back on top, so keep the faith!

Uranus in the solar first house affects everything you do, from your personal life to business matters. Don't let the erratic quality of Uranus ruffle you—go with the flow. It would be pointless to try to fight it—this trend is bigger than the both of us! Never forget that there is enormous cosmic clout behind you.

You wouldn't have been ready to manage energy this powerful without grounding from Saturn. Over the past few years, Saturn toughened you up while it was in Gemini, demonstrating that you were capable of handling more responsibility than you'd thought. This year Saturn will be in an ideal angle to your Sun, so you will easily assimilate Saturn's teachings this year.

Neptune, your ruler, will help you make any necessary transitions this year because it will be in "mutual reception" with Uranus. This means Neptune will be in the sign Uranus rules—Aquarius—at precisely the same time that Uranus will be in the sign that Neptune rules, Pisces. Remarkably, this exceedingly rare configuration will remain until 2011!

Neptune will be a position to boost your creativity—in fact, at times you will outdo yourself! For proof, note November 29, when Jupiter will come calling on Neptune. This will be a four-star date—you could profit enormously from something you develop from scratch.

If you've ever felt invisible—all Pisces do from time to time—that will change with Neptune and Uranus working so closely together. You will be conscious of your growing career status, and your confidence will grow as a result. Even if you felt a little uncomfortable accepting others' compliments (a common Pisces complaint), you will start to enjoy the respect and admiration that others have for you. You have a habit of concentrating so hard on your various projects—Pisces always has several going at one time—or on helping others that you often lose track of your own needs. Those days will soon be over!

Jupiter's position in Virgo this year can help you strengthen both your romantic and business relationships. In fact, your relationships have never had a better chance of success than in 2004.

To understand how Jupiter can help you, you need to know that the seventh house, where Jupiter will spend most of its time, rules all serious, committed relationships that are contract-based. (Marriage is a contract-based institution.) Relationships formed in the seventh house have weight and purpose, and are formed for mutual benefit. There are implied and explicit promises on both sides, which adds to a sense of security for both parties.

You will be anxious to move your closest relationship to the next level, no matter where it happens to be. If you want more, you can have more, since Jupiter often makes relationships grow quickly. For some, this might mean it's time to get married; for others, it may simply mean a decision to date exclusively. In business, this may mean signing a partner to help you expand your base. Anyone with whom you align yourself while Jupiter is in Virgo will likely meet or even exceed your greatest expectations, so start looking immediately! You will have until September 25. When Jupiter leaves it will not be back to this part of your chart for another twelve years. Your most divine time for a wedding will fall between September 14 and September 21.

If you are single and are tired of dating unsuitable people, you'll finally find a number of suitable partners. No Pisces will be left out! September should be your best month to marry or sign a new business partner. The first weekend of December should be enchanting, and if you meet someone new, the sparks of love should be practically visible!

Jupiter will be retrograde during the first four months of 2004, so if you don't see any progress in partnerships during that time, be patient. Jupiter's power will grow stronger once May arrives.

Your chart suggests that in 2003, you were the engine that drove everything in your life. You had ultimate control, and those around you may have been surprised by your intense sense of purpose and courage to try new ventures. The downside of this trend was that you had to achieve much of it alone. Only when Jupiter entered Virgo in late August 2003 did that situation change—help was on the way, and still is.

Jupiter's position through September shows that your very best opportunities will come via the efforts of your partners, so you should trust them enough to let go and let them work their magic for you. If you choose a partner during this very fertile time, you will forge a relationship that could last many years, or even the rest of your life. If you are already married, your spouse should do very well this year, and you will benefit.

Saturn's position this year will only enhance Jupiter's message, which is that you will soon adopt a serious attitude toward all your relationships, but particularly your personal ones. Saturn's contribution is also to make you more conscious of time. With Saturn in your solar fifth house (ruling true love, children, and creativity), you will be very aware of the need to make time count by spending it with people who share the same goals you do.

With Saturn moving into your fifth house of love, this planet will give you a serious approach to matters of love and romance. If you are single, you won't want to date someone for the fun of it—you want things to lead logically from first date to courtship to marriage and children. If you feel that this is not likely to happen, you will break up quickly, rather than hang on and hope things will get better. Some Pisces women will have a baby this year for the same reason—to make time count. Some women may feel, psychologically, that their time to do so is getting short.

Saturn's energy could manifest itself by strengthening your creativity. Saturn in the fifth house will give you a more a disciplined, careful approach to your craft. All creative endeavors require an intense focus—talent needs to be honed. Saturn will allow you to screen out distractions and give creative projects first priority.

If you don't work in a creative field, and if you have no hobbies, your flair for thinking along new and more innovative lines will still come out. Creativity can come in any form, from any source, for creativity is fanned as much by the heart, as attitude and intention, as it is by having talent. No matter what your profession happens to be, you will find a way to put your stamp of individuality on everything you touch. Of course you will—you are a Pisces!

This brings us to the question of finances, and although it is not like you to say "Show me the money!" you may be wondering about it. Like Aquarius, you are not a material-istic sign and would never put money ahead of creativity— the concept will always remain king for you, dear Pisces, as it should. The answer is that there will be a very powerful emphasis on money in the coming year, and all the influences are positive.

There are four eclipses this year, cosmic harbingers of change. Two will fall in different money sectors, the second and eighth houses, and are set to arrive, respec-tively on April 19 and October 14. Both eclipses should bring an immediate lift to your bank account. Being that there is a link between your creative house and your house of earned income this year, the time near these eclipses could bring sudden upbeat opportunities. Why? These are lunar eclipses, and the moon rules your fifth house of self-expression.

Eclipses usually ask us to give up one thing to gain some-thing else, so that may be part of the plan, but these two eclipses should bring good financial news, if not immediately, then within weeks of their appearance.

Adding to this bright picture is the presence of two new moons in your house of salary! This is very unusual. One will come in the form of the eclipse noted above on April 19, but there is one prior to that, on March 20, that will be quite energetic. Both new moons are in Aries, the sign considered to be the apotheosis of entrepreneurial efforts.

Once Jupiter moves into Libra in late September, you will begin to see even more money. Jupiter will remain in your eighth house of other people's money for a full year.

It's important to note that the area that Jupiter will light up is not the one usually connected with salary, but rather the eighth house. This house is associated with commissions, royalties, licensing fees, grants, taxes and rebates, bonuses, prize winnings, sponsorship, venture capital, inheritance, insurance payouts, divorce settlements, credit and loans, mortgages, court judgments, and so forth. This house is called the house of joint resources, so a "partner" (it could be a bank or someone you know, for example) could help generate this cash. This money appears to come in chunks rather than in a stream. There is a direct link between your house of career success and this house, so you could generate this money, rather than win it or have it given to you. Mid-October should astound you, for this money should be quite a bounty.

We talked about two of the four eclipses. The other two, both full moon lunar eclipses, will highlight both long and short-distance travel, as well as academic pursuits, both as student or teacher, and relationships with certain relatives (such as a sister, brother, cousin, aunt, uncle, or mother-in-law). These eclipses will fall on May 4 and October 28 and should be very refreshing and mind expanding.

These areas of your chart being affected are the third and ninth houses, which also cover contracts, publishing projects, and the legal system. In these areas something is coming to culmination or fullness. For example, your sister may announce she's getting married, or your aunt may say she's finally sold her house. The contract you've been expecting to sign may show up, or the book you worked so hard on may be published. These are intellectual houses that deal with the dissemination of information, travel, commerce, and legal agreements, so you should sail through them fairly easily.

Details of Your Year Ahead

PISCES WITH BIRTHDAYS FEBRUARY 18–26 TO FEEL EFFECTS OF URANUS IN 2004

Uranus' position encourages you to take yourself and your creative energies seriously. A project you believe in or are taking a hand in creating could have astoundingly strong mass appeal. Pisces always wants to help others, and you may do this through your artistic creations or directions, through writing, directing others, or by producing products or concepts.

You need not work in a traditionally "creative" area to take full advantage of Uranus in Pisces. You can make a difference to others through business efforts, social work, or work with a school, college, or charitable organization. You may do this through a current job or a new one, a business you start, or a voluntary position you accept. It really doesn't matter how you do it—only that you do.

You may also notice that you are more intuitive under this trend, as Uranus will raise your antenna to a higher level. At times you may pick up signals that you don't immediately understand. Take time to mull over them; you are being given the tools you need to navigate new waters.

Not only will Uranus help you reassess your point of view, it may coax you to give your looks a complete makeover. You may change your hairstyle or start to wear more fashionable clothing or even lose a great deal of weight. Uranus is the planet that modernizes everything it touches, including you! You may even decide to change your name, even if you don't marry (a pen name, perhaps, or a nickname?).

Never again in your life will you have a seven-year period so vitally important to your personal growth and development. It will seem that everything you ever learned or ever fantasized about is coming to fruition and catapulting you into a new realm. The opportunities that come your way will happen because you were at the right place at the right time—so much so that you might feel like it was fate.

Pisces born from February 19-26 were the first to feel Uranus' influence last year, and if your birthday is listed here, you will again be highlighted in 2004. You could radically change your lifestyle, and perhaps it will be something that you've always dreamed of doing. You may move cross-country, start a humanitarian organization, or develop a creative idea that quickly catches fire with the public, Whatever it may be, your past is receding into history—look to the future!

All Pisces will eventually feel Uranus' influence as it orbits into alignment with their Sun.

Pisces born March 1 will feel this trend more strongly in 2005. Those born March 7 will feel Uranus most powerfully in 2007. If you were born on March 19, at the very end of the sign, your main experience with Uranus will come in 2010 and 2011.

No matter what your birthday, you will feel tremors this year, because when a planet as massive as Uranus shows up in a certain neighborhood of the sky, the locals can't help but notice. Even if you are a late-born Pisces, you will start to see signs that Uranus is getting near, and enjoy all the upbeat changes we have been discussing.

If nothing else, remember this: the years when Uranus tours Pisces will be your best years for fulfilling those dearest dreams. Don't let this opportunity slip through your fingers!

SATURN IN CANCER THROUGH JULY 2005 BRINGS MATURITY

One Pisces I spoke to recently, Karen, gave a little sigh when she heard Saturn would spend all year in her solar fifth house of true love. "Oh, no," she said wearily. "I don't want Saturn anywhere in my chart, and I certainly don't want Saturn in my house of true love!" (The fifth house, which rules creativity, also rules romance, pregnancy, and children.) Nonetheless, Karen need not worry—this is not a difficult trend, and compared to having Saturn in your house of home and family relationships (which you just had), this one should be easier. That's not because your home is more important than your love life, but because of where that house fell on the wheel—at the very base, Saturn acted in a more forceful manner.

Saturn is the planet of serious commitments and responsibilities, and it generally provokes enormous personal growth in whichever house it visits. Nothing is given quickly or easily; this taskmaster planet will test your resolve and commitment. In the end, Saturn delivers insights that will remain with you forever.

For example, if you fall in love, you may have to deal with some sort of enforced separation. This separation may have to do with outside circumstances that can't be changed.

If you are single and dating, after a certain time, you will want assurances that the relationship has a chance for a proper future, perhaps one that will lead to commitment. If you sense that your romantic companion is not capable of even one of these steps, you are more likely to break off the relationship to pursue other attachments. This probably marks a new attitude for you, for Pisces is a patient and ultimately forgiving sign.

If you do find someone who interests you, there may a large age difference—but that won't matter (nor should it). Another possibility is that your new love interest lives in another city—again, that shouldn't be a problem. However, do be careful to ascertain whether your new partner is truly available—this person may be still married. Be circumspect and ask plenty of questions.

If you are attached, you will focus on children and may feel ready to start a family, as Saturn brings maturity. When I had your aspects, I had my first baby. Or you may decide to delay having a baby (Saturn often brings delays). If so, you would likely move forward after July 2005. Occasionally a medical problem concerning conception surfaces—a much rarer situation—but it usually can be helped with a medical specialist.

If you are adopting a baby, be prepared for plenty of paperwork—Saturn tends to be the king of red tape. That should not deter you.

If you have a baby, he or she may arrive when money is a bit scarce, so nights out with your mate may need to be planned and apportioned more carefully. Almost everyone goes through this at some time or another, but again, most people feel having a baby is such a blessing that some sacrifices are not a hardship. Remember, this would be a very temporary situation. Saturn often demands sacrifice so that you appreciate what you have all the more.

If you plan to remarry, take special care with the feelings of any children from a previous marriage (yours or your future spouse's), as they may be harboring fears or resentments that could cause problems later. Alternatively, if you are not getting along with your teenage child, Saturn's position suggests that it's you—not your child—that needs to find a new approach toward better communication, as this planet's place in a chart indicates where we will find our biggest learning experience.

We talked about how you may also begin to bring greater care and focus to your creative projects. Saturn's job is to derive tangible, successful results from intense concentration, and you seem to have that now, in spades.

Saturn almost always involves a major rite of passage, and this year, your maturity will come through your relationships with a lover, a spouse, or your children or through creating something of value. Your personal experience may be as simple as learning to be a mother or father when a first baby arrives, or learning what's involved in creating a first-class portfolio of photographs to show perspective clients. There is no reason to fear! Life is a learning process, and with each phase, we earn another star on our lapel.

This year, Saturn will support those Pisces born February 25 to March 17, but all Pisces will benefit in some way. Also, with Saturn in a water sign, you couldn't have a stronger supporter than Saturn!

2004 COULD BE YOUR BEST YEAR IN A DECADE TO WED

Your relationships will take a giant step forward this year. You are starting to view relationships not in terms of what they are now, but what they can be. This approach will allow your alliances to grow to the fullest. You have a sense of purpose this year, and you feel that with one person in particular you could conquer the world. As mentioned earlier, Jupiter, the great benefic planet, is visiting your seventh house of marriage and other close relationships.

In astrology, the fifth house governs true love and romance. It is where Cupid first shoots his arrow of love, and the house that we talked about earlier in regard to Saturn. However, once love begins to blossom, it becomes a seventh-house matter, for that is where marriage and other contractual relationships take place.

2004 is quite simply the best year in over a decade to marry—that is, until September 25, when Jupiter leaves to brighten another part of your chart. As you will see in the dates listed below, September will be positively bewitching for you. If you have no one in mind to marry, September may be when you decide to sign a joint-venture agreement or hire a publicist or agent. Whomever you align with this year, in mid-September in particular, will be a gem.

If you are already married, you will begin to gain substantially from your partner. Your other half is about to get a number of lucky breaks, and you will benefit as a result. If you are single, you will find someone of value to date. If you are dating seriously, you will crave greater stability, and for most people, that means engagement or marriage. Oddly, last year you were the dominant partner, but this year the roles reverse, and your partner appears to be the one who is pushing things forward. You may enjoy the change!

After Jupiter arrives in your seventh house, your interactions with others will be easier. That may be because your partners will be less tense, or perhaps you'll decide to switch partners and will find the going much smoother. You will sense a greater unity between you and your partner, which will ignite your spirit.

The seventh house describes not only your partner, but also how the outside world perceives you. With Jupiter there, you will be seen as optimistic and successful, which will give you certain magnetism.

If you have the kind of job where you could benefit from the help of a middleman, you should seriously think about signing such a person before Jupiter leaves this very positive position. You will do far better with an agent or representative than by yourself. Believe me, there will be times when you should represent yourself, but this is not one of them. Jupiter rules your tenth house of fame, and with this planet visiting your house of partnership, most of your status could be a result of the efforts of that special new partner.

If you choose to hire a doctor, lawyer, or other professional person, the one you find will protect your interests. If you are the agent or representative, you will attract superb talent this year.

Last but not least, if you are starting a business, you may want to take on a partner, for that person will add the missing element you need.

VENUS WILL RETROGRADE
FROM MAY 17 TO JUNE 29:
GIVE LOVE, FUN, BEAUTY, AND SHOPPING A REST

Venus rules love, romance, beauty, adornment, pleasure, and certain financial matters.

When Venus retrogrades, which it will do this year from May 17 through June 29, it is not a good time to buy expensive jewelry, clothes, or indulge in spa or salon treatments. Also, since Venus rules beauty, it would not be the right time to schedule plastic surgery.

Venus retrogrades for only a short time every two years, and is not due to go into another slumber until December 24, 2005.

If you are planning an important party, do so after Venus goes direct on June 29. Try not to marry during Venus retrograde—you want a strong Venus for that.

DAYS TO FALL IN LOVE, GET MARRIED, HAVE FUN!

January 7: The full moon is in your house of true love. Even though this day has a couple of aspects that might detract, it still gets a thumbs up. Jupiter is in your house of marriage and in perfect angle to the Sun, making this a winner. Saturn is close to the Moon, so promises made are promises kept. Give this full moon a range of plus or minus four days. Perfect for an engagement or marriage.

January 14–February 7: Venus glides in Pisces and your charisma is elevated. In mid-January, Uranus orbits close; love is surprising and fun.

February 20: The new moon is in Pisces, and your personal powers are at an all-time high. You are magnetic and irresistible. This date will initiate two weeks of energy. If you are single, circulate now.

March 6: This date brings a full moon in your wedding/commitment sector. With Jupiter giving a kiss to the Moon, this day rates four stars. This day also has a range of plus or minus four days.

May 7–June 23: Mars will tour your fifth house of true love, always an occasion you can count on for fun. Attached? Plan a vacation for two and revisit a spot you both used to love but haven't seen in some time. Single? Venus will be retrograde, so you may consider reconciliation with a former lover. However, this is not a time to wed.

July 17: This date initiates two weeks of golden energy thanks to the new moon in your fifth house. With the Sun and Moon conjunct Saturn, if you want stability and roots, you will get it. There could be a romance with an older person. Jupiter and Saturn are magically aligned, and even better, glamorous Neptune will be in perfect angle to Venus—this new moon rates four stars.

September 14–28: A magical four-star period, especially for an engagement or a wedding. All Pisces will benefit. See below.

December 4–5: A fabulous weekend when Venus and her lover Mars will embrace in your house of long-distance travel, so it's perfect for a long trip. This is the first and only time these planets will meet in two years. They will rendezvous in the sexy, compatible sign Scorpio. It's a four-star weekend!

December 26: This is a full moon in your eleventh house of friends and festivities, so this should be a social high spot at a time when your career is also flying. Give this date plus or minus four days.

Your Luckiest Day of the Year
Is September 21

Your luckiest day of the year—and everyone else's—will be September 21. Your luck will have to do with the magical part of your chart that we have been discussing: partnerships and marriage.

Everything starts with the new moon September 14. That new moon will open up two weeks of sparkling energy in your seventh house of committed partnerships and marriage. You can choose any day during the following two weeks. With five heavenly bodies in your house of partnership, if you have the urge to merge, there's no reason not to say "I do."

Things should really start to pop once you reach September 21 (or close to it). On that day, fortunate Jupiter will walk with the Sun, a once-a-year event that always portends happiness for committed love (or a solid business contract).

The New Moon June 17
May Be Your Best Time to Move,
Buy, or Sell a House

If you need to move, make repairs, or schedule a renovation, or if you want to buy, sell, or lease real estate or even change roommates, the following are your best dates to do so. Keep in mind that you can also make little changes at these times—such as buying new placemats and plants or painting your living room.

Your longest and most sustained period to find home-related options will be when Mars visits your fourth house of home from March 21 to May 6.

Within that period, from April 6 to April 30, Mercury will be retrograde, so don't sign any documents then—things will be in flux. If you do, you may regret making the deal later. You can go back to an earlier situation, which would work out well. For example, you submitted a bid for a house some time ago but were disappointed to hear that it was rejected. Now the owners of that house may invite you to make another bid. You may win the bid, and it may be at a price you like.

A Mercury retrograde period is also an ideal time to make repairs or paint. If you ask a contractor to do repairs or a renovation, get all estimates in writing, as Mercury retrograde may push some costs over budget—have a procedure in place if costs do climb.

Your next and best opportunity will come on the new moon on June 17. All new moons bring two weeks of energy, so you will have an ideal time to settle domestic projects. With Venus in this house, along with Mercury, the Sun, and Moon, it's an ideal time to give a party or barbeque at home.

Your parents also come under the fourth house, so perhaps your mom or dad will need your help. Many people are the prime caretakers for their parents, and knowing when you'll need to be "on call" is helpful.

Mercury, the planet that rules your house of home, will walk with benefic Jupiter on September 28. On this day you may see a generous profit from the sale or lease of property you own, or you may acquire a lovely piece of furniture—something you always wanted! Mercury will also be in good angle to Jupiter on June 25 and November 11.

December 26 brings a positive full moon in Gemini, and also falls in your house of home. Your place will be brimming with people at this time, and the atmosphere will be quite festive. In case you thought you were going to your sister's house for the holidays, think again—it looks like the gang's coming to you. Something is making your home—or family—the center of activity. Enjoy it!

WOULD YOU LIKE TO LOSE WEIGHT? BEGIN ON THESE DATES!

You have just come through a terrific year, in which Jupiter gave you a sterling opportunity to get healthier than you've been in years. If you took advantage of this opportunity you are entering 2004 in top shape. If that's not the case, you can always start now, as every day offers a fresh start.

Many people want to lose weight, but find that year after year their new year's resolution never works. Why not begin your program when there is a better chance of success? I have outlined your best dates to begin and will also introduce you to the astrological concept of weight reduction.

One should always begin a diet after the full moon. When I first read that advice, I was skeptical. Would it mean that I would lose only water weight? The answer turned out to be a resounding no. Try it and see for yourself, as I did. The weight you lose will stay off.

There is a full moon on February 6 in your sixth house of health. Begin your diet on this date, but only if you feel well and you have a doctor's blessing.

Here is the plan. Begin your sensible diet approximately four days after the full moon, which would make February 10 the start date.

Usually I tell my readers to begin exercising first; however, in your case, based on your chart, I will reverse that advice. On the new moon in Pisces, February 20, you can begin getting more active. However, a plan that doesn't combine exercise with a sensible diet won't work, so be sure to do both.

By the time you get to mid-year, you may be able to step up your sports or exercise program. One of your very best extended periods of the year will be from June 23 to August 9.

During this time, when Mars is visiting your sixth house, you will have energy to burn and a renewed enthusiasm for improving your health and fitness.

If you did not begin your exercise and diet routine earlier in the year, you will have a second chance on the new moon on August 15.

If you begin on August 15, you should get active first. Be careful not to overdo it, as Mars will oppose Uranus, and you could strain a muscle if you get overly enthusiastic.

Don't begin to cut back on calories until four days after the full moon, which will fall on August 29. Begin your diet on September 2. In short, first, get active for two weeks, and then begin your sensible diet.

If you follow that advice, you should be looking terrific by New Year's Eve! How much better to be celebrating your new look on New Year's Eve than to be making resolutions that never work! You'll feel in control and will look terrific. Enjoy!

JUPITER TO EXPAND YOUR FINANCIAL LUCK
SEPTEMBER 24, 2004, TO OCTOBER 25, 2005

You have worked for years toward a brighter financial future, but in some ways, the money has eluded you. No longer. Once Jupiter, the planet known to bring goodies to whatever house it visits, enters the eighth house, you should feel richer fairly soon. Jupiter has not been in this house for twelve years (and when it leaves on October 25, 2005, it won't be back for another twelve years), so this is something special.

We discussed earlier that the money that Jupiter will bring would not likely be money found in a paycheck, but money that arrives in other ways. It may come as a bonus, commission check, royalty, licensing fee, loan, prize, mortgage, scholarship, divorce settlement, grant, court settlement, insurance payout, tax rebate or refund, inheritance, child support, alimony, severance, or any other money that comes to you in ways outside of your normal earnings. However, Jupiter is also the planet that rules your tenth house of professional success, so I feel that this money is somehow connected to your efforts.

When aspects are this glittering you can afford to take some small risks. For example, if you regularly bid on jobs and your intuition tells you to bid a little higher than your competition, do so. The low bid does not always win. You will have to make your case for your ability to supply superior quality or better service, but if anyone can do it, it's you.

If you work on a freelance basis or as a consultant for clients, you should have no problem generating business. You may receive a very generous cash gift or be awarded quite a bit of money in a court settlement, workmen's compensation case, or insurance payout.

As soon as this cycle starts, if you are interviewing for a job and can't get the salary you want—or even if you can—try to negotiate for a better benefits package. Some companies offer different benefits to different employees. You can also try for a performance-based year-end bonus, or if you are in sales and are confident in your abilities, you can work on a straight commission rather than salary plus commission—don't worry, you'll come out ahead!

This glowing eighth house also rules money others owe you. If you have been waiting to be paid by a delinquent client, that money may arrive. If your ex-spouse has not sent child support, you may see those checks now. Contests are lucky—start sending those postcards in when you hear of a sweepstakes, and apply to be a contestant on TV.

Banks should be more willing to approve you if you apply for a loan. Of course, you have to be creditworthy, but if you have maintained a good credit history, you will benefit now.

If you were thinking of refinancing your mortgage, the time after September 25 might be ideal—check into interest rates. You might also do well with defaulted real estate that is being sold at auction.

DATES TO SEE FINANCIAL BENEFITS IN 2004

March 20: Your first date to star on your calendar. This is a new moon in your house of money, traditionally your very best period to see an influx of cash. This year the new moon is at zero degrees, considered a positive, critical degree for all sorts of entrepreneurial ventures. Venus also happens to be beautifully angled to Jupiter, another sign of success!

April 19: This new moon has the power of three, because it is an eclipse. A new source of income could emerge now or in the weeks that follow. You may have to give up a present source, but that should be fine with you because the new one looks more lucrative.

September 26: When it comes to salary, Mars sending greetings to Jupiter means you'll be batting a thousand. Try for a raise and you'll succeed. This is a Sunday, but you can give this day a plus or minus one day.

September 28: Coming two days later, this full moon falls in your second house of salary. Want a raise? Ask now.

October 14: This new moon solar eclipse is sure to be your golden financial day of the year, as many planets are crowded into this sector. All new moons bring two weeks of energy, but center your actions as close to this day as possible. This eclipse will appear in your eighth house of other people's money. No matter what type of funds you need, make your case now. Money should arrive soon.

November 4: Venus will dance with Jupiter in your house of other people's money. Here's another four-star day! While you are at it, why not pick up a raffle ticket for a charity function on the way home?

EXPECT TO COLLECT CAREER KUDOS AT YEAR'S END YOU MAY MAKE A COURSE CORRECTION IN EARLY AUGUST

Pluto has been shining like a beacon at the tiptop of your chart, in your tenth house of fame and honors, since 1995. Pluto won't move to another house of your chart until 2008. Pluto, being the slowest orbiting planet in our solar system, is also the most powerful, as it takes 246 years to orbit the Sun.

Pluto has an all-or-nothing quality that demands an intense, passionate response. Unlike Uranus, which sends surprising news suddenly, Pluto works in an opposite way, creating gradual changes over many years that turn out to be just as life altering, but less perceptible on a day-to-day level. One common effect of Pluto in your tenth house is that if you're not pleased with your career path, Pluto will make sure you find your true calling.

Pluto and Jupiter will be at odds this year, an aspect that will peak on August 6, although you may be aware of the need to make a major business decision as early as mid-July. Your wits will be sharpened, so you will be able to find ways around almost any challenge. You and your partner may not see eye-to-eye about a certain business idea initially, but if you are determined to move forward (and it appears you will be), you can identify common ground.

Alternatively, the obstacle you face in late July or August may have to do with a business or project you started in late 1994 or 1995. You have apparently reached a new phase in this endeavor's life cycle, and you need to assess your progress. If you would like to make any changes or embellishments, do so in August, or you may abandon it altogether.

Pluto will nudge you to make career changes if your birthday falls between March 9 and March 13. If your birthday falls before March 9, you'll have already faced and met these challenges.

Unquestionably, your very best time to change jobs will come at year's end. Your first day to watch is November 29, when Jupiter, the ruler of your solar tenth house of fame and honors, will send a beautiful vibration to your ruling planet, Neptune. If you work in a creative field or with artistic people, you will be doubly lucky, as Neptune is the planet ruling the arts. This is a four-star day, so plan to make a presentation or have an interview on this day.

Your next banner moment of 2004 will occur at the new moon December 11, and during the two weeks that follow. Try to get your interviews lined up within that period. December 11 is a Saturday, so be ready to roll on Monday morning, because all new moons deliver their best energy the moment they appear. Four heavenly bodies will be in your house of fame to help push you over the top, and that's the most you've had all year!

I know—it's holiday time. Don't let that stop you, as you will be able to persuade someone to give you that big break. You can land a new job or get a promotion despite the fact that most people have sugarplums dancing in their heads (or lampshades on their heads). If you are self-employed, you can land a new client or bring in new business.

Finally—here's the surprise—Mars will visit your house of fame and put your name in lights from December 25, 2004, until February 6, 2005. That will be an exceptional period, and one of your very best.

It certainly looks like you will have a career victory to celebrate by time the New Year's ball falls in Times Square!

Summary

It is a great time to be a Pisces! The move of Uranus into your sign (which began last year) will be the single most important change in your chart. If your birthday falls between February 19 and February 26, you are already feeling the shifts; all Pisces will have a turn at having a full dose of this powerful, life-altering energy.

Uranus will present you with options you never dreamed possible. Even the most casual experience could become a life-changing event. A visit from Uranus to your Sun even has the power to make you quite well known in your industry—or even in the world. Uranus is known to be erratic, so if you get a setback, a breakthrough is just around the corner.

In 2004 you are at the top of your creative game. Uranus and Neptune will work together to inspire you, while Saturn will teach you how to nourish your talents by using self-discipline, determination, and concentration.

This will also be a year that brings enormous personal development, particularly in the realm of romance and parenthood. Perhaps the biggest change is that you'll insist that your personal relationships have purpose. Saturn has made you realize that your time should count. If you sense a relationship is going nowhere, you will more likely leave than wait to see if things will work out.

If you are single, your relationship may be subject to some sort of temporary enforced separation, due perhaps to your sweetheart's work or study schedule or other circumstances outside your control.

If you have had difficulty meeting suitable partners, this year should bring a number of people that you will want to know better. Also, many attached Pisces may choose to have a baby this year—the time is right because you will be quite ready to commit to being the best parent you can be.

Travel, publishing, or higher education could give the year special sparkle, due to two of the year's eclipses on May 4 and October 28. One of my favorite dates for you to take an exciting long-distance trip would be on or after the new moon November 12. Short, fun trips are possible in February and March and late October.

This year is your very best in the decade for marriage and commitment! If you aren't ready to take that step, use this energy to form business associations, too, for those are equally favored. Cement an alliance on any day prior to Jupiter's departure from Virgo on September 25 (this cycle started in late August 2003). Mid-to-late September is your brightest period for forming any kind of lasting romantic alliance.

Financially, this year should be excellent as well. Two new moons, March 20 and April 19 (the latter also being a powerful solar eclipse), should start the ball rolling. When Jupiter, the planet of good fortune, moves into your house of joint resources in late September for a year's stay, you will see even more income. It may come in the form of a fat commission, bonus, court settlement, or prize. Mid-to-late October will bring your very best financial moment of 2004.

Happily, your career should take off like a rocket in the last two months of the year. Watch November 29—it will be an outstanding day if you are involved with any sort of artistic expression. The new moon on December 11 and the two weeks after may bring an opportunity to land a big promotion or new job that puts your name in lights. Remarkably, in the last week of December, Mars will begin to help you get ahead as well. If you want a new position, you will have all the cosmic support you need.

Dear Pisces, you can finally put the past difficult years behind you. You are looking at an exciting year, and future years will only pull you ahead faster. With all your stress levels going down, this is a year to be enjoyed to the fullest. Happy New Year, dear Pisces!

Cosmic Tools

The Planets, the Sun, and Moon

THE SUN

As seen from Earth, the Sun is the brightest star in the universe. It is the center of our solar system and the vital heart in any horoscope. Without the Sun, there would be no life. The Sun rules your will, your pride, your determination, your heart, health, and vitality, the recognition you receive for work well done, your sense of purpose, and motivation for future goals. The Sun is your ego and your self-esteem. This "planet" also determines how others view you. An essentially masculine force, the Sun also wields influence over the significant men in your life, especially those in positions of authority. This may be your father, your boyfriend or husband, a male friend, or a male boss or client.

The Sun rules all daylight. In the same way it rules public recognition and self-image by illuminating who we are, the Sun also clarifies the characteristics of any planet it touches and reveals truths about that planet. For example, if the Sun and Jupiter are involved a special configuration, Jupiter's goodness would be illuminated and made even more brilliant by the Sun. Under the nurturing light of the Sun, Jupiter's strengths would intensify, as would the benefits it bestows upon us.

The Sun takes one year to move through all twelve constellations (signs) of the zodiac. The Sun guards the heart. It is the ruler of the sign of Leo.

THE MOON

The Moon drives your deepest feelings, the fine-tuning of your character, your instinct and intuition, your emotions, and your reactions. The Moon also rules your private life, especially your home. Since the Moon is feminine in nature, it rules your mother and how you perceive her, and does the same for any other important women in your life, including your wife, girl-friend, grandmother, or a female boss.

If the Sun represents where you are going, the Moon signifies where you've been. More specifically, the Moon rules your history, your background, emotional development, and your roots. Your ability to get in touch with your feelings is dictated by planetary aspects to the Moon.

The dynamics surrounding the Moon also indicate the state of your health, especially if you are female. The Moon rules the sign of Cancer, the stomach and breasts, and the light of night (obviously, moonlight). The Moon, which takes approximately 28 days to orbit the zodiac, spends two to three days in each sign every month.

Every month there is a new moon. Depending where it falls in your horoscope, it shows which areas would be favored for new beginnings. A full moon arrives two weeks after a new moon; depending on where that moon falls in your chart, it could be time to reap the benefits or consequences of earlier actions.

MERCURY

This little planet is the mythological messenger, communicating information to one and all. Mercury represents non-emotional, rational, objective thought. Its placement in a sign determines that sign's intellectual style. As a quickly moving planet, Mercury is flexible, responsive, and adaptable. A big part of Mercury's job is to disburse information; as such it rules perception, language, writing, editing, research, speaking, learning experiences, and the assessment of data. It rules telecommunications, computing, software, electronic gadgets, the mail, shipping, couriers, and transportation. This planet has a lot of responsibility.

When Mercury retrogrades (something you can read about on my website, Astrology Zone, at *www.astologyzone.com*), it scrambles information, causing static and confusion. Its effects are felt universally. Mercury retrograde periods are bad times to sign contracts, complete important transactions, access accurate information, or make big decisions.

The sign and house in which Mercury resides in one's chart reveal a great deal about your style of gathering and giving out information. Mercury also rules sibling relationships, maps, letters, travel plans, appointments, roadways, vehicles, advertising, publishing, sales, and public relations.

Mercury rules Gemini and Virgo. Mercury spends about two to three weeks in each sign, but when it retrogrades, which it does three or four times a year, it can stay in one sign as long as ten weeks. Never far from the Sun, it takes about one year to circle the zodiac.

VENUS

Venus rules your affections, your heart, your love life, and pleasure. This feminine planet also rules gifts, beauty, fashion, adornment, and art. The planet of grace makes the world more attractive and fun. Venus' placement in a chart can also bring strong financial favor and material gain.

Venus is the governess of all that is beautiful. Venus can bring opportunities to hear music, eat good food, enjoy a beautiful perfume, appreciate a fine wine, or see a great art exhibit. Venus can even help you seduce your lover. What a dreary world it would be without Venus!

Venus is alluring, magnetic, and receptive, but never aggressive. (Assertiveness would be left to Mars, her cosmic lover; they make a great pair!) Venus is able to get her way by using charm instead of force. Some see this planet as hedonistic, as Venus tends not to be deeply thoughtful, ethical, or moral. Thinking about consequences is a job left to Saturn. Deciding what is just is left to Jupiter. Cold hard analysis of facts and data is Mercury's job.

Like Mercury, Venus stays close to the Sun. It remains in a sign for two to three weeks at a time—unless it retrogrades, in which case it can stay in a sign for as long as five months. This planet typically takes from ten to twelve months to tour all twelve signs, though it can take longer if it retrogrades. Venus is the natural ruler of Taurus and Libra.

MARS

Mars energizes other planets or houses of the zodiac. This is an aggressive, assertive, forceful, energetic, competitive, and daring planet.

The Red Planet governs the whole spectrum of masculine elements, from sex to war. Also known as the Warrior Planet, Mars is known for its courage, passion, strength, and stamina. As such, Mars is also famous for its ability (when in harmony) to help you outlast and outdistance adversaries.

Mars governs sharp instruments, fire, and anything combustible. Mars must be in a harmonious placement to be of help for any endeavor that requires endurance and determination. When its rays are positive, Mars lends survival instincts to any situation.

Mars allows you to keep progressing even when the going gets rough. If Mars is too energetic, an emotional outburst or physical accident could occur. If you are looking for a sense of spirit or gusto in just about any endeavor, Mars can provide it.

Mars takes two years to go around the zodiac, and stays in each sign for six to seven weeks. If it retrogrades in a particular sign, it can settle in for as many as seven to eight months. It is the natural ruler of Aries and the co-ruler of Scorpio.

JUPITER

Jupiter is known as the planet of good fortune. It expands opportunity and the benefits within the house it is visiting. This fortunate planet also rules wealth and financial or material gain.

Additionally, Jupiter brings vision, faith, optimism, loyalty, justice, confidence, and wisdom. Jupiter paints a broad picture and makes you think big.

Take all the planets in the solar system except the Sun (which is really a star), and put them together. Jupiter is physically larger than all the other planets combined. That's why we call Jupiter the expansive planet, or the Great Benefactor.

Jupiter allows us to philosophize and find a higher meaning or purpose in the sector it visits. It encourages reflection, study, and the attainment of higher education. Since long-distance travel is considered a factor of the education sector, having Jupiter in your sign may inspire you to travel far and wide or much more frequently than usual.

Jupiter is the natural ruler of Sagittarius. This happy planet takes twelve years to circle the zodiac. Each sign gets its blessings for one full year at a time.

SATURN

Saturn is the planet of concentration, permanence, tangible rewards, tenacity, ambition, and productivity. The taskmaster planet also rules caution, delay, constriction, limitation, responsibility, rules and regulations, pain, fear, authority, discipline, control, and denial.

Before you say "ugh!" consider this: without Saturn, we would see little or no progress. We live in a tangible world, and Saturn urges us to deal with it. Without Saturn we would have no gumption, no standards or controls, no structure—just chaos.

Saturn grabs us by the collar and forces us to confront reality. When Saturn touches a specific area in your chart, that area experiences a kind of slowdown or freeze. Saturn is cold and icy. This planet is also considered heavy or leaden.

However, Saturn, the great teacher planet, also brings maturity and teaches us the value of patience and sacrifice.

Saturn is the ruler of Capricorn. It rules the base structure of everything, from teeth and bones to the organizational hierarchy of a company. It governs historical, artistic, and archeological artifacts. It takes twenty-nine years to circle the zodiac, and stays in each sign for two and a half years.

URANUS

Uranus rules surprise and all things unexpected. It also rules the future and new technology, including things that are newly invented and all that is unimagined and yet to come. Uranus is the father of electricity.

Innovative, unpredictable, resourceful, imaginative, idiosyncratic, and experimental, Uranus also rules creativity and scientific genius. Uranus' job is to break rules and demolish established patterns or structures, creating sudden—even radical—change. Uranus works in sudden ways, and is called the Great Awakener.

Uranus gives a strong impulse for rebellion, independence, and even shock. Exciting and liberating, Uranus will overturn anything traditional or orthodox that it deems has outlived its usefulness.

This planet produces quick, liberating results, blending fact with intuition in its quest to discover universal truths. Uranus is considered the higher octave of intellectual Mercury, and is strongly objective and brainy, with no emotional side. People with strong Uranian influences in their charts are trailblazers and forerunners in their communities.

Since Uranus holds sway over social change, it also regulates mankind and humanitarian concerns, including environmental issues. Uranus rules Aquarius. Finally, Uranus rules astrology itself.

This planet stays in a sign for seven years and takes eighty-four years to circle the zodiac.

NEPTUNE

Neptune is the planet of inspiration. The higher octave of Venus, Neptune brings beauty to a higher, more spiritual level. It also holds sway over dreams, the subconscious, illusions, fantasies, and all things magical and enchanting.

Neptune intensifies intuition and teaches us to be deeply compassionate. It also often asks us to sacrifice for the greater good or for love of another.

Neptune refines, purifies, and cleanses any visitors. This planet cannot bear coarseness. Highly sensitive Neptune gets us more in tune with subtlety, and therefore increases the artistic side of one's personality. Neptune rules all visual communication, such as photography, movies, ballet and other dance arts, music, painting, and poetry.

Neptune also rules the sea and all other bodies of water. It governs rain, ice, and liquids of all kinds—including beverages and alcohol. Neptune also rules drugs—both the ones that make us suffer and the ones that make us well.

Neptune is known as the Planet of Mist. It makes us want to escape mundane, everyday reality and enter a more ideal, heavenly state. It urges us to excel and to reject limitations.

Neptune is the ruler of Pisces. It takes 146 years to circle the zodiac, with a stay of about fourteen years in each sign.

PLUTO

Pluto rules transformation. It is the father of the phoenix as it rises from the ashes, the symbol of rebirth. Pluto governs the act of ultimate survival in the never-ending cycle of beginnings and endings. Pluto's role as a catalyst for change and metamorphosis cannot be overemphasized.

When active in a chart, this planet can aid an individual in triumph over the odds. Pluto intensifies and strengthens any sector or planet it touches. It also rules obsessive behavior, taboos, and compulsions, even crises.

This planet rules many fundamental issues, including life and death, the ultimate transformation of energy. Pluto rules all that is hidden, unseen, or buried, including secrets, undercover work, strategic planning, and even the roots of plants. It also drives the unearthing or unmasking of that which is concealed.

Pluto takes 246 years to circle the zodiac, with a stay ranging from eleven years to thirty-two years in a sign! The sign of Scorpio is under Pluto's domain.

The Houses: The Building Blocks of Your Life

As each planet works its way through the twelve constellations (which make up the twelve signs of the zodiac), it passes through one of the twelve houses of each of those signs. Each house governs a different area of life, from relationships, marriage, and children, to career, co-workers, study, travel, and the home—one even rules your identity and appearance. At the moment of your birth, the planets were arrayed in a specific formation, each one located in a specific house. This pattern made by the planets and their locations, called the "natal horoscope," is nearly as individual to you as your fingerprint.

In your natal horoscope, some houses may have been full, and others empty. (There are eight planets plus the Sun and Moon and twelve houses, so there are not enough planets to go around.) It makes no difference if some houses are empty.

Everyone has one or more—at least an empty house doesn't have any difficult planetary energy in it!

Keep in mind that the planets continually move through these houses as they orbit the Sun. A house that is empty in your natal horoscope could be very full today! To know where the planets are at all times, check your forecast on my free website, *http://www.astrologyzone.com*.

FIRST HOUSE

The first house determines much of what makes you unique: your appearance, your personality, your drive, your goals, and your priorities. It covers your ego, your natural tendencies, the way you present yourself to the world, your energy, and your deepest desires.

The first house, when viewed along with conditions in the sixth house (more on that later), also reflects your health and vitality.

We look to the first house for any new, important trends and cycles. The first house is the hardest house for an astrologer to read, because your desires are so personal! It also rules your will, individuality, and determination.

The first house reveals the sign rising on the horizon at your birth, also called the ascendant sign. The only way you can find out your rising sign is to cast a natal horoscope chart for the exact date, time, and place of your birth. (All charts are converted to Greenwich Mean Time. Astrology is very concerned with mathematical measurements; everyone is converted to the same birth city to create a common denominator.)

The sign on your ascendant is the sign whose characteristics you express naturally. This explains why those born under the same sun sign are not alike; most of us are actually a combination of our sun sign and ascendant.

Once you know your ascendant, you should read both your sun sign and your ascendant sign, whether in forecasts or personality outlines; reading both will give you a more accurate picture.

The first house is ruled by feisty, entrepreneurial, energetic Mars and by the first sign of the zodiac, individualistic Aries.

SECOND HOUSE

The second house rules earned income, financial obligations, and material possessions. Material gains and losses are dictated by this house. It also presides over your sense of security and self-confidence.

This house is ruled by the planet of love and finances, Venus, and by the practical and stability-minded Taurus.

THIRD HOUSE

The third house rules your mind and intellect. It reveals how you approach and analyze problems, and how you perceive information. Basically, it drives your overall learning and communicative processes. For example, this house administers skills in writing, editing, speaking, thinking, and reading. It covers your ability and desire to learn, and brings opportunities to do so your way. Under the influence of this house, someone would decide to learn a language or become a teacher. Other endeavors covered here are the drafting of contracts and agreements, the presentation of ideas and proposals, and commerce, including sales, marketing, public relations, and self-promotion.

This house covers your neighborhood, short-distance trips, and local transportation and shipping.

The third house also regulates fundamental education (nursery school through high school), your relationships with siblings, cousins, and neighbors, and your perception of childhood experiences.

This house is ruled by the intellectual, communicative Mercury, and by the versatile Gemini.

FOURTH HOUSE

The fourth house covers your home—what it looks like, where it is located, and with whom you share your space. This includes anybody who stops by to visit, to help you with home-improvement projects, or to babysit. It also rules individuals who challenge domestic harmony.

Family life comes under this house, as do all property matters such as buying, selling, or renting houses or apartments. This house also rules your parents and your relationship with them. Finally, this house indicates the lifestyle you will have much later in life, for the fourth house is a metaphor for the end of the day.

The fourth house is ruled by the sentimental sign of Cancer and the Moon.

FIFTH HOUSE

Your love life, romance, fun, and pleasure are covered in the fifth house, as are children and pregnancy. This house also rules leisure activities, creativity, new ideas, hobbies, and sports. So do games of chance and finance, from gambling to investing in the stock market.

This house is ruled by creative Leo and our fun-loving, life-creating Sun.

Sixth House

The state of the sixth house indicates your daily routine and the methods you use to get work done. The cusp of this house describes the nature of your work and the general environment of your workplace. This house also rules people you employ, whether at home or at the office.

This house rules the conscious mind and the proactive measures we take to keep our bodies healthy. (The first house rules health in terms of overall energy level and vitality, so both have to be considered.) Diet, fitness, and exercise are covered in the sixth house, as are checkups with the doctor and visits to the dentist.

Finally, pets and small animals come under this house, too.

The sixth house is ruled by intellectual, news-gathering Mercury and by the meticulous and service-oriented Virgo.

Seventh House

The seventh house rules marriage, business partnerships, and any serious contractual agreement between two people or entities.

This house holds the possibility of both completion of or conflict with an agreement. Enemies and detractors are covered here, as are your staunchest allies.

This house also manages experts you hire: attorneys, agents, or others who collaborate with or represent you.

For most people, the seventh house indicates the status of their marriage. This house describes what you need most from your significant other, and the rapport that develops between you.

Please note that romantic love is reflected in the fifth house, but once a commitment is made, the relationship moves to the seventh house. The "contract" between two people, or two entities, may be written or verbal.

The seventh house is ruled by gentle, refined Venus and by the partnering sign of Libra.

EIGHTH HOUSE

This house is about rebirth, regeneration, and the transformation of energy. Joint financial matters also come under the eighth house. (To the ancients, money is a form of concentrated energy.) The financial dealings in this house do not include earned income (that would be in the second house), but do cover money you lend and owe others. Prizes, gifts, inheritances, tax payments and refunds, bonuses, commissions, royalties, child support, alimony, mortgages, credit, loans and venture capital are the kinds of transactions ruled by the eighth house.

Any time you need money to fund a big idea, your chances for success come under this house. This house also would indicate the state of your partner's prosperity.

Gifts and transactions of all kinds and physical love—sex and reproduction—are also included here. (Note that the fifth house is love, the seventh house is marriage, and the eighth house is sex.) Spiritual, highly intuitive, or even psychic experiences are often found in this house, too (along with the twelfth house). Finally, this house rules endings and things to be discarded. As such, surgery is covered here.

This house is ruled by Mars and co-ruled by catalyst Pluto and the intense Scorpio.

NINTH HOUSE

This is the house that encourages us to think big and bold, and to consider the future in the broadest terms. A certain amount of preparation is required before one can take full advantage of all that the ninth house has to offer. Long-distance travel, international communication, higher education, and interactions and relationships with foreigners, distant relatives, and in-laws are the key areas covered by this important house.

It also rules your attitudes and viewpoints, and your efforts to understand complex issues, including morals and ethics. This house drives discussions on philosophy, religion, publishing, and legal and academic matters. It emphasizes the higher mind and mental exploration.

The ninth house is ruled by fortunate Jupiter and by the philosophical and scholarly Sagittarius.

TENTH HOUSE

Fame, promotions, honors, career awards and professional opportunities, and your status in the community are covered by this high-powered house. Located at the mid-heaven (tip top) point of the horoscope, the cusp of this house (and the first house) indicates your profession and where you excel.

The eighth house also dictates your professional image. This house covers judges, high-level individuals, and government officials. It is here how such figures are determined to help you.

The tenth house is ruled by hard-working, serious Saturn and by the hard-working, focused Capricorn.

ELEVENTH HOUSE

Friendships and platonic relationships fall in this house, as do memberships in a group or club. Attendance at a trade show or a theme park—presence in any congregation of people sharing an interest—constitutes an eleventh-house activity. In that regard, even casual contacts, associations, and networking efforts are covered here.

This house can reveal clues about your employer's financial status. It can show you where you are most likely to make profits. This house governs humanitarian causes and any efforts to correct social ills and injustices.

Finally, this is the house of hopes and wishes, where higher aspirations and dreams come true. While that might sound overblown, when you have an important aspect occur in this house, you may be pleasantly surprised!

The eleventh house is ruled by creative and scientific Uranus and by idiosyncratic Aquarius.

TWELFTH HOUSE

The twelfth house rules the subconscious mind, dreams, intuition, instinct, and secrets. In fact, it dominates all that's hidden, including activities going on behind the scenes and confidential engagements.

Psychotherapy and psychic phenomena both fall under this house. Dynamics acting on this house can heighten hunches and intuition. "Self-undoing," meaning anything we do to undermine ourselves, also comes under this house. It governs rest and reaching the end of a long cycle, as well as the termination of any confinement, such as hospital stays, nursing home residences, or even jail sentences.

This is the house where we heal ourselves. It also rules self-sacrifice, inner suffering, limitations, and secret enemies. Lastly, this house rules charity, especially on a one-on-one basis.

A little-known fact is that large animals come under the domain of the twelfth house.

The twelfth house is ruled by spiritual and self-sacrificing Neptune and by compassionate Pisces.

The Four Eclipses in 2004

Aside from the movements of the big outer planets, such as
Jupiter and Saturn, the other key indicator of change in any
person's horoscope is the placement of the year's eclipses.
Some years have as many as eight eclipses, but this year has a
more typical number, four. Eclipses always come in pairs, in
the form of a new moon and full moon, and they always come
two weeks apart. Eclipses occur every five and a half months.
Their influence is wide—we can feel the effect of an eclipse
over the course of a full year (or in some cases, even more).
They are certainly not like normal new moons or full moons,
and pack much more energy.

Eclipses are the surest indicator of change of any cosmic
event, but in order to be affected by an eclipse, you need at
least one planet being touched (i.e., within 8 mathematical
degrees of any aspect), doubly so if they make a strong aspect
to one of the north/south/east/west angles of your chart. In

your individual forecast, you can find out specifically where each eclipse will fall in your solar chart, and whether it is due to touch one of these sensitive angles.

Eclipses fall in families—that is, two signs that fall opposite each other on the horoscope wheel, such as Taurus/Scorpio or Virgo/Pisces. Currently, two families of eclipses are activated at once: Aries/Libra and Taurus/Scorpio.

Subsequent eclipses will fall in the same two signs for an 18-month period. After that, they move into two other signs, and those signs are usually, but not always, exactly opposite each other in the zodiac. If you have had eclipses in your sign recently, after the 18-month period is over, eclipses won't come back to your sign for another nine years.

Every 19 years brings an almost exact repeat of an eclipse series, so that's why I suggest you look back to those years to see how the eclipses in that particular family worked out for you then.

I mention the magnitude of each eclipse so you can judge the relative strength of each one. The stronger the magnitude, the more powerful its effects. However, if an eclipse falls near your birthday, your world will spin a little faster!

Keep in mind that each sign will feel these eclipses differently. There are some general indications that you should add to the descriptions in your chapter, and those are listed below.

THE FOUR ECLIPSES IN 2004 IN DETAIL

1. April 19: a partial new moon solar eclipse in late
degrees (29 degrees) of Aries, magnitude .07

Readers born on the following dates, plus or minus five days, will certainly feel this eclipse: April 19, July 21, October 21, and January 18.

This eclipse may also positively change the lives of those readers born on: June 20, August 21, December 20, and February 17 (plus or minus five days).

Any eclipse falling in Aries urges us to show leadership skills and to pioneer into new, uncharted territories. It will also encourage you to put your stamp of individuality on projects, whether creative, academic, or business-oriented. The 29th degree of this eclipse signifies completion, so something you are doing may now reach a final stage. However, since it is a new moon eclipse, it also points to a new chapter beginning, and is more about what's yet to come than any ending.

Mars and Venus will be cuddled quite close at this eclipse, indicating romance (either immediately or within a few months) or gain from artistic endeavors. Lucky, financial Jupiter is in perfect angle to Saturn, too, lending stability and security to whatever you happen to be doing at the time. Mercury will send a wink to Pluto, indicating a favorable contract may be in the works.

Although these aspects are cheery for this solar eclipse, there will be one notable exception. Mars will also oppose Pluto, so a power struggle could break out as well. If this should happen, the person you will be dealing with will seem quite immobile; you'll need lots of determination, resourcefulness, and persistence to succeed. If you enter into a dispute or negotiation, it may take longer to resolve than originally estimated, and the strength or fierceness of the other party will amaze you. Don't crumble!

> 2. *May 4: a full moon lunar eclipse, falls in middle degrees (14) of Scorpio, magnitude 1.3*

Those who are sure to feel the effects of this eclipse are those with birthdays that fall on (or within five days of): May 4, August 5, November 5, and February 2.

If born on or within five days of the following dates you will benefit from this particular eclipse, even if initially this is not obvious: July 5, September 6, January 4, and March 4.

Scorpio is a highly financial sign, so there could be talks about money at this time, perhaps in regard to salary, commissions or royalties, insurance settlements, mortgages, home refinancing, child support, venture capital, licensing, or other means of cash flow. You may decide to reorganize your investment portfolio or change the way you spend your discretionary income.

Scorpio rules the eighth house of money you "share" with others, such as taxes or venture capital. Mortgages, credit cards, commissions, royalties, licensing deals, child support, alimony, proceeds from a split in a marriage or business, grants, scholarships, or workmen's compensation could become important for you as a result of this eclipse.

Scorpio also rules reproduction, transformational energy, and medicine and healing. In the latter sense, the eighth house also rules surgery. If you need an operation, schedule one near this eclipse. Don't worry—every indication is that you will benefit from this eclipse.

This is a mixed eclipse, with both positive and frustrating aspects. On the plus side, the Moon and Sun are in good angle to good fortune planet Jupiter. Also the Moon—always the key player in a lunar eclipse—will form a beneficial alignment with Uranus, the planet of surprise, and with Saturn, the planet that brings stability and security.

On the downside, this eclipse is not in friendly angle to Neptune, so you may feel disillusioned about a person or project. Or you may come away from an event feeling upset that you weren't told the whole story—until now. Do not agree to any new ventures under this eclipse, for you may not fully understand all the ramifications until later. In just a couple of weeks, the fog should lift.

Mars was opposed to Pluto during the last eclipse, April 19, and these two planets will still be within striking distance for this one. A difficult client may exasperate you, or a partner (current or soon-to-be-ex) won't give an inch in financially oriented negotiations. Mars opposed to Pluto is a hard aspect that will require a great deal of staying power from you—don't enter the boxing ring unless you have the stamina to stay many rounds!

3. October 14: a new moon partial eclipse, falling in late degrees of Libra, magnitude .93

Those that will be affected by this eclipse include people born on or within five days of October 14, April 10, July 13, and January 11.

Those with birthdays that fall on or within five days of the following dates will find ways to benefit from this eclipse: June 11, August 13, December 12, and February 9.

This eclipse will find the Sun, Moon, and Mercury in a hard angle to Saturn, the planet of obligations and long-term undertakings. You may be asked to make a serious decision or commitment. Or you may have to live up to a long-standing obligation, with no way to get out of it. You won't have much time to deliberate, but if you need more time to think about how to handle this challenging development, ask for it. Even an extra day or two may help.

Mars will be near the Sun and even closer to lucky Jupiter, which suggests lots of activity near this particular eclipse. You can expect some very upbeat developments. Uranus will be in a happy-go-lucky mood and lend its powers of creativity and innovation to the mix.

This eclipse falls in Libra, which rules partnerships, marriage, and one-on-one collaborations. This suggests that this eclipse will focus on these areas. This is especially true because no fewer than five out of ten heavenly bodies will be in Libra at the time!

As the sign that holds the scales, Libra also rules justice, balance, and the quest for fairness. Libra can be festive, so you may be planning a great party or wedding, or going to one. Ruled by Venus, Libra also governs the decorative arts, such as jewelry, flower arranging, and beauty treatments, including those that are spa-oriented. You might start a business in one of these areas or be involved with a charity gala or wedding, for example.

4. October 28: a total lunar eclipse, falling in early
degrees of Scorpio, magnitude 1.3

Those born on or within five days of the following dates will feel this eclipse most directly: October 28, April 24, July 27, and January 24.

Those born on the following dates will benefit from this eclipse: June 26, August 28, December 26, and February 23.

This is a full moon lunar eclipse, which suggests a final stage or an abrupt end. Life is filled with all sorts of beginnings and endings; new cycles are beginning all the time.

Sometimes, during an eclipse, we feel something has been taken away, but something better will replace it. Again, money seems to be an issue, whether directly or peripherally.

Lunar eclipses tend to be more emotional than solar eclipses, as memories, goals, and feelings usually come into play. That is not to say they always bring sad news—eclipses have been known to bring exciting, happy, life-changing events, too!

This eclipse has mainly happy, upbeat aspects. The Moon and Sun are in fine angle to unpredictable Uranus, suggesting a delightful surprise or that you will find a unique way to deal with a situation. Either way, this is good! You may find yourself at the right place at the right time, and be able to take advantage of some very fine opportunities as a result.

Neptune will be at odds with the Sun and Moon, however, indicating that a miscommunication is possible. Aim for clarity, and put off any pressing decisions or the signing of any contracts for a week or more after the eclipse if possible. (Try not to make a decision under an eclipse, as there is plenty of static in the air.)

Mars and Pluto patch up their dispute (found in earlier eclipses) and decide to work cooperatively this time around. And best of all, Jupiter will dance with Neptune in the midnight sky, a gorgeous and glamorous vibration. This indicates that a happy, profitable ending is attainable if you ride out some of the more difficult parts of the eclipse. Focus on the positive elements of the situation as much as possible.

CLUES TO THE ECLIPSE PATTERNS LIE IN THE PAST: A LOOK BACK 19 YEARS IS HELPFUL

An eclipse delivers a unique message; no two will bring identical results. Even so, you can get a general idea of what these eclipses might bring by looking back approximately 19 years, for that is the length of time it takes to repeat an eclipse to exact mathematical degree.

Accordingly, look back to 1984 and 1985 to see what themes emerged. In those years were eclipses of similar degrees. (Keep in mind that all the other planets have since changed position in relationship to those eclipses. As you see, astrology is very complex!)

Here is an example of an eclipse's effect on me. I noticed that the part of my chart ruling children, the fifth house, was being aspected by a major eclipse on the very day my daughter Diana was going away to college for the first time. I began to wonder if everything would be all right on the drive up to Boston from New York. She was 18 at the time, so I figured that the last eclipse to this degree could not have been about Diana. Boy, was I wrong.

I looked up the date of the eclipse and learned it fell during the very week that I discovered I was pregnant with her, 19 years earlier. Hence, it was clear that the current eclipse was teaching me to let her go, just as the first eclipse 19 years earlier taught me how to welcome her to our little nest. I got goose pimples when I saw that, and indeed, that turned out to be the message of this eclipse. Diana has since graduated from college. The eclipse proved to be a positive learning experience for Diana, but probably more so for me as her mother! (The eclipse had aspected my planets, not hers, proving I was the one who had to make the adjustment, not Diana!)

If looking back 19 years is a bit too far to remember, see if you can remember back nine years. This year's eclipses will be similar to the ones that happened then. (However, the ones that occurred 19 years ago will match 2004's more closely. Still, it's worth checking out the ones that fell in late 1995 and early 1996. If those were powerful years for you, chances are this one will be, too.

Keep in mind that everything depends on where these eclipses fall in your own chart. Good luck, dear reader! Remember, change is good and necessary. Without it we simply can't grow!

Mercury Retrograde in 2004

————◯————

WHAT IT MEANS FOR YOU

You may have heard friends say, "Oh, no—Mercury is about to retrograde again!" If you don't know astrology, you may have wondered what they mean. Of all planetary aspects, this one seems to
garner the most attention from the general public, including
those who have only the most casual understanding of astrology.
The reason is clear—this phenomenon is one of the few that
affects everyone in a fairly uniform way, and its effects are always
quite obvious. Once you begin to pay attention to how events in
your life change during these phases, you will soon see evidence
of the pandemonium that this planet can create.

Keeping track of Mercury retrograde periods can allow
you to increase your productivity and avoid at least some of
the frustration they can bring about. Let's look closely at
Mercury retrograde and what it means to you.

IN 2004 THE PERIODS AND SIGNS IN WHICH MERCURY WILL RETROGRADE

December 17, 2003, to January 6, 2004
In Capricorn and Sagittarius

April 6, 2004, to April 30, 2004
In Taurus and Aries

August 10, 2004, to September 2, 2004
In Virgo and Leo

November 30, 2004, to December 20, 2004
In Sagittarius

DOES MERCURY REALLY MOVE BACKWARDS?

Mercury doesn't actually move backwards. If you do a bit of stargazing, you will see Mercury appearing to move backwards, just as the ancient astrologers did thousands of years ago. After a while—in Mercury's case, a three-and-a-half-week period—the planet will reverse itself and move "forward" again.

Being that Mercury is the planet situated closest to the Sun, its orbit is much shorter than Earth's. About three or four times a year, Mercury speeds past Earth, and that is when we experience a Mercury retrograde period. If you were standing on Mars watching Mercury and Earth, Earth would appear to be moving backwards, because Mercury is so quick, leaving Earth "in the dust," so to speak. As Mercury speeds by, it is like a train flying past, creating a powerful, turbulent gust of "wind" in its wake. The turbulence and disruption Mercury creates when it retrogrades are similar to what we feel on Earth in our everyday lives.

In astrology, we always feel "as above, so too below," and by that we mean there is a fractal relationship between the orbits in the heavens and human activity down here on Earth. That idea pervades all of astrology and is a very good concept to keep in mind.

AREAS OF LIFE MERCURY RULES

Mercury rules all types of communication, including listening, speaking, learning, reading, editing, researching, negotiating, selling, and buying. Mercury also rules all formal contracts and agreements, as well as important documents, such as book manuscripts or term papers. Included under this planet's domain are all types of code, including computer codes, as well as transportation, shipping, and travel. When this planet retrogrades, these areas tend to get scrambled or spin out of control.

Why does this happen? When a planet retrogrades, astrologically, it is in a resting or sleep state. Hence, while Mercury naps, the activities that it governs don't have the benefit of a well-functioning, wide-awake planet supervising them. Expect a certain degree of pandemonium to ensue!

Don't make any important moves when Mercury is retrograde. Nothing will be settled successfully for the future during these periods anyway—you will find it nearly impossible to nail down a plan. During a retrograde period, you will find it hard to get decisions from others. Even if a decision is made, it will be subject to change, whether just after Mercury turns to direct motion or else much later.

It would not be a good time to do anything communications-oriented, such as launch a magazine, website, or an advertising or publicity campaign.

Mercury retrograde periods are considered poor times to launch any new endeavors, even if they are not related to the communications industries.

Similarly, it is not a good time to sign any contracts or to even shake hands on any new agreements. The environment will be quite fluid and changeable, no matter what you are told—or what you think. It's not that the people you are dealing with are necessarily duplicitous; it's just that nobody can fully predict what conditions will be like later. If you start a new job, it won't necessarily be the position you thought it was when you accepted it. If you are a manager, you will have difficulty choosing the right candidate for the job, so hold off hiring anyone if you can.

WHAT IF YOU CAN'T PUT OFF A DECISION TILL A LATER DATE?

What if you can't wait a few weeks? In that case, you may have to sign or make a decision anyway. Do so knowing that the conditions around the situation will probably change, so be flexible. For example, if you are looking at a great apartment, you may have to sign the lease or risk losing it. However, before you do, ask lots of questions.

However, if you are going back to a past situation, you can do so with a free and clear mind. Mercury allows us to find closure with the past. Say you were going to sign a contract, but for whatever reason, it was delayed and now a retrograde has started. Or you are going back to the past to reconnect with someone. If you knew this person previously, or had dealt with this company before, you may give your answer with a clear conscience.

What Other Specific Things Should I Watch Out For?

Since Mercury rules the mail and the conveyance of information, be extra careful when sending important documents. If you send a fax, be sure to call the person at the other end to let them know your document is waiting for them. Otherwise, they may never see it! If you work in an office and have to photocopy an important document, be sure to retrieve the original. Be equally careful about whom you send email to—you don't want to send a private email to the wrong person or have a sensitive email forwarded to others.

Your client may suddenly change direction on a project you have been working on and give you new instructions, which may require you to discard some of the work you did. Miscommunications abound, so during these periods keep summarizing what you think the other person has just told you. Go the extra mile—you will be glad you did!

Mercury retrograde periods are notorious for causing computers to crash and for machines to show signs of wear, requiring urgent repair. Back up your computer in advance of any Mercury retrograde period. If you had planned to install new software on your personal computer (or, if you work in IT, on your network), wait until the retrograde period is over to do so. Weird things happen during these periods. For example, you may suddenly discover that you were sold a defective hard drive—even though it may never have given you problems in the past.

As Mercury also rules trade and commerce, don't buy or sell anything expensive during its retrograde phases, either. Often you will find that the item you want is out of stock. Or if you do purchase something—a car, a computer, or jewelry, for example—you may regret your decision later. If you are buying or selling a house, expect problems and delays to crop up. The only times you can buy something expensive during a retrograde period is if you are returning something you already bought.

The November to December retrograde period in 2004 will be especially frustrating because it is gift-giving season. Not only is it a bad idea to buy expensive things, it's also a bad time to ship things, as the address could be wrong, or the packing may not protect the item sufficiently. Do yourself a favor and shop very early for the holidays in 2004!

If driving, bring extra maps, ensure that you have enough gas, and verify that you have the correct address and clear driving instructions. If your car is making strange sounds, have it checked before you leave—you don't want a problem when you are on the road! If you are flying, check with your airline to make sure your flight is going to take off on time. Have your luggage well marked so that it won't get lost or sent to the wrong airport!

Some people put off travel altogether, and perhaps that would be wise if your trip is business-oriented. However, pleasure trips are great during these periods—you get away from it all, and everyone back home misses you! Try traveling to a place from your childhood that you loved but haven't seen in a long time during a retrograde phase. It could be lots of fun!

Forgetfulness can be a problem during these phases. You are more likely to leave your airline ticket or passport on your desk rather than put it in your pocket. Or you leave your cell phone or gloves in the back seat of a cab, or lock yourself out of your car or house!

Even romance tends to go haywire during these periods. Couples misunderstand each other and create a comedy of errors. Try not to jump to conclusions—keep striving for clarity. Your sweetheart or spouse could also have a change of mind. For example, if your boyfriend or girlfriend says, "I want to break up," he or she could say later, "No, let's not! I didn't really mean it!" That's because people aren't always thinking straight during these phases. Mercury retrograde is notorious for creating confusion.

Keep in mind that Mercury retrogrades in one or two of the 12 zodiac signs during each retrograde period. If it retrogrades in your sign, delays and frustrations will become even more noticeable than usual. In this case, try to be even more vigilant and double-check proposals, ideas, creative efforts, and other plans to root out flaws or incorrect assumptions.

WHAT IF I WAS BORN UNDER MERCURY RETROGRADE?

People who were born under Mercury retrograde are said to be immune from much of the mayhem of this phase, but I am not so sure this is true. (It has not been for me—I was born under Mercury retrograde, and I always find these periods quite difficult, perhaps because I work in Mercury-ruled publishing!)

You can find out if you were born under these phases by checking your horoscope. Mercury will have a small "R" under it on the wheel.

People born under this phase are said to have philosophical and reflective natures that help them think through complex concepts quite creatively. Never worry having a baby during one of these periods—it is always a good time to have a child!

MERCURY'S IMPENDING SHADOW PERIOD

As Mercury approaches its "switch point" (the day it actually turns retro), it will cover a path that it will later re-trace in the sky over the next few weeks. The two- or three-week period prior to Mercury retrograde is called the "impending shadow period." If you initiate anything important during that shadow period—that is, before Mercury begins to retrograde—you may still encounter problems, but probably not as serious.

Once Mercury has reached its last day of retrograding, however, you are free to push forward. Mercury is more powerful on the onset and finish dates. Move forward with vigor a day or two after this planet moves to normal direct speed.

IS MERCURY RETROGRADE ALL BAD? NOT AT ALL!

Although these Mercury retrograde periods can be frustrating, these periods are often useful, too, for they allow us to reassess, revisit, readdress, redo, and redesign our plans. Sometimes we rush along in life without fully considering our basic assumptions or actions. Mercury retrograde allows us to stop, look, listen, and redirect our energies more productively. Mercury also helps us find closure to certain situations.

Reconnecting with old pals and relatives is very common during retrograde periods, and that can be one of the most positive and fun sides of this planet's retrograde orbit.

We can all benefit from taking a closer look at situations with greater depth, which happens with Mercury retrograde. Even if you want to rush, you will find it almost impossible to do so. Mercury retrograde periods are like walking through glue!

Here are some common ways Mercury retrograde can help you:

○ Perhaps you have been working on a project that seems to have gone down the wrong path. When Mercury retrogrades, it could become evident to the team or client that the project needs to be tweaked or redirected. If you argue your case persuasively, things could go your way.

○ You stall on accepting a job offer, and lo and behold, a better one comes your way.

○ You don't buy a certain big-ticket item, and within a few weeks the coveted item goes on sale.

○ If a meeting is postponed or canceled, you have more time to garner additional information, and it probably will come in quite handy.

○ Missing objects are found. That beautiful bracelet wasn't lost after all—it was on your bookshelf, behind your favorite book!

What else should you do during Mercury retrograde periods? It would be a great time to reorganize your files or closets. Pack up clothes you haven't worn in a while to give to charity. Polish shoes and decide which ones need repair, and while you are at it, decide which appliances need to be taken in for repair as well. Oddly, as busy as we are, during these phases, we always seem to find more time to get things done.

Mercury rules anything that begins with "re"–redo, reassess, repair, repeat, redesign, or revisit. As you see, Mercury retrograde is not all bad—you can count on it!

About Susan Miller

Susan Miller is an internationally known accredited astrologer, author, and columnist with twenty-five years of experience. Her website, *Astrology Zone®* (*www.astrologyzone.com*), reaches millions of readers around the world each month. Her books include *Planets and Possibilities* (Warner Books, 2001), *The Year Ahead 2002* (Barnes & Noble Publishing), and *The Year Ahead 2003* (Barnes & Noble Publishing).

Susan writes a monthly horoscope column for *Self* and has written countless cover stories for a variety of consumer magazines. Her newspaper column "Signs of Love" is a weekly feature in the New York *Daily News*.

Susan is also a regular television guest on such shows as *20/20*, *The View*, CBS' *The Early Show*, *The Other Half* and CNN's *American Morning*.

OTHER BOOKS BY SUSAN MILLER

Planets & Possibilities

The Year Ahead 2002

The Year Ahead 2003